North West Civic Trust

Published by   The North West Civic Trust
The Environmental Institute, Greaves School,
Bolton Road, Swinton, Manchester, M27 2UX,
England

First published 1983

ISBN 0 901347 35 3

Illustrations by   Stephen Essex, BA

Photographs by   Robert Kemp, LIIP, MMPA
Brian Bower, FRPS
Tony Redford, ARPS
Norman Bilsborough, MA

Text by   Norman Bilsborough, MA

Printed by   H. Shanley (Printers) Ltd., Bolton

Front Cover: *Styal Village*

Back Cover: *Little Moreton Hall*

PREFACE

I am delighted to be able to write the preface to this splendid book. In many ways it should be written by Viscount Leverhulme but it is characteristic of his Lordship to have made the book possible and then to have modestly asked that someone else should write the preface. When we discussed the book it was Lord Leverhulme's wish that it should reflect credit on the county he loves and the North West Civic Trust which he has encouraged throughout the years. I believe the book does both and we are most grateful to Lord Leverhulme's private trust which has sponsored it.

We are also indebted to many other people for making the book possible. Particularly, we should like to thank those who were prepared to share their insights and knowledge about this locality — parish clerks, farmers, school teachers and secretaries of societies. Many people acted as guides or suggested others who would, many wrote into the Trust's office with information that enabled 'flesh' to be put on the bones of our basic knowledge about Cheshire. All their names must necessarily go unrecorded, but their contribution has been vital. Acknowledgements are made elsewhere to the photographers and artist involved, and we are grateful for their skill and thoroughness.

Finally I should like to express the Trust's very own appreciation to Norman Bilsborough for his diligence in seeing this project through from start to finish. I am sure the expressions of appreciation that he will receive from the book's readers will reward him for his endeavours and I trust that all those who read it will find in it the kind of treasure that is priceless.

Graham Ashworth
Chairman, North West Civic Trust Executive Committee

FOREWORD

This book is about the environmental treasures of Cheshire — its landscape and settlements, its beauty spots and historic buildings, its hidden corners as well as its wide open spaces. By virtue of the wealth of such features to be found in this fascinating county our account has necessarily and regrettably been selective, for one book on its own could hardly do justice to all Cheshire's towns and villages, its mansions and churches, its parks and gardens and its lovely countryside. Each of these would merit a volume of their own, but we hope that 'The Treasures of Cheshire' will not only give you a taste of the character of the county but also move you to discover much more for yourself. For those who know Cheshire well it will refresh their recollection of many places with which they are familiar, while for others we hope that it will not only develop their appreciation of the county but also kindle their enthusiasm to venture forth for themselves. In some measure too we trust that this book will not only stir the heart but also excite the senses, for Cheshire is supremely a place to be experienced — not only through its sights, some of which are recaptured here, but also through its scents and sounds.

This book is not exhaustive in its treatment of Cheshire's treasures and neither is it authoritative, for others have written at greater length and certainly in greater scholarship about different aspects of Cheshire. Our purpose is to draw together these different threads in one complete and colourful tapestry, to present as faithfully as possible in words and photographs the many facets of this gem of England. Where possible the text endeavours to give some of the historical background to buildings and places, enabling the present to be viewed and interpreted in the light of the past.

Chapter I
CHESHIRE
— a county of contrasts

A Picturesque County

"Please would you tell me", said Alice a little timidly, "why your cat grins like that?" "It's a Cheshire cat", said the Duchess, "and that's why".

Lewis Carroll

Everyone of course has heard about the Cheshire Cat, one of the characters created by Lewis Carroll in his fascinating story of 'Alice in Wonderland' and now immortalised in stained glass at Daresbury Church. Perhaps the cat was grinning simply because it came from Cheshire, surely one of the most attractive and picturesque parts of England's fair and pleasant land. Similarly there can be few people who have not heard of Cheshire cheese, a product which is synonymous with the county and which has been famous since Elizabethan times. Yet Cheshire has so much more to offer than these two 'home-grown' features which are traditionally associated with it.

Cheshire is more often than not thought of as a predominantly rural county which is mostly flat and consequently a little uninteresting. Certainly the Cheshire Plain covers a large part of the area, although it is more in the nature of a shallow basin extending southwards into Shropshire which is dissected by streams and rivers and further broken up by occasional higher ground. An unexpected face of the county is to be found on the eastern side where one is confronted with the wild and dramatic foothills of the Pennines which link up with the Derbyshire Dales just across the border, a landscape of steep-sided cloughs and fast-flowing streams which is a rebuke to one's traditionally-held views of Cheshire. Yet even the Cheshire Plain has its hills in the form of the central sandstone ridge, a narrow spine of higher ground running from Runcorn in the north down to Malpas in the south — although perhaps not as dramatic as the hills to the east this central ridge offers superb views of the surrounding countryside and at the same time is a lovely feature in itself, the occasional red sandstone cliffs on more exposed fronts mingling with softer wooded slopes. The ridge is made up of the Peckforton and Bickerton Hills to the south with the Frodsham and Helsby Hills further north, and throughout Cheshire's history it has been a strategic defensive location as witnessed by the line of Iron Age hill forts found here and the presence of Beeston Castle situated on a rocky crag overlooking the valley below. So without having perhaps the scenic grandeur of some counties, Cheshire is nevertheless a picturesque and lovely place with considerable variations in its landscape as well as a fascinating history.

As with most other counties Cheshire can be divided up into a number of distinct geographical areas. In the north-west (and as close to the sea as one can get in Cheshire) is

Hang-gliding from Bosley Cloud ▶

◀ *Cottages at Styal*

1

CHESHIRE

the Wirral, although only the southern half of the Peninsula is now included within the realms of the county following a revamping of the boundary as part of local government re-organisation in 1974. Rightly known for its delightful villages the Wirral is also the location for various industrial complexes, which while being economically important are not quite so acceptable from a visual standpoint, even though at night their illumination presents a fascinating sight. Eastwards of the Wirral is the Metropolitan Fringe, the northern part of the county which looks across to its metropolitan neighbours of Merseyside and Greater Manchester. Here can be found industrial towns such as Runcorn, Widnes and Warrington together with commuter villages such as Lymm and Prestbury, places which have grown largely in conjunction with developments of the 19th and 20th centuries. Along the eastern edge of Cheshire is the Pennine Border, a more isolated and remote part of the county where the land rises to well over 1500 feet from the line of the Red Rock Fault which divides the soft red sandstone beneath the Cheshire Plain from the harder millstone grit underlying this particular area. The more exposed conditions here seem to have encouraged the hamlets and villages to huddle together for protection within the wooded valleys hidden in the folds of the hills. By way of contrast the Deep South is a rich agricultural area adjoining the border with Staffordshire and Shropshire, characterised by its verdant landscape, while to the west are the Welsh Marches which historically have been far less settled. In earlier times it was an area protected by a line of fortified castle sites stretching from Chester down to Malpas, but

even so the border with Wales frequently moved back and forth in response to the activities of maurauding Welsh bands. Then finally, at the heart of the county, is the Cheshire Plain with the higher ground of the Central Highlands to the west, an important agricultural area but one where the salt towns of Northwich and Middlewich have also played a significant role.

A slightly different division of Cheshire can be made on the basis of history rather than geography. The area in the west of the county, for example, seems to have been important from the very earliest times, and in pre-historic days the Central Highlands were probably the most thickly populated part of the region (demonstrated by the fact that most of Cheshire's hill forts lie within this area, the work of Iron Age man). At a later date Chester itself received prominence as an important Roman settlement, a prominence which it has maintained right up to the present day. A second area to be distinguished centres on the Cheshire Plain where the salt towns of Nantwich, Northwich and Middlewich developed as the principle centres of salt production from well before the Norman period right through the Middle Ages, bringing a flourishing prosperity to the Weaver valley. Then in the 18th and 19th centuries the emphasis shifted again to the eastern part of Cheshire with the growth of the silk and cotton spinning industries. Congleton, Macclesfield and Bollington all achieved special significance at this time through the invention of textile machinery which could be harnessed to power produced by the water wheel. The development

A typical village scene ►

◄ *Eastgate Clock, Chester*

CHESHIRE

of the chemical and oil-refining industries led to yet another shift in emphasis, this time towards the area around the Mersey with the emergence of Widnes and Ellesmere Port as major centres. In very recent years the designation of Warrington and Runcorn New Towns as focal points for growth has further consolidated the importance of this area.

Holford Hall near Plumley ▶

A word needs to be said about the characteristic building materials used in Cheshire, for these have influenced the overall appearance of villages and towns as much as their setting in the physical landscape. Cheshire is rightly famous for its 'black and white' buildings, and few counties have so many timber-framed houses as this one — a situation which developed by virtue of the fact that the occurrence of extensive forests and marshy reedbeds on the Cheshire Plain meant that oak-framing, in conjunction with wattle and daub panels and thatch roofs, was the cheapest and easiest form of construction for domestic buildings up to the 17th century. What we have now is a heritage of some of the loveliest buildings in England, perhaps best typified by such gems as Little Moreton Hall, their classic 'magpie' appearance being obtained by blackening the timbers with tar or pitch and whitening the infill panels. From the 17th

Decorative brick cottage ▶

◀ *Little Moreton Hall*

century onwards bricks came to be the commonly-used building material, made from the clay deposits found on the Cheshire Plain. At first they were only a substitute for stone (used for the chimneys of houses that were otherwise half-timbered) but by the Georgian period they had become the norm in central and west Cheshire, producing some lovely individual brick houses as well as elegant terraces and churches. The other characteristic building material of Cheshire is sandstone, with the western half of the county being dominated by the use of soft red Triassic sandstone which outcrops at various points throughout the Cheshire Plain while the eastern half is characterised by the buff-coloured gritstone from the Carboniferous series of rocks which proved suitable not only for building walls but also in slab-form as a roofing material. Both types of sandstone have been used to great effect in their localities, enhancing the particular style of vernacular architecture being practised.

A Potted History

The earliest remaining evidences of human settlement in Cheshire are the hill forts which have been found on the central sandstone ridge, dating from the early Iron Age. Seven of these forts have been located on the ridge, which as well as providing better settlement sites than the marshy plain below would also have been a major route for pre-historic travel. With the coming of the Romans travel was greatly facilitated by the network of proverbially-straight roads which was established across the Cheshire Plain, Chester being the focal point to which these roads were directed, and for the first time the Plain was recognised as an important corridor of communications. The Romans also brought about many other advances in the area, such as the growth of trade and the mining of ores as well as the extraction of salt, while an important cultural legacy was the adoption of Christianity and its transmission to the Celtic church. When the Romans left Cheshire the territory reverted to the native British, with the Church maintaining its position as a centre of learning.

The general prosperity which Cheshire seems to have enjoyed in the Anglo-Saxon period came to a rather abrupt end with the coming of the Normans, for many villages and large areas of farmland were laid waste by William I in his reprisals following the insurrection which arose here. Consequently the Norman period saw Cheshire develop only as a military zone, with most of the remains from this time being those of fortifications such as Chester Castle, the later castle at Beeston and the baronial castle at Halton. Since the Normans did little

CHESHIRE

Rostherne Mere ▶

Doorway at Chester Cathedral ▶

to stimulate trade and industry little has remained of the domestic architecture, and even ecclesiastical buildings are limited with only the chapels at Prestbury and Shocklach surviving to the present day. Chester was seemingly the one place which maintained any importance, developing its role as a military base and a major port as well as an administrative and judicial centre.

The conquest of Wales in the 13th century was a significant event for Cheshire since the peace which this brought about encouraged both the improvement of farming and the growth of trade. Castles were also improved, church building was increased and monasteries extended their sphere of influence. Continuing prosperity in the 14th and 15th centuries brought about the further growth of towns and villages, and it is from this period that the oldest halls and manors in Cheshire have survived (including Gawsworth Old Hall and Little Moreton Hall) together with some of the county's finest churches.

The 16th and 17th centuries saw the consolidation of this growth, particularly in towns such as Chester and Nantwich where many of the oak-framed houses from this period still remain. There was also a greater variety of buildings constructed to meet developing social needs, including inns and almshouses as well as schools. Farms and farmland were considerably improved in the late 17th and early 18th centuries, with the result that there is a proliferation of farm buildings from this period which have survived into the 20th century. Yet the wind of change which was about to bring in new architectural styles was already evident in buildings such as Lyme Hall where the emphasis was very much upon the classical design. Significant advances were also being made in transport at the same time, particularly in the development of canals — the Mersey and Irwell were improved to

CHESHIRE

Daresbury nuclear research laboratory ▶

provide a route for barges between Liverpool and Manchester, the Weaver was made navigable for salt barges as far as Northwich, and in 1765 the Bridgewater Canal was completed. Later the Trent and Mersey Canal was constructed which, together with the Shropshire Union and Grand Union Canals, joined Cheshire and Liverpool with the Midlands.

The introduction of textile machinery in the 18th century led to a dramatic growth in manufacturing industry and the consequent inception of factories with Macclesfield and Congleton among the first towns to feel the effects of these changes as they developed into important silk centres. Yet the growth of population generally combined with growth in agricultural production also encouraged the expansion of Cheshire's market towns (particularly Chester, Knutsford and Sandbach), demonstrated by the large number of attractive houses which were built during the Georgian and Regency periods. Further changes in the towns were experienced in the Victorian era as a result of new transport developments, such as the coming of the railways and the Manchester Ship Canal, and the change and growth of the salt and chemical industries. It was the latter which led to the rapid expansion of the Weaver salt towns (Northwich, Winsford and Middlewich) and the Mersey chemical towns (Widnes, Warrington and Runcorn), compared with the more stable conditions experienced in the textile and market towns. Changes in the Cheshire countryside during this period were somewhat less dramatic, with the most important being the consolidation and improvement of the

major country estates such as the Grosvenor estate at Eaton near Chester and the Egerton estate at Tatton near Knutsford.

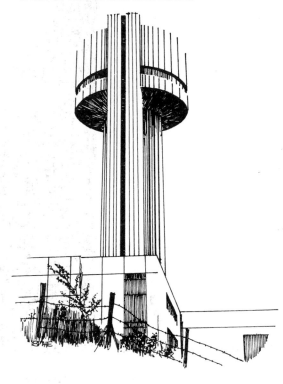

Perhaps it remains to be seen what developments of the 20th century will have the most significant impact upon the face of Cheshire, yet those associated with transport and technology are the ones which spring immediately to mind — particularly the steel arch road bridge across the Mersey at Runcorn, the radio telescopes at Jodrell Bank and the tower of Daresbury nuclear physics laboratory.

Medieval packhorse bridge, Hockenhull Platts ▶

Chapter II
CHESTER

*— Roman foundations
and Victorian imitations*

Chester has quite rightly been described as 'the jewel of the north-west of England', and it is pre-eminent among the treasures of Cheshire. Perhaps the most fascinating aspect of this city is that within a very small area one can see physical evidence of every period of history from Roman times — the street pattern of the Roman fortress, Anglo-Saxon fortifications, medieval churches, Elizabethan timber-framed town houses, Georgian terraces, Victorian restorations and some sensitive 20th century architecture which has respected all that has gone before it. Chester has always prized its architectural heritage, and it was the first city to levy a Conservation Rate to assist with the work of restoring some of its more neglected buildings. Yet it is certainly no static museum piece, but rather a vibrant and lovely place full of people which maintains a faithful witness to its varied and colourful history.

One of the best ways to appreciate Chester is to take a walk around the City Walls, looking inwards along the busy main streets and outwards towards some beautiful surrounding countryside. The continuous walkway on top of the Walls, a circuit of nearly two miles, is unique in this country and encompasses the area of the medieval walled town. The city was originally established and defended as a fortress by the Romans, who enclosed it with a ditch and rampart; this was later replaced by a stone wall using the local red sandstone, and parts of the original Roman wall still survive in the north and eastern stretches. Later expansion of Chester in medieval times led to the demolition of the western and southern Roman walls and the building of new

ones nearer the river, while further repairs and realignments have meant that the walls are now a complex mixture of work from many periods. The towers and gates which are situated at various points along the Walls have also been replaced over the years — in the late 18th and early 19th centuries the Roman and medieval remains of the gates were replaced by elegant new gates in the form of bridges to preserve the walk along the top.

It seems that the condition of the Walls has always been a concern to the people of Chester — even back in medieval times repairs were financed by a special local tax (murage) and the task of maintaining them was the responsibility of the 'murengers', whose accounts can still be seen in the archives of the City Record Office.

An excellent place to start one's walk along the City Walls is at the Watergate on the western side, just above Chester Racecourse. When Chester was a flourishing port in the Middle Ages, the Dee flowed close to the Watergate and all goods entering the city from the port passed through this gate. As early as the 12th century Monk Lucien was declaring:

"Our Chester has also, by the favour of God, a rich and graceful river beneath the City Walls, beautiful and abounding in fish, and on its south side a harbour for ships coming from Aquitaine, Spain, Ireland and Germany, which by Christ's guidance and by the labour and skill of the merchants come and unload at the City bay with many goods, so that comforted in all ways by the grace of God, we may drink wine more often and more plentifully . . ."

Chester Castle ▶

◀ *Grosvenor Bridge*

CHESTER

In 1788 the medieval gate at this point in the Walls was replaced by the present elegant arch, built in attractive red sandstone to the design of Joseph Turner. From the superb vantage point offered by the Watergate one can look eastwards along the line of restored Georgian buildings towards the city centre, catching a fine view of Trinity Church steeple, while in the opposite direction one can look out onto the beautiful green expanse of the racecourse with the tree-lined banks of the River Dee in the distance. The racecourse is known as The Roodee, and like the Walls is a feature unique to Chester — it takes its name from the rood, or cross (the base of which can still be seen), and the word 'eye' which means 'land partly surrounded by water'. In the Middle Ages the people of Chester used the area as a place to graze their cattle, as a place of recreation and as a training ground for soldiers. In the 16th century the football match between the Shoemakers and Drapers Companies began at the Cross on the Roodee, but football violence (obviously not just a modern phenomenon) caused the City Assembly to ban the match in 1540 and replace it firstly by footraces and then by horseraces. This makes Chester Racecourse one of the oldest in the country.

Walking southwards from the Watergate and its elevated position above the queues of traffic on the street below, one has the opportunity to enjoy the peaceful scene of The Roodee contained by a loop in the river. Crossing over Grosvenor Road, the stone-flagged walkway on top of the Walls continues around the southern end of the impressive Chester Castle; rebuilt between 1788 and 1822 to the designs of Thomas Harrison, the central block and two separate wings surround a massive parade ground. As one passes the Castle on the left there is a beautiful view of the Grosvenor Bridge, gracefully spanning the Dee in one single arch. It was again designed by Thomas Harrison and opened by Princess Victoria on 17th October 1832.

Following the Walls round the southern tip of the Castle grounds one comes very close to the slow-moving river, and in the distance there is a view of the Old Dee Bridge which connects Chester to the suburb of Handbridge. It is completely different to the Grosvenor Bridge, its seven irregular arches being built of a deep red sandstone which has been weathered and eroded over a long life. The Old Dee Bridge is probably Roman in origin, although the present structure dates from the 14th century, and up to the 19th century it was the only bridge crossing the river at Chester. It has had quite a chequered history, having fallen down twice in the 13th century and then been considered 'very narrow and dangerous' in the 18th century, but today traffic still makes its way across the bridge and it is a lovely feature of the river, with seagulls wheeling overhead and the roaring weir on its northern side which is said to have been built in the 11th century.

Old Dee Bridge ▶

Siddington Church

Great Budworth

Astbury

CHESTER

At this point the route along the City Walls passes over Bridgegate, originally a medieval gate which guarded the Old Dee Bridge and this particular entrance to the City. The present archway was built in 1782, and from it one can look along Lower Bridge Street to the centre of Chester down the line of one of the original Roman roads. This ceased to be a principal thoroughfare when Grosvenor Street was built in the 1820's, but from Bridgegate one can still see a number of buildings which indicate its former importance. On the left hand side the Bear and Billet Hotel is especially prominent, a black and white timber-framed building dating from 1664, while on the opposite side Bridge Place is an attractive row of Georgian houses.

Bridgegate ▶

From Bridgegate the walkway follows the river up to the south-east corner of the City Walls, and here again there is another splendid view of a third bridge over the Dee. This is the Queen's Park Bridge, a gossamer-like suspension bridge first built in 1852 to link Chester with its new suburb of Queen's Park, whose desirable residences attracted many of Chester's more prosperous citizens. In between the Walls and Queen's Park Bridge is an area known as The Groves, a shady promenade along the riverside which is one of the city's most popular recreation areas. Regattas have been held here since the early 19th century, there is a delightful Edwardian bandstand, and pleasure boats have been cruising up the river to Eaton Hall for more than a hundred years. Access to The Groves from the Walls is by way of the Wishing Steps, constructed in 1785, and then by the Recorder's Steps, named after Roger Comberbach who served as Recorder of Chester from 1700 to 1720.

Further northwards the Walls are punctuated by the Newgate and the Wolfgate, overlooking Pepper Street which follows the line of the south wall of the Roman fortress towards Bridge Street. This particular area of the City is a very interesting mixture of ancient and modern — in one corner just outside the Walls are the Roman Gardens and the northern half of a Roman amphitheatre, while inside the Walls to the north of Pepper Street is the thoroughly modern Grosvenor Shopping Precinct. The Newgate is also modern, its wide stone archway flanked by two towers having been opened in 1938, but it was built alongside the Wolfgate or Pepper Gate which dates from 1608 and is the oldest gateway of the many to be found in Chester.

Back on the Walls again and progressing northwards the walkway becomes more enclosed by buildings on both sides as it reaches the Eastgate and the Eastgate Clock, one of Chester's most photographed features. The Eastgate itself, from which there is a very good view up towards the Cross at the centre of Chester, marks the principal entrance to the City. The present structure was built in 1786 - 89 to replace a narrow medieval gateway, while the highly ornate wrought-iron clock was erected in order to commemorate Queen Victoria's Diamond Jubilee in 1897. Along Eastgate Street, and St Werburgh Street running off it, one is impressed by the number of black and white buildings, but most of them are the result of Victorian restoration work. Prior to 1850 Georgian brick probably predominated, but in the second half of the 19th century an almost complete transformation took place creating a Victorian street of unique character. Several architects were involved, but John Douglas played a particularly important part — the whole of the east side of St. Werburgh Street, with its highly detailed and decorative treatment, was designed and built by him in 1895-9. On the south side of Eastgate the story is very much the same — the Grosvenor Hotel is again a Victorian design, its architect T.M. Penson being one of the first exponents of the half-timber revival and the clients (the Grosvenor family of Eaton Hall) being responsible for much of the 19th century rebuilding of Chester. One other very interesting building is that occupied by Brown's of Chester, with three distinctive architectural styles — one part has a classical facade in the Greek Revival style, another part is an early example of high Victorian Gothic (erected in 1858) while yet another part has a half-timbered frontage also dating from the mid-19th century. Foregate Street, the continuation of Eastgate Street outside the city walls and at one time the Roman Watling Street, also displays a wide variety of building styles along its length.

From Eastgate the City Walls pass by the Cathedral precinct on the left hand side, and the first feature to be seen is the new Bell Tower in the south-east corner. A very impressive concrete structure with brick infilling and clad in slate, it is the first free-standing bell tower to be built for an English cathedral since the 15th century. Beyond it is the Cathedral itself, even now

CHESTER

Chester Cathedral and the new bell-tower ▶

somehow retaining the atmosphere of sanctified seclusion which is must have enjoyed when it was first founded as an abbey in 1092 by Hugh Lupus, Earl of Chester. For five centuries the building remained a monastery with widespread lands and considerable power, and it was not until after its dissolution in 1540 that it was made a Cathedral. The fine cloisters and refectory of the abbey still exist, providing an insight into the manner of life and surroundings of the monks who lived there. Although the Cathedral illustrates architectural styles from almost every century — and as such is a microcosm of Chester as a whole — its appearance today owes much to Sir Gilbert Scott who carried out extensive repairs and restoration work during the latter half of the nineteenth century.

Just beyond the Cathedral a separate footpath takes the visitor down from the Walls into Abbey Street, a detour well worth making since this is a very picturesque cobbled street running between Abbey Square and the small Kaleyards Gate. Tradition says that in 1275 the monks at the Abbey were allowed to make this gateway in the wall to give them access to their vegetable gardens, provided that the gate was locked each night — a rule which is still observed even now. Abbey Street has some fine Georgian houses on the northern side, including the Bishop's House (dating from the late 18th century) with its walled garden in front. The lovely cobbled road continues into Abbey Square and draws the inquisitive visitor into

this quite delightful and secluded space tucked away behind the busy Northgate Street. The Square was built by the Church Authorities between 1750 and 1830 as an adjunct to the Cathedral, and although all the houses were built individually and differ in detail they form a unified composition and are the nearest approach to a formal Georgian square in the City. On the north side three of the houses have particularly fine large doorways, while the whole area is beautifully complemented by a central walled green with trees and a tall stone pillar which came originally from the late 17th century Town Hall known as the Exchange which was destroyed by fire in 1862. Jealously guarding the tranquility of the Square is the Abbey Gateway, a sandstone arch dating from the 14th century with the Muniments Room above where Abbey records were stored. In medieval times the annual abbey fair was held here and it was also the first location of the Whitsun Mystery Plays.

Back on the Walls, the walk follows the stone parapet in a straight line northwards to King Charles' Tower, so called because it was from here in September 1645 that King Charles I watched the closing stages of the defeat of his forces by the Parliamentarians in an area between Hoole Heath and the City, a battle which had started earlier in the day at Rowton Moor. This 70-foot high sandstone structure was built on the site of the north-eastern tower of the Roman fortress, and although it has been altered and restored over the years it still

CHESTER

King Charles' Tower on the Walls ▶

retains its medieval appearance. It was originally called the Newton Tower and then later on the Phoenix Tower, the phoenix being the emblem of the Painters, Glaziers, Embroiderers and Stationers Company who used it as a meeting house in the 17th century. Above the small door opening out onto the Walls one can see a phoenix and the date 1613 carved into the stonework; there is also a phoenix on the weather vane, but this is probably much more recent.

The Walls now turn westwards to the Northgate, and along most of this section they are bounded by the Shropshire Union Canal which is set in a deep ravine cut out of solid rock well below them. Like the other entrances into Chester the Northgate was rebuilt as an archway, erected in 1808 to the designs of Thomas Harrison. From it one can look away from the City and see the Bluecoat School on the left hand side, founded in 1700 by Bishop Stratford to house and educate poor boys in an attempt to combat the growth of vice and debauchery. The southern wing of the school housed the Chapel of Little St. John, to which condemned criminals were taken from the City Gaol which occupied the old Northgate, and the two were linked by the graceful single-span sandstone arch across the canal known as the Bridge of Sighs. Although now disused, this can still be seen from the road-bridge over the canal at this point.

CHESTER

From Northgate the Walls make a gradual descent to the north-west corner of their two mile circuit, the canal veering away slightly on the northern side to the Canal Basin. Although the views into the City from this section are not especially significant, there are some excellent panoramas of the Welsh Hills in the far distance. A little way down on the right hand side, just before the modern St. Martin's Gate over the Inner Ring Road, one can see the old watch tower called Morgan's Mount. Named after the commander of a gun battery which was placed on this tower during the Siege of Chester in 1644-46, this point would have been the north-west corner of the Roman fortress. Further beyond St. Martin's Gate is the Goblin Tower, also known as Pemberton's Parlour because of a ropemaker who worked there. Originally a circular tower straddling the wall here, it was rebuilt in a semi-circular form in the early 18th century and again in 1894. On the tower there is a stone tablet commemorating the repairs which were carried out between 1701 –1708 and mentioning the Murengers, the officials responsible for administering the tax required to maintain the walls.

A flight of narrow steps leading down from the Walls, just past the railway line, provides the opportunity for another little excursion to investigate a different facet of Chester's history. Passing along the tow path beneath a bridge one enters the Canal Basin with its fascinating collection of buildings from Chester's industrial era. At one end is an Iron Roving Bridge, built to enable a barge horse to cross over to the opposite side of the canal without the towing rope being detached. To the left of this bridge is a dry dock which was built in 1798 in conjunction with the nearby boatyards, while on the far side is a footbridge over Bridge Lock which descends into the Dee Basin where a last series of locks gives entry to the river. Walking back towards the Walls away from the Canal Basin, one can see the Northgate Locks on the left hand side — these form the junction between the Shropshire and Ellesmere Canals and were built by Thomas Telford. Cut out from solid sandstone, the locks originally formed a staircase of five levels but were later enlarged to form the present three locks rising steeply to the Northgate section of the canal.

The north-west corner of the medieval walls is marked by Bonewaldesthorne's Tower, really little more than a defended entrance to a spur wall leading to the Water Tower. Although now standing in the midst of some beautifully landscaped grounds, this tower once served as the main defence for Chester's harbour when the River Dee flowed below and ships were moored alongside. As the river silted up and

The Roman Garden ▶

◄ *The Water Tower*

changed its course the Water Tower ceased to have the significance for which it was built, but it survives as an important medieval monument and a reminder of Chester's former significance as a port. Now standing about 75 feet high, it was built (together with the spur wall) between 1322 and 1325 by John de Helpeston at a cost of £100.

The last part of our round-Chester tour takes us south along the Walls back towards the starting point at Watergate, with the appropriately named City Walls Road running alongside. Immediately on the left hand side is the Royal Infirmary, dating from 1761 but added to several times; it was supported by subscribers who had the right to recommend patients for treatment. Further down on the same side is Stanley Place, its two elegant terraces making up one of Chester's few planned Georgian developments. Dating from 1778 it is composed of individually-built merchant houses conforming to an overall pattern three storeys high. On one of the houses a fire insurance plate can still be seen, a feature repeated on several other Georgian houses in different parts of the City. Finally, just before arriving back at the Watergate, one of the last houses along City Walls Road has a rare sedan chair porch. A more common feature of the Georgian period, this porch with a door on each side allowed the passenger to enter the chair direct from the house.

The City Walls provide both the casual and the serious visitor with a marvellous opportunity to get an almost 'bird's-eye' view of the different parts of Chester and its wide range of building styles. Yet it is also important to develop an historical perspective of the City's development, since one of its special features is its vast architectural heritage stretching back across the centuries. To begin with the Roman remains which can be observed in Chester include the main street pattern of the legionary fortress which was built here — the present Eastgate Street and Watergate Street correspond to the Via Principalis, Bridge Street follows the line of the Via Praetoria and Northgate Street the line of the Via Decumana. The fortress was called Deva and was the base of the 20th Valeria Victrix legion which served here for 200 years; it was typically Roman,

15

CHESTER

Roman amphitheatre viewed from the Walls ▶

Part of St. John's Church ▶

being rectangular in shape and having the principal buildings at its centre. Although the fortress was smaller than the present day walled area of the City, a substantial section of the existing walls are Roman in origin and open to view (especially around the north-eastern corner). Another feature of Roman origin is the amphitheatre, to be found just outside the City Walls to the south-east — this oval arena must have played an important role in the social life of Roman Chester and is thought to have measured 190 feet by 162 feet with accommodation for about 7,000 people. On the other side of the river in Handbridge are the remains of a quarry which began to be used about AD100 when the Roman fortress was largely rebuilt in stone (originally having been of timber). Here is a unique Roman monument within a small recess in the sandstone rock, a shrine to the Roman goddess Minerva.

Chester was also a significant settlement in Anglo-Saxon times, and at the beginning of the 10th century it was refortified after having been deserted for several hundred years. It was probably about 907 when the walls of the old Roman fortress were extended to the line of the present City Walls. St. John's Church to the east of the Roman amphitheatre is also from the Anglo-Saxon period, probably being founded in the early 10th century. It was obviously extended over time, and from 1075 to 1102 it was the Cathedral church for

Chester. With disuse part of the church on the eastern side collapsed, and now remains as a dramatic ruin.

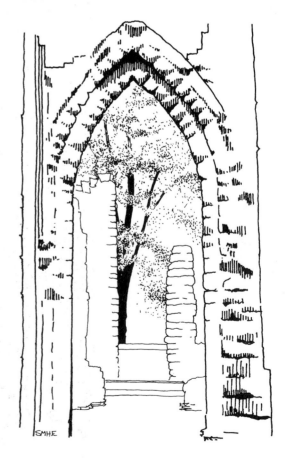

CHESTER

Much more has been left to us from medieval times in Chester, the City achieving some prominence because of its strategic position in military campaigns against the Welsh and the Irish. Probably the most important feature is the Cathedral, having originally been founded in the 11th century as the monastery of St. Werburgh and then becoming a Cathedral after the Dissolution. Particularly impressive are the great nave and the woodwork of the choir stalls, as well as the chapter house and the refectory which remain from the old monastic buildings. A number of other Chester churches have medieval roots too, including the very small sandstone church of St. Olave on Lower Bridge Street and St. Peter's Church at the junction of Watergate Street and Eastgate Street. This latter church was probably an Anglo-Saxon foundation but it has an interior dating from the 14th or 15th century; it is quite unusual in that it is almost square in shape and has no nave. Hidden behind St. Peter's is its tiny churchyard, now a quiet paved 'oasis' which is a short-cut for the pedestrian between Northgate Street and Watergate Street.

Surrounding this secluded corner are some very attractively restored buildings which have given an old part of the City a new lease of life.

Among the most important features of Chester, as important as the City Walls, are the Rows. These two-level shopping galleries are unique to Chester and are thought to have first developed during the Middle Ages. They provide not only a very civilised shopping environment but also some superb vantage points from which to view different parts of the City, and the best examples are to be seen on Bridge Street, Eastgate Street and Watergate Street. Reached by steps from the pavement, the Rows consist of covered galleries above the shops at street level; each section of the Rows has a 'stall' where goods are often displayed and from where people can watch the street scene below. It appears that the origin of the Rows has never been explained in a satisfactory way — one theory proposes a gradual development while another one suggests that they could have been built as a town planning exercise after the fire of 1278 which destroyed most of Chester.

The Rows ►

CHESTER

Documentary evidence, however, seems to support a gradual development lasting from the 13th until the 18th century, with the three components of the Rows (stalls at street level, cellars and the Rows themselves) all being in existence by the 14th century. Whatever their origin, the Rows are a wonderful endowment to the City from the medieval period — people are able to shop in comparative peace free from the bustle of busy streets below, and the centre of Chester has remained compact and personal.

The steady growth of Chester in the 16th and 17th centuries was characterised by many fine timber-framed houses built at that time, now an important and well-known feature of the City with their crisp black and white facades which were the source of inspiration for later Victorian imitations. The 'Bear and Billet' Hotel on Lower Bridge Street is a classic example which has already been mentioned, but a little further up on the corner of Grosvenor Street and Lower Bridge Street is 'The Falcon', its newly restored timberwork faithfully bringing to life this fine example of 17th century architecture. The elevation looking out onto Lower Bridge Street is particularly attractive, with its long continuous line of windows on the first floor and underneath this is a row of 'clover-leaf' decorative patterns. It was at one time the town house of the Grosvenor family and in 1643 Richard Grosvenor petitioned the City Assembly for permission to enlarge this house by enclosing the Row beneath it. Another example, again on Lower Bridge Street, is Ye

The Bear and Billet Hotel ▶

◀ *The Falcon,*
Lower Bridge Street

CHESTER

Gamul House ▶

Olde King's Head which was the town house of a prominent landed family. Again dating from the 17th century, its top timber-framed storey underneath three gables overhangs the pavement below. More buildings of the same period are to be found on Watergate Street, with the highly decorated Bishop Lloyd's House being one of the best timber-framed buildings in Chester. Although God's Providence House was reconstructed in 1862, it still has the original date of 1652 inscribed upon it together with the inscription 'God's Providence is Mine Inheritance' which celebrates the fact that the inhabitants were spared from the plague. Towards the bottom of Watergate Street and just across the other side of the Inner Ring Road is Stanley Palace, built

in 1591 by Peter Warburton and then becoming the town house of the Stanleys of Alderley in the 17th century.

From the 17th century onwards a greater variety of buildings emerged in Chester as the use of brick and stone became much more commonplace and new architectural styles developed. Gamul House on Lower Bridge Street is a fine Jacobean town house which marks the transition between two of Chester's distinctive architectural forms, its 18th century brick facade with large iron casements and elliptical windows concealing a timber framework. The building dates from about 1620 and was the home of Sir Francis Gamul, a wealthy City merchant who was also Mayor of

CHESTER

Chester at one time, and it is thought that Charles I stayed here during the Siege of Chester in 1645. The front doorway of the house is really at first-floor level, confirming other evidence that a typical Chester Row once passed through the building, and along the raised pavement are the cottages of Gamul Terrace which were built in the middle of the 19th century. Gamul House is a classic example of how much history can be revealed through careful restoration, the building being rescued from the point of collapse in the early 1970's — a considerable section of oak framing with wattle and daub infill has been uncovered, stone-framed doors and windows have come to light and in repairing the 18th century front door it was found that this had been planted upon the face of a fine oak-studded 16th century door which has now been re-used elsewhere in the house. There is also a carved 17th century sandstone fireplace, only brought to light after many layers of paint had been stripped away, and a plastered segmental ceiling ornamented with carved oak decorations.

Although Chester's significance as a port had been diminishing throughout the Middle Ages, its steady growth as an administrative and market town encouraged further developments in the form of Georgian squares, terraces and many attractive individual buildings. Abbey Square within the Cathedral precincts has already been mentioned, and it is probably the best piece of Georgian urban design within the City; while King Street, sloping gently from Northgate Street towards the Inner Ring Road, also has some very attractive houses from the 18th and 19th centuries which have been recently restored and have made this part of Chester a highly desirable residential area. The most distinguished Georgian buildings in Chester were designed by Thomas Harrison, who was responsible for the group of buildings which now occupy the site of Chester Castle, overlooking the River Dee. According to Pevsner and Hubbard, what Harrison produced here is one of the most powerful monuments of the Greek Revival in the whole of England — a fitting replacement for the original Castle which had been founded by William the Conqueror on the site of the Saxon fortification and had become the seat of the Earls of Chester and the centre of government of the County Palatine.

The Georgian era was marked not only by beautiful and majestic architecture but also by the coming of the canal, largely developed with the hope of attracting trade from Liverpool and the Midlands. Some attempts had been made in the 17th century to improve the navigability of the River Dee, by this time heavily choked by silt, but with little success. Then in 1737 an eight mile stretch of the river was canalised in an endeavour to create a tidal channel, but the

Abbey Square ▶

CHESTER

estuarine sands continued to accumulate. Finally, in 1771 the idea was hit upon of a canal to link the new cut of the Dee with the new Trent and Mersey Canal at Middlewich, but this proved to be economically unsuccessful and by 1790 it had fallen into disuse.

A new scheme was then proposed for a waterway to connect the Mersey, Dee and Severn and in 1793 an Act of Parliament authorised the building of the Ellesmere Canal, so-called after the town of Ellesmere in Shropshire which was at the heart of the system. Branch lines were to be cut east and west to serve agriculture and industry, and the first part of the canal to be completed was between the Chester Basin and the River Mersey in 1795. Sixty one years after the first cut of the Chester Canal a link was made with the Trent and Mersey Canal near Middlewich in 1833, thereby connecting the Ellesmere — Chester canal to the main network. Yet in the end these efforts proved too late in the face of competition from the steam engine, and the canal gradually lost trade to the railways. Despite this rather unhappy history there are some very interesting features associated with

the canal and several of these have been mentioned already (e.g. Tower Wharf and the Iron Roving Bridge by the Canal Basin). Close to the Basin is Harvest House, a fine early 19th century building which was once the headquarters of the Shropshire Union Railway and Canal Company; this and the adjoining buildings contained warehouses, offices and a hotel for the passengers of packet boats.

The Victorian influence upon Chester has been undeniably significant if not immediately obvious to the casual visitor. This is because much of the architecture from this period is an imitation of medieval half-timbering, and in some cases it is difficult to distinguish Victorian reproductions from the real thing. Indeed, it has been estimated that 95% of the 'black and white' architecture in Chester is Victorian and after. Yet the quality and standard of the 'mock' medieval is such that in no way can one feel cheated; rather, the Victorian contribution has created an overriding unity to a city which has a tremendous diversity of architectural styles. Eastgate Street is the example 'par excellence' of Victorian intervention — prior to 1850

Tower Wharf by the Canal Basin ▶

CHESTER

St. Werburgh Street ▶

Georgian brick predominated, but in the second half of the 19th century an almost complete transformation took place. This is particularly true of the north side of the street (between Northgate Street and St. Werburgh Street) where the work of four different architects can be seen along one frontage. The east side of St. Werburgh Street is another example of reproduction 'black and white' architecture, this being John Douglas (the Duke of Westminster's architect) at his best and most decorative.

As well as their distinctive interest in rebuilding and restoration, Victorian architects also produced a variety of individual buildings which are good in their own right. The railway station is especially attractive, built of brick and stone in an Italianate style, while the Town Hall in Northgate Street is 'imitation Gothic' in red and grey sandstone with a central tower rising to a height of 160 feet.

Meanwhile, the twentieth century is making its own quiet contribution to the high quality of Chester's architectural heritage, fitting in with much older buildings and paying a very real respect to the City's past. The Grosvenor Shopping Precinct is an excellent example, tucked away between Bridge Street and the City Walls yet very accessible to the pedestrian, a modern development with an intimate environment – even the multi-storey car park is as unobtrusive as one could wish. By virtue of

23

CHESTER

the classically-styled St. Michael's Arcade, the Grosvenor Precinct is effectively an extension of the Rows, and as such is an example of architectural good taste and ingenuity.

Perhaps the last word in this description of Chester should deal with The Cross, since it has had great significance in the City's history. The High Cross stood on its present site at the junction of Chester's four principal streets from 1407 until the English Civil War (when it was demolished), and it was here that merchants would make their bargains. For centuries it was the centre of City government, with the Mayor and Aldermen meeting in the Pentice — originally a timber-framed structure built against the south side of St. Peter's Church.

From the Pentice they watched performances of the Mystery Plays and celebrated the defeat of the Spanish Armada in 1588. Yet this was also the scene of riots and disturbances — master weavers and their journeymen fought at The Cross in 1399 and during the 1732 election the Pentice was stormed by an angry mob. Although the Cross was demolished during the Civil War, most of the pieces were preserved and after a period in the Roman Gardens it was eventually restored to its present and rightful position in 1975. So once again The Cross is very much the focal point of Chester, presiding over a city which embraces within its Walls the marks of every significant period in our history since Roman times.

The Cross

View down Eastgate Street ▶

◀ *St. Michael's Arcade*

Ancient and modern in Macclesfield

Snow-covered fields near Rainow

Little Moreton Hall

Town Crier in Chester

Chapter III
THE TOWNS
— medieval and modern

Much of the diversity in architectural style as well as in social and economic development which is particularly found in Chester is repeated in Cheshire towns generally, capturing a flavour of the county's history in their streets and buildings — although it is perhaps rather surprising for those who do not know Cheshire well that many of the towns owe their present significance to industry rather than to agriculture. For example, the towns of Macclesfield, Bollington and Congleton grew up largely through the textile industries which were established there, and consequently the dominant impression is one of mills and terraced streets, but set very pleasantly against the backcloth of the Pennine Hills. At the heart of the Cheshire Plain are the salt towns of Northwich, Middlewich and Winsford lying in the midst of a characteristic landscape of flashes and meres, while not far away to the south is Crewe whose existence is solely due to the railways and to the engine works which were established here to serve them. By contrast its near-neighbour Nantwich is very largely Elizabethan in appearance, a lovely town full of black and white oak-framed buildings linked together by narrow winding streets and tantalising passageways. Then there is Knutsford, a Georgian market town with an appearance of elegance and prosperity which is particularly evident along its two main streets leading up to the impressive entrance into Tatton Park. Runcorn, Widnes and Warrington are clustered along the banks of the Mersey and are towns largely of this century, especially the first and last which were designated as New Towns in the past two decades. Then finally there is Malpas, a small but rather appealing country town which is just quietly minding its own business in the south-west corner of the county. So each of the Cheshire towns has its ambient characteristics peculiar to itself, as will be discovered from the selection included here.

Whereas Chester affords the visitor a glimpse into just about every period of history, **Macclesfield** offers the opportunity of discovering in detail how people lived and worked at one particular point in time. In this small town one can clearly discern the life and times of the early industrial era within a fascinating display of old mills, terraced cottages, town houses and non-conformist churches. Walking along the narrow streets and back passages one is soon aware of Macclesfield's Georgian glory and its former pre-eminence in the silk industry which heralded much of the later Industrial Revolution.

Macclesfield's origins actually lie in the Middle Ages, and its medieval heritage is still evident from the Parish Church and the street layout which has largely remained unaltered. This medieval core — embracing the church, the Town Hall and the Market Place — is still very much the focal point of the town, its elevated position on the bluff of an escarpment giving superb views out across to the surrounding hills. From the valley below the position of the church looks spectacular, occupying a site which was obviously chosen for its defensive qualities and even now is accessible only by a steep climb up attractively cobbled walkways or along the winding stone-flagged pavements of Church Street. The change in levels, the dominance of the church and the 'wild' banks of the hill upon which it stands all contribute to the atmosphere of a medieval town which this part of Macclesfield still retains.

Macclesfield was mentioned in Domesday Book and received its charter in 1261, constituting it as a free borough with a merchant guild and according certain accustomed privileges to the burgesses while at the same time imposing the usual obligation of grinding corn at the King's mill and baking at his oven. The Parish Church (originally known as the Chapel of All Saints and All Hallows) was founded in 1278 by Eleanor of Castile, the wife of Edward I, although it was largely rebuilt in the 18th century and again in 1901. Now the oldest part is the intricately decorated Savage Chapel on the southern side, having been built by Thomas Savage (the Archbishop of York) between 1501 and 1507. The church is perhaps most famous for its interior features, having more large monuments than any other church in Cheshire — of particular interest are the alabaster effigies of the Savage family, the splendid late 17th century canopied figure of Earl Rivers in black and white marble, and the Pardon Brass of Roger Legh from 1506.

Adjoining the churchyard is the triangular-shaped Market Place, this arrangement being a typical medieval form. Still the recognisable centre of the town, it must have been the social and business 'hub' even in the earliest days and the market stalls which formerly filled this space extended down Church Street to the lower market at Waters Green. The Market Cross, still standing in the centre of the Market Place but now in a somewhat truncated form, was the place from which proclamations and public notices were read out to the townspeople, and it was here that the yeomen and archers of the borough must have assembled before marching to the Battle of Bosworth Field and again to Flodden Field in 1513. The site now covered by the present Town Hall was once occupied by the ancient Guildhall while nearby was the King's Oven where the people were compelled to bake their

THE TOWNS

bread. Just behind the church were the Gutters — a fitting name for what were in medieval days the slums of the town. It was probably in this period that the low-lying Waters Green was connected with the upper part of the town by the series of steps and terraces now known as Step Hill, the 108 steps and Brunswick Hill — although the latter was originally known as Goose Lane Hill since it was down here that ducks and geese were driven to the river below.

So for much of its early history Macclesfield was a market town, its medieval origins even today evident in the atmosphere to be experienced around the Parish Church — particularly enjoyed by the visitor on foot wandering down the picturesque Church Street with its stone setts and original shop fronts, or round the back of the church along the quiet Churchside with its two rows of terraced houses which are now largely the offices of well-to-do solicitors. The elegant Greek Revival style of the Town Hall, first built in 1823, introduced a new element of grandeur to the scene and provided a new focus for the town, indicative of Macclesfield's later prosperity as an industrial centre.

Just as topography was very much the deciding factor in the development of medieval Macclesfield, so it was with Macclesfield's early industrial growth which was centred upon the Park Green area to the south of the old town — water power available from the River Bollin here encouraged the construction of mills which replaced the domestic methods of production prevailing before 1750. Park Green

Doorway of 36 Park Green ▶

itself developed as a second centre of Macclesfield by the end of the 18th century, and with its mix of churches, public buildings, shops and large houses grouped around the Green it forms a striking image of Macclesfield's industrial history. It was here that Charles Roe, the father of industrial growth in the town, first set up his business as Silk Button and Twist Manufacturer on Parsonage Green in 1744, the site now occupied by the modern office building named Silk House. In 1756 he introduced machinery into his mill and so brought the Industrial Revolution to Macclesfield, and in the course of the next hundred years the town became the acknowledged centre of the silk industry in this country.

Park Green is an excellent starting point from which to begin one's journey of discovery into Macclesfield's industrial past. At the southern end of the Green itself is the Georgian Mill, built in 1785 with dignified Georgian proportions and an elegant clock face, while on the opposite side is 36 Park Green, a large Georgian house with an impressive doorway which became the town's first lending library in 1770. Georgian doorways are a particularly characteristic feature of Macclesfield, and wherever you go they can be seen in a tremendous variety of styles — some with bold columns and pediments, some with decorative fanlights beneath rounded arches, and others with steps and handrails leading to the door itself. It would be hard to find a more interesting range of doorways anywhere else, and all of them seem to extend an invitation for the casual passer-by to stop and take a closer look.

Just around the corner, at the junction with Sunderland Street, is Park Green House which was built by Charles Roe for the first vicar of Christ Church towards the end of the 18th century. It is a particularly attractive town house with unusual curved gables and a fine Venetian window with an open balustrade above the door. Sunderland Street itself was developed in the early 19th century as a commercial street serving the lower part of the town with small shops — here again one can see more interesting doorways and also the Wesley Chapel, built in 1779 and an example of the town's many non-conformist churches. Mill workers in this area lived largely to the south and west of Park Green and on the south side of Park Street one can still see an example of a late 18th century industrial community consisting of weavers' cottages, chapels, schools and shops.

Up the hill from Park Green is Roe Street, where there are other buildings to be found

THE TOWNS

Park Green ▶

Doorway at the Sunday School on Roe Street ▶

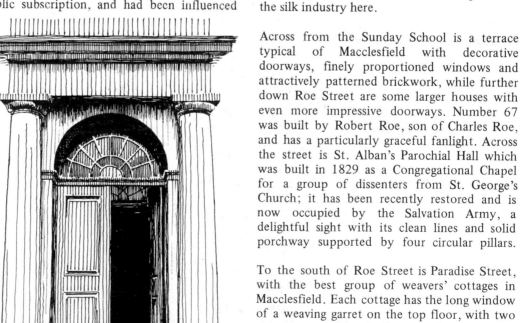

which are indicative of the town's industrial fervour and history of religious dissent. On the right hand side is the massive Sunday School, four storeys high and said to have accommodated 2,500 pupils. It was built in 1814 by John Whittaker, the cost of £5,639 being met by public subscription, and had been influenced by the break-away movement centred upon Christ Church which was founded by Charles Roe. Now no longer filled with the chatter of children, the Sunday School is being converted into a Heritage Centre focussing upon the history of Macclesfield and the development of the silk industry here.

Across from the Sunday School is a terrace typical of Macclesfield with decorative doorways, finely proportioned windows and attractively patterned brickwork, while further down Roe Street are some larger houses with even more impressive doorways. Number 67 was built by Robert Roe, son of Charles Roe, and has a particularly graceful fanlight. Across the street is St. Alban's Parochial Hall which was built in 1829 as a Congregational Chapel for a group of dissenters from St. George's Church; it has been recently restored and is now occupied by the Salvation Army, a delightful sight with its clean lines and solid porchway supported by four circular pillars.

To the south of Roe Street is Paradise Street, with the best group of weavers' cottages in Macclesfield. Each cottage has the long window of a weaving garret on the top floor, with two stone steps and handrails up to the front door, and the whole terrace has been beautifully restored down to the very last detail.

Christ Church, built by Charles Roe at his own expense in 1776, is a rather austere brick

THE TOWNS

Jordangate House ▶

Charles Roe House ▶

building standing in its own expansive grounds on Bridge Street. The existence of this church was really due to Roe's own involvement in the religious differences which seem to have characterised Macclesfield during this time — having fallen out with the established church he commissioned the building of Christ Church with the instruction that the tower should be higher than that of St. Michael's. Obviously a classic case of one-upmanship if ever there was one! Inside the church the most notable feature is the exceptionally fine monument to Roe himself, depicting in relief his enterprises within the town (the church, the old Park Green Mill with its water wheel and the copper works with their smoking chimneys). Further along Bridge Street one has a view of St. Alban's Church away to the left, with probably the finest interior of any church building in the town. Designed in 1838 by the leading Gothic Revival architect A.W.N. Pugin, its large west tower was unfortunately never finished, but inside the very slender stone piers add to the impression of height and space.

Bridge Street continues northwards to Chestergate, a narrow shopping street which was an important thoroughfare even in medieval times. Little of its medieval character remains now, with most of the frontages being substantially altered in the 18th and 19th centuries, but there is a very satisfying view of the Town Hall at the far end of the street with its classical facade completely dominating the scene. Along Chestergate is the house which was most likely the home of Charles Roe (number 62), a provincial version of a Baroque town house built about 1700, and one of the most impressive in Macclesfield. The front

doorway has even more decorative touches to it than usual, while inside there is a massive carved staircase. A similarly-proportioned building is Jordangate House on Jordangate, the main entry into the town from the north bringing the visitor swiftly and dramatically into the Market Place. Built in 1728, this is a beautiful Georgian house with large windows and an intricately detailed door-surround looking out imperiously onto the street below.

It was at one time the residence of John Brocklehurst, grandfather of Macclesfield's first MP and a member of the famous silk manufacturing family. The Brocklehursts had come to prominence in the button trade of the 1740's, and by the 19th century were the most important local family and the largest silk firm in the country. Standing opposite is another 18th century residence, Cumberland House, so called because in 1745 the Duke of Cumberland stayed here as he pursued Bonnie Prince Charlie after the defeat at Derby.

One of the most interesting churches in Macclesfield, and certainly the most unobtrusive, is the Unitarian Chapel hidden behind other buildings on King Edward Street, along which a neat porticoed entrance guards the narrow passageway leading to the chapel and the tiny stone-flagged courtyard in front of it. This small and friendly stone building is the oldest dissenting chapel in the town and is an intriguing reminder of the religious struggles of the 17th century, having been built in 1689 immediately after the passing of the Toleration Act which granted freedom of worship to non-conformists. The style and design of the chapel is exactly the same as in other Unitarian churches built at this time (for example in

THE TOWNS

Knutsford and Wilmslow) — two storeys with mullioned windows and entrances at both ends of the building with doorways into both the upper and lower storeys, the upper storeys being reached by narrow staircases running along part of the front of the chapel. The simplicity of the exterior is matched by the intimacy of the interior, with a good deal of attractive woodwork and an organ dating from 1876.

More Macclesfield doorways . . .

▶

. . . on Bridge Street

. . . on Roe Street

From King Edward Street one can return to Chestergate by the side of the new Council Offices and through a narrow passage under the archway of Bate Hall Hotel. This appropriately takes us back in time to our medieval starting point, since the small lead-paned mullioned windows at the rear of Bate Hall and the carved beam over the passageway show that this is a 16th or early 17th century building. Although the front has been greatly altered, its antiquity is evident from the timberwork inside. It was at one time the town house of the Stopford family, later the Earls of Courtown, who founded the Courtown Ironworks which were situated in the area where the new Council Offices now stand.

. . . on Chestergate

In many respects Macclesfield is a delightfully surprising place. Delightful because of its small market-town intimacy which it still retains, and surprising because here within sight of the lower Pennines is a precious picture of early industrial life as it encompassed ordinary working people. Thankfully, the value of

Macclesfield's heritage is coming to be recognised for its true worth and is being preserved by local people for the appreciation of future generations.

The small town of **Bollington**, just three miles north of Macclesfield, has much in common with its larger neighbour, since it also owes its present form to the Industrial Revolution. Yet Bollington's heritage stems from cotton rather than from silk, and with its impressive old mills

31

THE TOWNS

and attractive stone-built houses it is a unique spot in a predominantly rural county such as Cheshire. One of its most endearing features is its location, delightfully enclosed by the surrounding hills and acting as a natural gateway to the Pennines. If Macclesfield is a lively reminder of the silk industry in Georgian times, Bollington must be a picture in miniature of Victorian enterprise and the more enlightened aspects of the cotton trade. It bears its title of 'The Happy Valley' proudly and justifiably, unconcerned that it is perhaps a little less well-known than it really deserves, and thankful that a large part of old Bollington has been appropriately designated as a Conservation Area on the basis of its valley location, its natural stone buildings and its historical associations with the Industrial Revolution.

Although those who compiled the Domesday Survey ignored Bollington, it is fairly certain that a settlement existed in the area in Saxon times. Its name is probably derived from two Saxon words meaning the town, settlement or farm of 'Bollo' — not directly from the River Bollin which runs three miles to the west of the town. Up to the 18th century Bollington was a peaceful agricultural community made up of a string of hamlets along the main road from Macclesfield to Pott Shrigley and included within the ecclesiastical parish of Prestbury. A number of farms from this early period have survived to the present day, including

Bollington Hall Farm on Wellington Road which is probably the town's oldest building and was the site of the Black Prince's corn mill built around 1360. In the late 18th century the first stirrings of industrial change began to be felt when a number of water-powered mills for cotton cloth manufacture were built in the area, following the example of Arkwright's famous mill at Cromford near Matlock. A number of mills and pools from this period are still to be seen in the area to the south of Bollington known as Ingersley Clough, and one of the mills here had a 56 foot-diameter water wheel which was the second largest in the country at the time. Bollington's early industrial development was really the result of the enterprise of one or two significant families, with the Gaskells and the Mellors being particularly important. It was the Gaskells who built Ingersley Hall and White Nancy, Bollington's well-known landmark on the top of Kerridge Hill which was erected to commemorate the Battle of Waterloo. Yet it was the Swindells family which eventually came to have most influence upon the fortunes of the town among the leading cotton manufacturers — Martin Swindells acquired the lease for the Ingersley Vale and Rainow mills early in the nineteenth century and then went on to build two much larger mills by the side of the canal, the Clarence Mill and the Adelphi Mill. These magnificent examples of industrial entrepreneurship, with their tall red-brick chimneys reaching to the skies, have dominated

Bollington seen from Kerridge Hill ▶

THE TOWNS

this small town for nearly one and a half centuries — their location by the Macclesfield Canal, built above the rest of Bollington, accentuates their huge but nicely balanced proportions as they admire each other from either side of the valley. Even until comparatively recently these two mills were the principal employers of labour in the town, but the recession in the textile industry put an end to this as mill after mill closed down or had to be turned over to another use.

The effect of the Industrial Revolution upon Bollington was dramatic and was reflected in the rapid growth of the town in the first half of the 19th century. At the height of its prosperity there were thirteen mills packed into this little corner of Cheshire's green and pleasant land, built by the Swindells family, the Greg family (also involved in Quarry Bank Mill at Styal) and by other entrepreneurs such as George Antrobus, Joseph Brooke and Thomas Oliver. Further stimulus to local industry came with the construction of the Macclesfield Canal, its massive viaduct stretching over the main road dominating the town visually while effectively separating one half of the town from the other. Most of the buildings in the older part of Bollington (to the east of the canal) date from this period of rapid industrialisation and population growth between 1800 and 1850. Local sandstone from small quarries in the town and from nearby Kerridge was available as a building material which was not only attractive and weathered

well but which split easily into thin sheets for roofing and paving. It is this predominance of local stone which gives Bollington its distinctive atmosphere, reminiscent of other mill towns in the valleys of Lancashire and Yorkshire. The beginning of the 19th century saw the construction of many of the terraced cottages which survive today, such as those along Queen Street and the lower part of Church Street and Lord Street, while in Ingersley Road one can see the whole history of the town's accommodation for its cotton workers since the houses here were built progressively from 1820 to 1865. At one end the cottages are small and simply built, while at the other end the houses are larger and more detailed in style, reflecting the greater prosperity of the mid-Victorian era.

There are many other interesting features in Bollington from this same period, particularly among the terraced streets which huddle together in the valley bottom. The old core of the town around Water Street and High Street has remained remarkably intact — a delightful little area with its rows of terraced cottages interspersed with old shops which still have their original shopfronts. Here also is the Market Place, just off High Street, with the unusual market booths along one side of the square facing onto a central green. In a somewhat more regal style are the mill owners' houses, such as Limefields House and Rock Bank (built for the Brooke and the Swindells families respectively), enjoying a more detached situation higher up on the hillsides above the valley.

Market Place ▶

33

THE TOWNS

As in Macclesfield, there is a wealth of churches and chapels which were built in the last century to serve the new congregations of this mushrooming town — St. John's parish church, the Catholic Chapel, the Primitive Methodist Chapel and the Congregationalist Church — while church schools were built to accommodate increasing numbers of children.

Bollington is quite unique in the history of the Industrial Revolution in that it experienced the best that the 19th century had to offer rather than its worst excesses. Throughout the whole period it remained a civilised place to live and work — each family had its own house, rather than having to suffer the deprivations of multiple-occupation; married women no longer had to work in the mill once they had their first child; and the mill owners were philanthropic and enlightened in their dealings with their employees. It was a place which saw little of the poverty which prevailed in other cotton towns, largely because its physical location placed a limit upon its growth and ensured that Bollington remained comparatively small and manageable. Its small size encouraged a strong local identity, neighbourliness and a real community spirit within the hearts of the people living here — and these are features which have continued right up to the present day. Some of these elements are well represented in the hamlet of Lowerhouse, a little removed from the main town on the western side. The mill here was built by George Antrobus, who also provided a terrace of houses known as Long Row for his workers. These attractive and intimate stone-built cottages with their long front gardens are indicative of the concern which many of the mill owners had for the welfare of their employees.

The best place from which to view Bollington is without doubt Kerridge Hill, immediately to the south of the town. From the lee of White Nancy, protected from the winds sweeping along the ridge, one can look out over the whole town stretched out just below in the valley of the River Dean. On one's right hand side the green slopes of Kerridge lead down to wooded Ingersley Clough, the early water-powered mills which were built here providing the basis of Bollington's industrial growth. Following the line of Ingersley Clough one's eye is drawn to the heart of the town in the middle distance, with the clustered rows of terraced houses and narrow streets winding out of the valley up the adjoining hillsides. Then one can see the line of the canal, cutting its way through Bollington at right angles to the very marked linear settlement pattern which is evident from this elevated viewpoint. The prominent Adelphi and Clarence Mills stand as sentinels on guard, their chimneys raised in salute like sabres, while beyond the town are open green fields hemmed in only by Alderley Edge in the distance. Then in the blue haze of the far distance one can just glimpse the tower blocks of Stockport and Manchester, much less attractive twentieth century counterparts of the nineteenth century stone-built houses and cottages gathered together just below. Although the Industrial Revolution led to the growth of a town here, it has retained the heart and character of a village which can be experienced and enjoyed even by the casual visitor.

In many respects well-known **Knutsford** is a complete contrast to both Macclesfield and Bollington, having been very largely by-passed by the Industrial Revolution. It still exhibits the character of a prosperous Georgian country town and the variety of architectural styles to be found here gives it an unusual individuality. Surrounded by some lovely countryside, with the wooded Tatton Park on its doorstep, Knutsford is a classic market centre which enjoyed the title of 'Capital of Mid-Cheshire' in the 18th century. Among the best features are the intimate spaces and narrow passageways, particularly between the two main shopping streets, which provide some intriguing perspectives and encourage the visitor to explore further. The long view down King Street is especially impressive, with its fine Georgian buildings and 19th century shop fronts displaying traditional signs and plaques. It is undoubtedly the architecture of Knutsford which catches one's attention most of all, ranging from the many handsome 18th century buildings of local red-brown brick with stone arches and doorcases to the unusual Italianate-style houses built in the late 19th century with their red pantiles and painted plaster work. This rich architectural experience is complemented by two large open areas within sight of the town centre (The Moor and The Heath) and by the many trees which retain

White Nancy, Kerridge Hill ▶

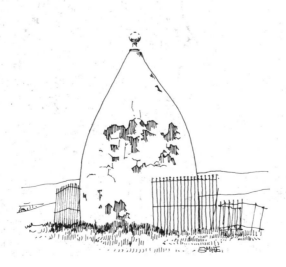

34

THE TOWNS

a feel of the countryside. If the town lacks a focal point, the quality of the town centre in general more than makes up for this. Knutsford has also had its fair share of important people connected with it, the most important being the novelist Mrs. Gaskell who as a child lived with her aunt in the road now known as Gaskell Avenue. She was a close observer of 19th century Knutsford, and many of the buildings which she knew and portrayed (especially in her novel 'Cranford') can still be seen today.

Historically, Knutsford drew its name from the Danish King Canute, or, more correctly, Knut, who is said to have forded the stream dividing Over Knutsford from Nether Knutsford. How true this is may be open to debate, but there do seem to be many names of Danish origin in the area eg Thorley Leigh, Ravenscroft and Branden. The town was granted its first charter by William de Tabley in 1292, providing for a Borough Court and empowering the burgesses to elect a Bailiff or Mayor, while the right to hold a Saturday market was derived from a Royal Charter granted to William de Tabley by Edward I. During the Middle Ages Knutsford grew steadily along the line of the two main parallel streets (now Princess Street and King Street), and by the 17th century it was already a prosperous market town — William Webb noting "the market greatly frequented and the town extraordinarily

Enticing passage off King Street, Knutsford ▶

THE TOWNS

well-traded" in his 'Itinerary of Cheshire' of 1621. It gained further status as a parish in the 18th century, this being a time of considerable development and new building as it became a popular residential area for wealthy county families. At this point it also developed into an important coaching place, Pigot's Directory of 1829 listing numerous services which had posting houses at the local inns and taverns. One of these was the Royal George Hotel on King Street, its attractive covered coachway under a wide arch indicating its former role as an important coaching stop.

The fact that Knutsford attained no prominence as an industrial town was due in the first instance to the lack of water power and then later to the lack of a canal or railway. There was, however, a thriving cottage industry during the 18th century for the making of silk buttons and an early silk mill was built in 1753, giving its name to the present Silk Mill Street. Any other movements towards the building of factories and mills were probably nipped in the bud by the Egerton family of Tatton Hall, who seem to have actively discouraged the development of industry in Knutsford — a number of houses and workshops near the north end of King Street were actually pulled down by the Egertons in order to improve the entrance to Tatton Park. So the end result was that Knutsford was protected from the adverse effects of industrial growth and nurtured instead its pleasant residential character which it retains to this day.

An appropriate place to begin a tour of the sights of Knutsford is the southern end of King Street, with the Unitarian Chapel just across from here set back a little behind a small shaded garden. Identical in style to the Unitarian Chapel in Macclesfield it is one of Knutsford's oldest buildings, having been completed in 1688 and opened for worship by Dissenters on the passing of the Toleration Act in 1689. It seems that a congregation had actually been in existence as early as 1672, and prior to the passing of the Act it had been necessary to post a man with a musket to keep guard while the faithful worshipped. The chapel is a humble two storey red-brick building with stone mullioned windows and two outside staircases giving access to a first floor balcony through tiny porches. The interior is equally unpretentious, with whitewashed walls and old oak pews reflecting the simplicity of the chapel as it watches over its lovely cobbled yard dotted with clumps of ferns. It was here that the famous Mrs. Gaskell was buried in 1865, her grave mounted by a stone cross.

King Street proper begins from just behind the railway bridge. Known locally as 'the bottom street' it curves gracefully away to the right towards Tatton Park, its considerable length emphasised by the narrowness of the street as the buildings either side tiptoe almost to the edge of their pavements and reach out towards one another. There is probably no other street anywhere else in Cheshire where one can see such an exciting and almost bewildering variety

Unitarian Chapel ▶

◀ *Gaskell Memorial Tower and La Belle Epoque*

THE TOWNS

Weaver's Cottages, King Street ▶

of architectural styles — just about every conceivable type of building is represented here, even though the overall impression one is left with at the end is that of Georgian elegance. To start with, on the left hand side just before the graveyard of the parish church is a group of traditional 17th century Cheshire cottages, timber-framed and dressed in the usual black and white livery but lacking the expected thatch roofs. Then a little beyond Church Hill is another black and white building of the early 1660's with some of the original timbering still evident along the side passage. Beyond this is the first of those famous (or perhaps infamous) buildings constructed in an Italianate style for Richard Harding Watt, a Manchester businessman who introduced a Continental flavour to Knutsford's architecture towards the close of the 19th century. Built in 1907 — 8, the Gaskell Memorial Tower and La Belle Epoque (originally known as the King's Coffee House) create an indelible impression of distant and romantic lands, although Pevsner and Hubbard comment that this is just the start of Watt's remorseless imposition of crazy grandeur on poor Knutsford. Built largely of stone with a red pantile roof, La Belle Epoque carries several carved inscriptions from a variety of writers together with a list of the kings and queens of England, while the Gaskell Memorial Tower has a bust of Mrs. Gaskell in a niche just above the street. Then there is the courtyard to the rear, an attractive place to discover with its two tall Doric columns, a raised garden with stone balustrade and a Flemish lamp hanging above.

Georgian doorway ▶

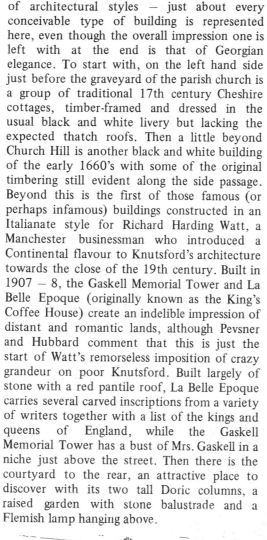

◀ *The Ruskin Rooms*

Further along King Street, past a variety of shops occupying 18th and 19th century premises, is the Royal George Hotel, one of the most prominent buildings in this part of the town. Originally named 'The White Swan' and then 'The George', this late 18th century brick building was an important old coaching house; inside, the 18th century ballroom and circular card room decorated in the Adam fashion reveal the leisurely lifestyle of a former age. On both sides of King Street from here can be seen a variety of 18th and 19th century red-brick buildings with some interesting details such as the rainwater head dated 1785 at No. 78 and the rather fine Georgian doorway with oblong fanlight at No. 98. Opposite this latter house is an early 18th century dwelling with an archway leading under the building to an interesting little cobbled courtyard which was the original location of The Angel Hotel (now across the street) — the old buildings have since been converted to houses and offices, although the former mounting stones can still be seen outside some of them.

The northern end of King Street finishes with a flurry of architectural interest. On the west side is a block of five weavers' cottages, the last evidence of the small silk 'industry' which existed in Knutsford at one time, while across King Street at the top of Drury Lane are the Ruskin Rooms. This building is another by R.H. Watt, its Italianate or Moorish style heavily underlined by the octagonal turret, arched windows and wavy pantiles. Next door is a block of brick cottages also by Watt, their Art Nouveau features such as towers, cupolas and overhanging balconies separating them completely from the silk weavers' cottages less than a hundred yards away. Yet in the midst of all this can still be sensed the paternal presence of the Egertons of Tatton, their estate coming right down into the very heart of Knutsford with the Lodge and gateway forming an impressive entrance to Tatton Park within sight of King Street. Built in 1810, the gateway is particularly imposing with its triple arch stone screen, iron gates and fluted Doric columns.

THE TOWNS

Princess Street is the other main thoroughfare in Knutsford, known locally as 'the top street', but it seems to have been developed much later than King Street and consequently has fewer older buildings. Yet between the shops and houses spanning the period between the 18th and 20th centuries there are several very interesting passageways of varying widths connecting one street with the other, including the cobbled yard at the rear of the Royal George Hotel, the well-used Silk Mill Street and also Church View leading down to the Coffee House Steps with a sight of The Moor in the distance. Right at the southern end of Princess Street is the former Knutsford Town Hall, built by Alfred Waterhouse in 1871 and a comparatively small affair by his standards (he was the architect for Manchester Town Hall and Eaton Hall). Constructed of dark red brick in the Gothic style, the ground floor was planned as a market under five open arches with the Council meeting room above. Another impressive public building close by is The Sessions House, built at the start of the 19th century in a classical style with a four column central portico. This is the only remaining building of the former Knutsford Gaol, the prison having been situated behind the Sessions House where there is now a coach park.

The most attractive route between Princess Street and King Street must surely be Church Hill, with its narrow carriageway of stone setts and its uneven flagged pavements. On one side the Georgian parish church of St. John the Baptist stands quite aloof in the midst of its extensive churchyard, tidily hemmed in by an elderly brick wall, while on the other side near the top is a good group of early 18th century houses which have been sensitively restored. The church itself, with its Georgian interior of Tuscan columns and a gallery on three sides, was built in 1741 – 44 at a cost of £4,000 to replace earlier Chapels of Ease since Knutsford had once formed part of the Parish of Rostherne. One of these Chapels (the Chapel of St. Helena) was situated across the fields in the Mobberley direction and was built in 1316; its foundations have been marked out in stone and can still be seen, together with some old gravestones and what were presumably the altar steps, in a railed-off enclosure. Another Chapel stood at the foot of Church Hill in King Street. Many of the materials from these Chapels, including four bells from the one dedicated to St. Helena, were used in the construction of the present church.

The other areas of interest in Knutsford are just a little removed from the town centre and really focus attention again upon Knutsford's most famous characters, Mrs. Gaskell and Mr. Watt. To the south-west is Gaskell Avenue, an attractive tree-lined road with some smart 18th and 19th century houses which look out onto The Heath, an open tract of land about 30 acres in extent. Halfway down is Heathwaite, the three storey Georgian house where Mrs. Gaskell lived as a girl with her aunt, while a little further on is another classically-fronted house with historical and literary connections from the early 18th century. It used to be known as the Cann Office, where weights and measures were officially tested, and for several years it was the home of Gentleman Highwayman Higgins whose adventures were terminated at the end of a rope in 1767. The select Victorian houses also to be found on Gaskell Avenue are indicative of the high-class residential character which Knutsford has always enjoyed.

Across the way, The Heath has been the scene for many town events which have taken place over the years. It was once a racecourse with a fine grandstand, and races were held there continuously from 1729 to 1875. Now it is better known for the Royal May Day Festival which began in 1864 and takes place every year with a long procession (mainly of children) winding its way round the town on the first Saturday in May. An ancient custom which is peculiar to Knutsford is carried out in the early morning hours before the Festival really gets under way — the streets of the town are swept and the pavements then covered with sand of different colours to form elaborate patterns. Other features include the crowning of the May Queen with great pomp and ceremony, dancing displays and the decoration of the whole town with flags and bunting.

To the south of the town centre is an area between Toft Road and Chelford Road which was developed in the late 19th and early 20th centuries with large houses set in the midst of generous landscaped grounds, and the resulting character has been one of great maturity with an 'arcadian' atmosphere about it. Particularly significant are the series of extraordinary houses on the west side of Legh Road built by Mr. Watt, their turrets and towers turning the traditional English suburban style of architecture on its head. Yet perhaps the architectural historians Pevsner and Hubbard were a little too unkind when they wrote that Legh Road boasted 'the maddest sequence of villas in all England'.

Despite the bustle of its main shopping street Knutsford still displays all the attributes of a quiet country town, and is probably the most attractive place of its size in Cheshire. It is full of Georgian gracefulness and Victorian

THE TOWNS

virtue, its cobbled courtyards and passageways opening up secret areas for the visitor to discover and marvel at. Even its architectural 'quirks' are to be enjoyed, providing extra (if unexpected) interest and demonstrating that the noble family in nearby Tatton Hall did not always have things their own way.

If Knutsford was seen as the 'Capital of Mid-Cheshire' at the height of its prosperity, **Nantwich** would be justified in claiming to be the capital of the south – not only because of its importance over the centuries but also because of the fact that its Parish Church is often referred to as the Cathedral of South Cheshire. It is a delightful ancient market town, still with an intrinsic 'olde-worlde' character about it due to the profusion of half-timbered buildings and the narrow streets with names which are reminiscent of a bygone age.

If Knutsford is predominantly Georgian, Nantwich is principally Elizabethan and thankfully its lovely black and white houses are very much the genuine article rather than the results of Victorian restoration. The town's early importance was due to the production of salt here, and from Roman times right through to the 18th century it was very much the centre of the English salt industry.

Lying in a rich farming area and on the main route through to Chester, Nantwich has always been a focal point for settlers since the time of the Roman occupation. It has had several names in its long history, beginning with Hellath Wen in the pre-Saxon era. The Saxons themselves called it Warmundestrou, the Normans Wich Malbanc, and then in the 16th century it was known as Nauntwych. Its importance as a market town was recognised in 1283 when King Edward I granted the town the right to have an annual fair for three days at the Feast of St. Bartholomew, and it was of strategic significance too since it was the last outpost in the area before the Welsh border.

Yet it was the town's role in the production of salt which was probably the main factor in its influence over the surrounding area. Salt production was the major industry in Nantwich and historically salt was a very valuable commodity since it was the only method of preserving food in the days before refrigeration. The contribution of the salt industry to the town's prosperity is reflected in both its old Welsh name, Hellath Wen – meaning 'The White Salt Pit' – and the name Nantwich itself, meaning The Salt Pit (Wich) in the Riverside Vale (Nant). The Romans made use of the town as a source of salt for their settlement at Chester and the industry continued to thrive until the 18th century when Nantwich was one of the largest salt producing towns in England. In addition to its preservative properties the salts were said to alleviate fits, chronic

Welsh Row, Nantwich

41

THE TOWNS

indigestion and rheumatism, and during the 18th century people travelled from far afield to take treatment here. In the area around the River Weaver in Welsh Row to the west of the main town there were a multitude of brine houses to which the brine was conveyed in wooden channels and poured into lead pans under which fires were lit to produce the salt by evaporation. At the end of the 16th century there were 216 of these 'wich-houses' in use, this being a maximum limit imposed in order to maintain high prices. Then gradually competition with other sources and the mining of rock salt in the Winsford and Northwich areas made the process used in Nantwich uneconomic, and by 1792 there were only three salt houses left in the town. In 1856 the industry finally died out with the closure of the last of the salt works.

Thankfully the prosperity of the town was not dependent soley upon salt, since cheese-making and tanning had both been important in the Middle Ages. There were also other trades employing significant numbers of people, including shoe-making and glove-making, and Nantwich later became an important stopping-off point in the coaching era — by 1792 there were 34 inns and public houses, 12 malt kilns and malt houses, 127 stables and 5 smithies. Right up to the present century farming had always been an important aspect of the town economy, and from the main streets running out from the central market place lanes extended into the arable fields which lay immediately around the settled area. It was even said that the streets were so filled with sheep, cattle and pigs that women and children scarcely ventured out of doors.

Present-day Nantwich is with us as it is only because it has managed to survive a number of near-catastrophes. After the Norman conquest in the 11th century one of the last stands by the natives was made at Nantwich and the town was almost totally destroyed, with only one house left. Then later in the Middle Ages the town was attacked several times by the Welsh and devastated. In 1583 what was known as The Great Fire broke out on a site near to Welsh Row bridge and encouraged by constant winds laid waste most of the town. The fire lasted for an amazing twenty days, the efforts of the fire fighters being hampered by four bears roaming the town which had been freed from their cages in the town's bear pit. It was estimated that £30,000 (an enormous sum in those days) would be needed to rebuild the town, and Queen Elizabeth herself held a collection over all England together with her own contribution of £2,000 towards the town's reconstruction. Nantwich also had its share of troubles during the Civil War in the 17th

century, when it was the only Cheshire town which held out for the Parliamentarians. It was beseiged for weeks by the Royalists who bombarded the town with red-hot shot hoping to burn down the buildings, but eventually Nantwich was relieved when Sir Thomas Fairfax and Sir William Brereton joined forces to defeat Lord Byron's army. The townspeople celebrated the victory by wearing sprigs of holly in their hats, and every year Holly Holy Day is still remembered on the nearest Saturday to 25th January with a colourful festival and mock battle re-enacting the siege of Nantwich.

The focal point of Nantwich is The Square, to which all the roads coming into the town are directed. It is a quite delightful central feature of the town, with a lovely view down to St. Mary's Parish Church across a tree-lined green and bordered by some antique oak-framed buildings.

The church itself is historically the most interesting building in Nantwich, being largely of the fourteenth century but incorporating the foundations of much earlier structures. It is particularly splendid by virtue of the many unique and unusual features which are exhibited in this one building, including the crowning octagonal tower, the magnificent lierne vault above the chancel, the beautiful triple-canopied choirstalls which are among the best examples of medieval woodcarving in the country, and the stone perpendicular pulpit. The exterior of the church is decorated with some fascinating stone carvings, including leering gargoyles and many representations of 'Jack in the Green' or 'The Green Man'. There is also a humorous sculpture of the Devil flying away with a woman whose hand is in a pitcher — it seems that the craftsmen employed in the construction of some parts of the church

Replica of the town pillory ▶

◀ *Crown Hotel*

returned to their lodgings one night to find their landlady dipping her hand into a jar where they kept their money and took it upon themselves to immortalise her in stone.

The flagged footpath leading from the west doorway of the parish church passes alongside the pleasant churchyard (not used for burials since the cholera epidemic of 1848) and ends at The Square, with High Street off to the right and Pillory Street away to the left. High Street was the area where the town's wealthiest merchants lived and worked, and centuries later it still retains an air of affluence and prosperity.

Queen's Aid House ▶

All the timber-framed buildings here were rebuilt after the Great Fire, an event which is recorded by an inscription to be seen on the appropriately named Queen's Aid House (No. 41 High Street):

> "God grant our Ryal Queen
> In England longe to Raign
> For she hath put her helping
> Hand to bild this towne again."

This is an excellent example of a medieval merchant's house, built of three storeys which overhang each other and decorated in the best Elizabethan style. The house opposite was rebuilt after the Great Fire at a cost of £120, and its panelling, plasterwork and carved figures beneath the overhanging floors are good examples of Elizabethan craftsmanship. Perhaps the best timber-framed building among the many on High Street is the Crown Hotel, its three overhanging storeys reeling a little with their great antiquity but still managing to present a dignified appearance to passers-by. Also rebuilt after the Great Fire, its most striking features are the very long upper storey window (which gave light to the Assembly Room inside) and the closely spaced vertical members of the timber-framed walls. The interior is well preserved and a section of a wall in the bar has been cut away to exhibit the original wattle and daub construction, while other relics include an old coach converted into a telephone kiosk.

A little excursion up Churchyardside from the top end of High Street brings us to Dysart Buildings, a beautifully proportioned Georgian terrace of nine houses set in sylvan surroundings with the usual combination of elegant doorways and windows. Built in the latter half of the 18th century, Dysart Buildings represents the first expansion of the town into the area of meadows and town gardens known as The Crofts. Then to the north of Churchyardside and running into High Street is Beam Street, the eastern entrance to the town along which the town's livestock were driven up to the common land on Beam Heath. The most interesting buildings here are the Crewe and Wright Almshouses: the former were built in 1767 by John Crewe on the site of a 'house of correction' and were specifically intended "for Seven Decayed Tradesmen", while the Wright Almshouses standing alongside them were originally sited at the junction of London Road and Hospital Street but were moved brick by brick to their present position together with an attractive stone archway. They had been built in 1638 by Sir Edmund Wright, a native of Nantwich who went to London as a boy and became a wealthy grocer and then eventually Lord Mayor.

Hospital Street on the southern side of the town is also an ancient thoroughfare like Beam Street, and here are to be found some of the oldest buildings in Nantwich. The well-known Churche's Mansion, now a restaurant, was built in 1577 for Richard and Margery Churche as a symbol of their wealth and is a very fine example of a town house of that period as well as being an outstanding piece of decorated half-timbered architecture. The front of the house has four gables together with the usual overhanging upper storeys, and the decorative

◀ *Dysart Buildings*

emblems on the carved brackets depict a lion, a salamander, an ape and the Devil. Inside there are some lovely domestic features which are characteristic of the late medieval period — a buttery, a large inglenook fireplace in the kitchen, and some beautifully-carved panelling in the Long Withdrawing Room (now the main dining room for the restaurant). Opposite Churche's Mansion is The Rookery, a stately Georgian brick house with two projecting wings, while adjacent is Combermere House, a very good example of an early eighteenth century merchant's house with a classically designed doorway. Further along towards the town centre is 140 Hospital Street, standing on the site of the Hospice of St. Nicholas which was founded in 1083. The seventeenth century facade hides a timber-framed building which was the house of John Crewe, a tanner who died in 1598. Despite its Georgian exterior, 116 Hospital Street is in fact medieval and contains two 15th century stone fireplaces; it is likely that the roof is also of the same period.

Halfway along Hospital Street, next to an historic footpath called The Gullet, is the venerable Sweetbriar Hall which was built in 1450 and fortunately escaped the ravages of the Great Fire. Timber-framed like many of its neighbours, the ornamental panelling on its front consists of curved braces forming diamond shapes and timbers placed diagonally forming a herringbone pattern. One of the people who lived here was Dr. Joseph Priestley, famous for his discovery of oxygen. Right at the end of Hospital Street closest to The Square is The Lamb Hotel, originally mentioned as a mansion house in 1551 when William Chadderton was granted a licence to keep a tavern there. It was used as the Parliamentary headquarters during the Civil War, but its character was considerably altered by changes carried out in 1861.

Across the town centre and just beyond the bridge crossing the River Weaver is Welsh Row, the best and prettiest street in Nantwich, down which the Welsh drove their Blackhorn cattle to trade for the salt needed for the long winter months. It was previously known as Frog Row, either after a row of houses which stood on the south side of the road or more probably because of Frog Channel which ran down its centre. Like Hospital Street it is lined with many interesting buildings which have been important in the town's history — buildings such as The Three Pigeons Inn, once a centre of cock fighting, and The Cheshire Cat, a black and white timber-framed building originally known as the Widows Almshouse after Roger Wilbraham converted three cottages in 1676 to house six widows as a memorial to his wife and two sons who died on the same day. There

are also many excellent examples of Georgian architecture on Welsh Row, including Townwell House with its five bay frontage encompassing a big pedimented stone doorway and The Archway with its display of skilled craftsmanship in the use of gauged and rubbed brick. Then a little further along are the Tollemache Almshouses, built in 1870 in the traditional pattern embracing gable ends, large chimneys and diamond-lattice windows. They replaced an almshouse which was built in 1613 by Roger Wilbraham for six poor men, and it was recorded that the recipients of alms received £2 per annum, shoes every year and gowns and caps every two years.

Narrow winding streets, traditional timber-framed houses in the best black and white style, elegant Georgian buildings which complement their older neighbours, an impressive sandstone church which watches over the whole town and above all a pervading sense of history — these are the elements which set Nantwich apart as one of the loveliest places in Cheshire.

A charming little town tucked away in the south-west corner of the county, **Malpas** is a microcosm of the best features of Cheshire life and history. Unpretentious without being too old-fashioned, this is a place with a character which far outstrips its size and a variety of buildings each with their own story to tell. It is arranged quite simply around the intersection of four main streets, with the magnificent 14th century parish church of St. Oswald presiding sedately over affairs from its elevated position above the rest of the town. It is particularly impressive as one approaches from a distance, with the stone battlements and pinnacles of the church rather more suggestive of a fortified castle than a spiritual haven. Interestingly enough the churchyard was probably the bailey of the timber Norman castle which was built here, with the castle mound still evident just to the north of the church, and St. Oswald's may well have started life as a private chapel. The lovely mellowed Perpendicular style of the architecture is matched by the elegant 18th century gateways and steps which are in Church Street, extending a warm invitation for passers-by to make a miniature pilgrimage into this sacred plot.

Gathered around the church, like children around a mother's skirts, are some lovely houses and cottages spanning the generations. Immediately to the west are some timber-framed cottages clad in local brick and painted in the black and white style, while a little further down Church Street is the old Tithe Barn — probably the best 17th century timber-

◀ Churche's Mansion

framed building in the town. Converted to a house about 35 years ago, it was originally used to store the tithes (or taxes in kind) which were levied by the church upon local inhabitants. Just across the road is The Bolling, a fine example of an early 18th century brick house which became the Lower Rectory for Malpas. For a large part of its history the town has had the 'blessing' of two rectors rather than the normal one, with two of the old established land-owning families (the Drakes and the Cholmondeleys) having the right to nominate one each. Although the true origins of this division lie in medieval times, local legend has it that the situation arose from King James I's visit to the town while travelling incognito. The rector at that time is reputed to have been slack in his hospitality and as a result James split the living and granted the second part to the curate. It would be difficult to imagine such an informal royal visit in our own generation!

Next door to The Bolling is a house named 'Scholes', of local red brick and Welsh slate which at one time was probably a thatched barn; the decorative brickwork along the eaves is typical of the 18th century. As in many towns and villages, changing uses of buildings are part and parcel of the cycle of growth and decline, and several buildings in Malpas have experienced this. Further up Church Street and almost opposite St. Oswald's is the appropriately named Church View, an excellent example of a 17th century box-framed house,

which at one time was the Gryphon Inn, while Wycherley's shop in the market place was another inn named The Wyvern. These hostelries belonged to the two major landed families, the Cholmondeleys and the Drakes, and the gryphon and the wyvern were two mythical heraldic beasts incorporated into their coats of arms. Representations of both these creatures can still be found painted on panelling from old box pews preserved in the parish church. Both families had houses for their stewards in Malpas, that of the Cholmondeleys being the Old Printing House built in 1733 immediately opposite the church on the corner of Parbutt's Lane, with the figure of a gryphon being carved on to the pediment, while the Drakes' steward lived a little further away in a house named Woodville, built in 1765 close to the junction of High Street and Chester Road. This 18th century house is a very good example of many similar houses which the Drakes and Cholmondeleys were building all over the area at this time.

Prior to this burst of building activity at the centre of the town, Malpas probably had a large cobbled market place, looking up towards the church at its top corner. The medieval market cross would have been located at its lower end, on the line of the old Roman road from Chester through to Whitchurch. This road is now the High Street, and although the base of the cross standing close-by is still original its top part is Victorian. The southern corner of the market place was probably marked by the Old Hall,

Market House, Malpas ▶

THE TOWNS

the present building having replaced the original timber-built hall which had been burnt down in 1768. This had been the home of the Breretons, the Lords of the Manor, from whom the Drake family had inherited two-thirds of the Barony of Malpas in the 17th century.

The importance which Malpas once held as a market town in the midst of the surrounding countryside is still evident from its impressive Market House, occupying a key position by the church steps with their ancient iron handrails. Built in 1762 of local brick, this lovely building with its double gabled facade has an unusual colonnade of eight slender Tuscan stone columns which support the overhanging upper storeys above. These columns seem to be rooted into the sandstone blocks upon which they stand, as though determined to hold this building up for at least another two centuries. As far back as medieval times Malpas had been given the status of a borough with permission to hold fairs and markets, but by the 19th century these ancient rights had gradually died out — yet despite this, the atmosphere of the country market town lingers on.

The very strong influence which the land-owning families exercised in the town also lingers on. Their philanthropy is particularly demonstrated by the one-storey Cholmondeley Almshouses in Church Street, founded by Sir Randle Brereton during the reign of Henry VIII but with the present building dating from 1721. The Breretons also endowed a Grammar School in 1527, partly financed by the revenue from salt works in other parts of the county. At first it was not very successful but then flourished after it was re-endowed under the influence of Lord Cholmondeley at the end of the 17th century. The school survived until the end of the 19th century and was housed in buildings (now used as shops) near the Cross. Another benefactor was Richard Alport of nearby Overton Hall, who endowed a Bluecoat charity school. Its successor is the present primary school, but the original Alport School building at the top end of the High Street has been converted into some very attractive cottages.

The town's position on the main Chester to London road meant that it developed into an important coaching stop, and it was the Red Lion on Old Hall Street which was the main coaching inn during the 18th and 19th centuries. In the 1830's the 'Albion' from London and the 'Hero' from Shrewsbury called every day except Sunday on their way to Chester — and the local history society make the interesting remark that even 150 years later Malpas still has no Sunday service passing through it! The coming of the railway to this

isolated neck of the woods in the 1870's meant that a greater diversity of building material was available rather than just those at hand locally, and this ushered in a fuller expression of Victorian architecture (but in a quite homely form). On High Street one can see some splendid decorative cast iron on the front of the chemist's shop just opposite the Cross, while further up the road Rock Terrace is a good example of Victorian housing making use of mass-produced materials. Then towards the bottom of Church Street the Red House has a splendid facade of red Ruabon brick, a material first produced about 1870, while next door The Hayes also has some good examples of Victorian decorative brickwork.

Yet Malpas in the twentieth century seems to remain largely undisturbed by the threats of progress — even the railway, that 19th century forerunner for industrial growth, was dismantled some years ago and the town continues as a quiet little backwater in the midst of some of the richest and most beautiful countryside in Cheshire. It is a place where the march of time has slowed to an amble, providing both the resident and the visitor alike with the opportunity to absorb the town's historic atmosphere and enjoy glimpses of the surrounding hills which can be caught between the brick and timber-framed houses.

Sandbach is an ancient town in the south-east of the county whose main feature is a lovely cobbled market place surrounded by historic buildings and looking in towards two famous Saxon crosses which represent one of the oldest Christian monuments of its kind in this country. Despite its recent growth the centre of Sandbach has really changed very little over the centuries, encompassing a magnificent old hall and St. Mary's Church as well as the timeless Square.

Sandbach (the name means 'sandy brook') was referred to in the Domesday Book but had already been in existence as an Anglo Saxon settlement as early as the seventh century. It was about this time that the Saxon crosses were erected, their original site being the same one as they occupy now. The town developed steadily through the Middle Ages and provided for the material as well as the spiritual needs of the surrounding agricultural population — a stone church has existed on the site of St. Mary's Church since 1200 and before that a timber and thatch building is thought to have stood there. By the 16th century Sandbach was already noted for its excellent malt liquor and the quality of its worsted yarns, and it was probably these things which encouraged Sir John Radcliffe of Ordsall in Lancashire to obtain a market charter from Queen Elizabeth I

THE TOWNS

giving the right to hold fairs and markets in the town and also the right to establish a Court Leet and a Court of Pied-powder.

Sandbach had its own share of troubles during the English Civil Wars of the 17th century, like many other places in Cheshire. Scots' Common just to the north of the town centre gets its name from the skirmish that took place there on September 3rd 1651 when a troop of Scots, retreating after the Battle of Worcester, reached Sandbach and rested on this open ground. The townspeople, fearing the same fate as that which had befallen the inhabitants of Barthomley, set upon the Scots with poles from the market-stalls. Many of the soldiers were killed and many more were taken prisoner — so many, in fact, that they had to be kept in the church and the following Sunday services had to be held in the churchyard.

By the early 19th century Sandbach was a busy coaching point with 'The Royal Sovereign' coach running daily to London, 'The Rocket' to both Liverpool and Birmingham and another coach called 'The Nettle' journeying daily to Manchester and Nantwich. The George Hotel just across from the Square was a particularly busy coaching inn, and sometimes even prisoners in ball and chains could be seen outside on their way to Liverpool and deportation. It was the advent of the railway in the nineteenth century which facilitated the establishment of industry in the area on a greater scale than had previously been possible, with the result that Sandbach developed an extensive silk trade, made boots and shoes for the Manchester and Liverpool markets and also enjoyed a considerable trade with salt works and corn mills.

Standing at the centre of the Square, with its undulating but decorative cobbles underfoot, one is amazed by the number of old established inns and pubs which seem to jostle for space — from the right spot one can see a grand total of six! On the western side is Ye Olde Black Beare, a particularly attractive inn with its thatched roof and half-timbered upper storey proudly displaying the date of 1634 beneath a latticed window. There is no evidence that it was ever a coaching inn, but it was here that the poor bear was baited. The Market Tavern and The Crown stand close to each other in the northern corner of the Square, both of them having been built about 1680 but considerably altered since then, while down a narrow road leading off the eastern side is the very pretty Lower Chequer Inn. This building claims to be the oldest in Sandbach, dating from 1570, and it is said that the chequered board was used to help uneducated customers to count their money — many landlords also acted as money lenders in medieval times. From Hawk Street at the side of the Lower Chequer there is a marvellous view across St. Mary's churchyard, looking through the open archway beneath the prominent west tower, especially in autumn

The Crown Hotel ▶

◀ The Saxon Crosses against the setting sun

THE TOWNS

The Lower Chequer Inn ▶

when the gentle sunlight casts long shadows from nearby trees and accentuates the uneven cobbled surfaces. Back in the Square the buildings on the eastern side are a mixture of old and new, while just across the High Street are the two remaining pubs in this unusually tight-knit collection of half a dozen within sight of the Crosses.

The Saxon Crosses naturally occupy pride of place in the Square, although they are really stone pillars rather than 'Crosses' as we know them in the normal sense. There are some interesting ideas as to their age and the reasons for their being here — some sources suggest that they were erected by Peada (son of King Penda of Mercia) after his conversion to Christianity, since it is believed that he and his Court were baptised by four travelling priests on the spot where the Crosses now stand, while another source suggests that the presence of the Crosses and other monuments of the period indicate that the town was the site of an old Saxon minster served by a community of priests responsible for the conversion of the district. Another suggestion is that they were erected in the ninth century as a monument to King Egbert. Unfortunately the Crosses were badly damaged by religious extremists sometime between 1585 and 1621 — except for the platform, base stones and a large part of one shaft, fragments of the Crosses were scattered far and wide. Then in 1816 these fragments were recovered and the Crosses largely rebuilt

to be restored to their original site. The taller of the two has carvings and embellishments on all its four faces, and once stood 25 feet high. The east face has angels in circles, a figure of Christ and other figures representing the transfiguration, the nativity and the crucifixion; while on the west and north faces are many small panels with single figures and a dragon at the top. The southern or smaller cross (10 ft 9 in high) has a plaited border of human masks on the east and west faces and panels with single figures on the other two faces. Although these Crosses resemble similar Saxon monuments found elsewhere in this country they are unique in that no others have so many carved figures.

Beyond the historic Square with its ancient Crosses Sandbach has a number of other very interesting features, including St. Mary's Parish Church which stands on a spur boldly projecting into the valley of a small stream running down to the River Wheelock. Although there has been a church on the site for many centuries, the existing building of local sandstone is very largely a reconstruction by the famous Victorian architect George Gilbert Scott. The church tower, with a public right of way passing right through the high open porch at its base, is said to be an exact replica of the original Perpendicular tower which it replaced. The oldest parts of the main building are the oak roofs above the nave and side aisles, erected in 1661, while on the left of the

◀ *Part of Hawk Street*

nave is an old font dating back to 1200 A.D. Outside the church can be seen the defaced fragments of another two Saxon crosses.

Opposite the bottom end of the churchyard and across the High Street is the Old Hall Hotel, a beautiful black and white building which was built in 1656. An oak-framed house originally erected to a square plan using wattle and daub, it also has a long wing which was added at a later date. Inside there are three Jacobean fireplaces, the one downstairs being very ornate and having the added attraction of a secret door on the right, while the oak panelled dining room is supposed to be haunted by the ghost of The Grey Lady — could this have any connection with the skeleton of a baby which was found behind one of the panels some years ago? Another interesting feature is the little door on the landing which hides a spiral staircase leading to the attic where the servants would have lived. The Hall is thought to have been the residence of the Lords of the Manor of Sandbach.

Sandbach could rightfully lay claim to more recent architectural significance in that it has other examples of George Gilbert Scott's work besides St. Mary's Church. The Literary Institute was built in 1857 to a typical Gothic design produced by him, incorporating a well-balanced brick facade with stone dressings, while next door is the Trustees Savings Bank which is also in Gothic style and again by Scott. Another church with which he was involved is St. John's at Sandbach Heath — dating from 1861 and in Scott's favourite 'Second Pointed' style reflecting the 13th century, it is a handsome church with a fine tower and some beautiful screens. Scott also had a hand in some of the buildings for Sandbach Grammar School midway through the 19th century, including the Gothic gatehouse and the main parts along the front.

Although not as unspoilt as some other places in Cheshire, Sandbach nevertheless still has a pleasant country town atmosphere, particularly around the Market Square with its narrow cobbled streets, black and white timbered buildings, old inns and small shops. It is a place worth venturing out to see, particularly for those famous Saxon Crosses.

Close to the county border with Staffordshire, the town of **Congleton** has very much the same close-knit character and atmosphere as its more northerly neighbour Macclesfield, since it also has retained its medieval street plan with the later addition of some very attractive Georgian buildings. As with Macclesfield, the influx of industry in the 18th century was an important feature of the town's development, with silk weaving being particularly significant and then cotton spinning coming to the fore at a slightly later date. Yet Congleton has an identity of its own created by the pleasant blend of public buildings and private houses which exist together in quiet harmony.

The earliest reference to Congleton is in the Domesday Survey of 1086, when the manor was approximately two-thirds the value of Newbold Manor to the south. Interestingly enough Congleton remained part of Astbury parish until 1868, by which time the former had far outgrown its 'parent' settlement. During the 13th century the manor of Congleton was held as part of the estate of the de Lacy family, and it was Henry de Lacy who granted the town charter in 1272 authorising the right to hold markets and a fair as well as establishing the positions of mayor, catchpole (the sheriff's officer) and aletasters. The burgesses were entitled to form a merchant guild and hold rights over land, but they were equally bound by obligations to the manor which included compulsory use of the mill. The nucleus of the medieval town at this time consisted of the Main Street from Duke Street to High Street running west-east along the south side of the valley and burgage plots running off this to the north and south.

By the time of the Tudor period the town had an upper chapel, a lower or bridge chapel (where travellers who crossed the bridge prayed), a Moothall and a Grammar School. It also had a market, held three fairs a year and had a flourishing industry in lace making and leather working. The town was also noted for 'Congleton Points', the metal tags put on to the ends of laces. Steady employment was available and the town was recognised as being moderately prosperous. Then in the 17th century Congleton was disturbed both by plague and by war. At least two occurences of the plague are recorded — 1603-4 and 1641-2 — and during the former period normal life was disrupted so badly that grass grew in the streets. The Civil War left Congleton unscathed as far as actual fighting was concerned but there were political disputes in the town, soldiers were garrisoned there and local levies were requisitioned.

It was in the 18th century that the town prospered once again, starting with the building of the first silk mill by John Clayton in 1752. At about the same time ribbon weaving began, to be followed by cotton spinning in 1784. Communications around the town were also gradually improved through the introduction of turnpike roads in the 1760's, the completion of the canal by Thomas Telford in 1831 and the

THE TOWNS

arrival of the railway in 1848. Yet by this time another decline had set in due to the recession of the silk trade, and Congleton was only saved by the development of fustian and velvet cutting which employed the surplus labour and made use of idle mills. At the peak of this latest phase there were thirty-four fustian mills in the centre of the town. The textile trades continued to be the main industry in Congleton in the earlier part of the 20th century, but gradually these have given way to the light engineering to be found in the town today.

Many of Congleton's most interesting buildings are to be seen around the triangular area at the heart of the town bounded by High Street, Moody Street and Chapel Street. The focal point of High Street is undoubtedly the Town Hall, built in a monumental Venetian Gothic style which only a Victorian architect could have produced. Its high tower and clock spire overshadow the street below, while the three stone statues of Henry de Lacy, Edward I and Queen Victoria project outwards from the brick facade above a series of arches. Also on High Street is the 17th century White Lion pub, timber-framed in black and white with an irregular front and herringbone bracing. Moody Street is a very pleasant residential thoroughfare leading up the hill from the town centre to just above the Parish Church, its western side being particularly imposing with the large detached Moody Hall and a fine row of rendered Georgian and Regency houses. Where Moody Street joins Chapel Street there is an excellent view of St. Peter's, the parish church, a little down the hill and set at an oblique angle to the other buildings here. Built of brick with a stone tower in 1742, the style of this sizeable church is typical of the Basilican parish churches of the 17th and 18th centuries. The three galleries and Tuscan columns are part of a fine and largely untouched Georgian interior, while other interesting features include a 'Venetian' east window and a Jacobean pulpit. Winding its way back down to the Town Hall, Chapel Street has a mixture of 18th and 19th century buildings along it with a highlight being the delicate Regency front of 'Homefield', while its visual interest is enhanced by the way in which the street narrows between the old Sunday school and the church. Just behind St. Peter's is an interesting little footpath known as the 'Cockshoot' which runs in a dog-legged fashion from Chapel Street through to Canal Street.

Another area of some architectural distinction is around the junction of three streets on the western side of the town. Swan Bank (originally known as 'Claybank'), Little Street and West Street form part of Congleton's ancient street pattern and their coming together was probably the 'crossing' of the north-south and east-west routes. Little Street is one of the quaintest streets in Congleton, largely retaining much of its original character and scale with a good view up towards the 17th century Lion and Swan Inn on West Street. West Street itself is lined with some good examples of Georgian domestic architecture, including Damion House with a Gibbs suround to its doorway and Overton House with a nice front garden and fine gatepiers.

Although not perhaps the most stunningly beautiful place in Cheshire, Congleton's pleasant mixture of Georgian domestic architecture and Victorian public buildings make it worthy of inclusion among the long list of places which one ought to see, particularly as it is surrounded by lovely hills and a ring of pleasant villages.

One of Congleton's ancient inns ▶

THE TOWNS

Northwich is important to Cheshire not because it is particularly attractive but because of its significance as the centre of the salt industry. It is a town which has quite literally, as well as metaphorically, been built upon salt and it has suffered more than any other place in the county from subsidence due to the extensive pumping of brine from the rich salt deposits in the strata beneath it. The timber-framed buildings to be seen in the town centre are not medieval in origin as at Nantwich, but rather stem from the late 19th and early 20th centuries when they were specially constructed to withstand the effects of subsidence — many of them have been jacked up several times to stop them from slipping below street level, although the subsidence has now largely ceased due to the improved methods of extraction.

Northwich has had a long history and was one of the three original 'wiches' or salt towns of Cheshire, the others being Nantwich and Middlewich. Salt was being dug out of the ground here even before the Romans set up an auxiliary fort (named Condate) in 70 AD, located to the south-west of the present town centre, and by the time of the Domesday Survey the salt houses of Northwich were valued at the considerable sum of £8 a year. During the Middle Ages the production of salt remained uppermost in the local economy, and as a basic necessity of life it was in constant demand. It was only in the late 17th century that changes in the methods of salt extraction set Northwich above its competitors, with the discovery of rock salt in 1670 which dealt the final death blow to the salt industry at rival Nantwich. Northwich became even more important when navigation up the River Weaver was improved in 1721, with the result that Lancashire coal could easily be brought in and salt could just as easily be sent out. In 1781 deeper mines were sunk and by the early years of the 19th century there were twenty-three local salt mines producing 100,000 tons of rock salt each year. Improvements to the River Weaver had played a significant part in this growth of the salt industry — whereas before pack-horses were limited to loads of 200 lbs, now barges drawn by a single tow-path horse could convey up to 100 tons. The coming of the Trent and Mersey Canal in 1777 was also important — although its prime purpose had been to serve the Potteries, salt works were soon built along its banks to take advantage of this cheap form of transport. Remains of some of these can still be seen from the canal between Anderton and Marston, including the Lion Salt Works which is the only traditional 'open pan' salt works still in operation.

By the middle of the 19th century the Northwich mines were producing 284,000 tons of salt each year, in addition to the salt produced from a host of small works by the evaporation of brine. Then in 1873 came the event which was to revolutionise the entire salt industry, when Brunner and Mond came together to establish a chemical works at nearby Winnington to which brine was pumped from springs throughout the district. The new company expanded very rapidly indeed and eventually Brunner-Mond became a part of I.C.I., the largest salt makers in what was then the British Empire. Today brine from the salt deposits is used at the I.C.I. works to manufacture alkali products which are used in the glass, soap, rayon, paper, drug and dyemaking industries, and the chemical industry far outweighs in economic terms the older salt industry from which it stems.

The price which Northwich has had to pay for its prosperity is seen most clearly along the main street running through the town, with its many comparatively modern timber-framed buildings which have replaced much older ones destroyed by subsidence. Yet the overall effect is quite pleasing, particularly around the curve of the High Street as it slopes down towards the River Weaver. At the far end of Witton Street is the Post Office with its four-storey gabled frontage in black and white which was built in 1911, while a little further down is the timber-framed and symmetrical Brunner Public Library. This building (dated 1909) replaced an earlier one built in 1886 which was demolished because of subsidence damage; both were given to the town by Sir John Brunner. Nearby is the White Lion Hotel, a superb example of the disruptive effects of the salt industry — although timber-framed it was not jacked up when the street level was raised, with the result that the building has effectively lost a storey. What are now the cellars were formerly the ground floor, with the outside doors and windows still evident. Then down the hill and around the corner in High Street can be seen some of the best timber-framed buildings in the town, mostly dating from the 1890's. All of them have been jacked up, notably during the 'big lift' of 1920-22 when the Bull Ring (originally the location of a weekly market in the 17th century) was raised six feet. Parts of the High Street have been raised over 20 feet in the battle against subsidence. Even bridges were not safe from this threat, and the Town Bridge running over the Weaver from the junction of High Street and London Road is an adjustable water-supported swing bridge which replaced the former stone structure. Over the river is Castle Street, the scene of one of Northwich's most famous incidents — it was here in 1920 that a complete timber-framed house fell back at an angle of 45 degrees and almost

THE TOWNS

disappeared intact into a cavernous subsidence hole. Similar things were happening all over the town at this time, with buildings not only sinking but being torn apart as the subsidence forced them into some precarious positions. Only the Parish Church remained untouched by the dramatic effects of subsidence, due to being located quite unusually well away from the rest of the town. Although heavily restored three times during the 19th century this visually impressive church standing on a hill overlooking the new dual carriageway is mainly a Perpendicular-style building erected between 1498 and 1525, and is the oldest building in Northwich. Its most prominent features are the vast eastern windows creating 'walls' of glass and the splendid nave and chancel roofs dating from about 1525.

The best place to discover the whole history of salt in Northwich is the Salt Museum on London Road to the south of the town. Completely devoted to the explanation and interpretation of the salt industry, this Museum run by Cheshire County Council occupies Weaver Hall which was built as a workhouse in 1837. Here one can find some fascinating displays and models which illuminate the growth of the salt trade and its quite unusual effects on the town. An equally fascinating place is the Lion Salt Works at Marston, the last remaining establishment producing salt by the original 'open pan' method and run by the Thompson family since 1721. The process used within these timber and brick buildings to produce salt is very largely the same method as has been used over the centuries. Brine (a concentrated salt solution eight times saltier than sea water) is pumped up from underground streams 150 feet beneath the works into a large iron salt pan (up to 80 ft by 24 ft in size) and then heated by oil-fired burners (charcoal and coal were used originally) until the salt crystals begin to form. These crystals are raked to the side of the pan where they are shovelled into tubs to form 14 lb blocks of salt which need to be slowly dried for two weeks in the 'stove' area before they can be cut and wrapped for sale. The landscape surrounding the Lion Salt Works is typical of an old salt-producing area, and the effects of natural brine pumping (as opposed to the more modern and safer 'controlled' brine pumping) can be seen all around — subsidence is a serious problem, many buildings tilt or have collasped leaving odd gaps, and waste ground and flooded 'flashes' are a common occurrence.

The last feature of interest in the area is the Anderton Boat Lift, a marvellous piece of Victorian ingenuity and engineering skill which connects the Trent and Mersey Canal with the River Weaver just to the north of the town. Originally the two were linked by loading chutes down which salt and other commodities were poured, but then in 1875 this massive iron structure was erected to speed up the movement of cargoes, raising and lowering boats hydraulically in two counter-balanced water filled tanks. By 1908 the lift had been electrified so that the tanks could be operated independently, and although very few boats now use it the lift is operating as smoothly and efficiently as the day it was first opened.

Anderton Boat Lift ▶

Halton Castle

Prestbury in the snow

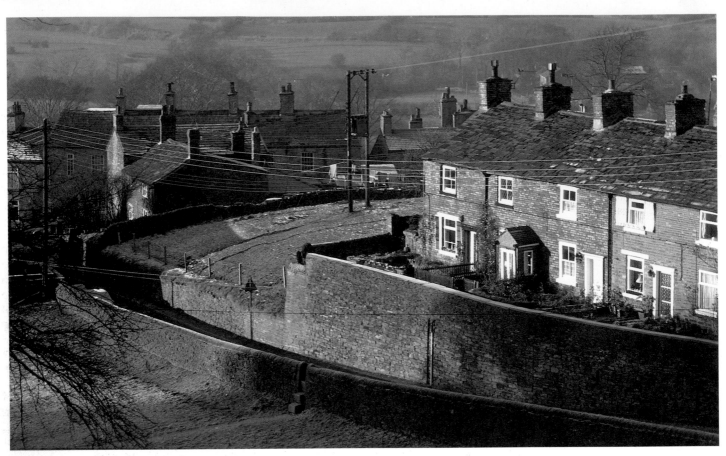

Stone built cottages in eastern Cheshire

The Shroppie Fly at Audlem

THE TOWNS

Runcorn is an appropriate place to end a survey of Cheshire's towns, since its special character is very largely the result of the industrial era bringing us right into the twentieth century. Its most significant features are some impressive transport achievements, such as canals and bridges, and the housing developments of a modern New Town. Yet the best place from which to view these is undoubtedly the ruins of Halton Castle, built on a rocky hill with superb sweeping views of the surrounding area stretching right across the River Mersey to Widnes. From this ancient ruin, with the old stone cottages of Halton village just below, one can pick out a collection of dramatic modern features which are to be seen nowhere else in Cheshire — the stark cooling towers of Fiddlers Ferry Power Station across the Mersey, the more graceful tower of Daresbury nuclear laboratory, the delicate-looking superstructure of the Runcorn suspension bridge and the outline of several chemical works over in Widnes.

The history of Runcorn as a settlement dates back to Roman times, although the first fortification was built in 916 overlooking the river where the railway bridge now stands. Following the Norman conquest the area was largely laid waste but then given over to Nigel, the constable of Chester — at that time the Barony of Halton included land on both sides of the Mersey. It was later in the twelfth century that a stone castle on Halton Hill was built, largely to keep watch over the surrounding plain and the river estuary, and at the same time the first ferry across the Mersey was established for local people and pilgrims en route to the Shrine of St. Werburgh at Chester.

During the Middle Ages Runcorn was

Part of the castle ruins ▶

comparatively prosperous, with two fairs each year, a weekly market and the presence of two windmills, yet it remained a small place. It was the arrival of the Canal Age in the 18th century which dramatically changed this situation, largely due to the Duke of Bridgewater who wished to increase the sales of his coal which he mined at Worsley. By 1765 he had completed the canal connecting Worsley and Manchester, and in 1766 he managed to get an Act passed allowing him to extend this to Runcorn and thus provide a connection to the open sea and to the major port of Liverpool. The canal had the distinction of being the first totally constructed canal in England i.e. it did not use a river or estuary as part of its course. Yet before work on the canal really started the Duke had Bridgewater House built as a temporary residence from where he could keep his eye on the construction of the canal terminus with its ladder of locks. Still standing at the heart of Runcorn's dockland, this three-storey building is a picture of Georgian elegance in a most unlikely spot. Right from the very beginning the canal was a success, its construction bringing industry, prosperity and people to Runcorn. Yet soon much congestion was caused by boats waiting to enter the locks, and to relieve this the Waterloo Basin was built in which boats could assemble.

By the mid-nineteenth century Runcorn had slate works, a timber yard, three shipyards and an increasingly important tanning industry. For part of the nineteenth century it was also well-known as a health resort, with its boarding houses and day trips from Liverpool, yet this feature of the town naturally declined as the soap and chemical industries became well-established. Then in the 1890's Runcorn experienced a boom as thousands of labourers arrived to work on the Manchester Ship Canal. This was built between 1887 and 1894 for the purpose of enabling ocean-going vessels to gain access to Manchester and avoid paying the heavy dock dues and transhipment costs at Liverpool. Yet once the canal was built Runcorn Docks began a long slow decline, since boats now sailed past Runcorn on towards Manchester which began to experience a consequent increase in its prosperity.

Over the years there have been numerous attempts to bridge the gap across the Mersey between Runcorn and Widnes, and the present iron railway bridge with fortress-like stone pylons was the first structure to be erected. Built in 1868, the bridge has three 305 ft spans with foundations which are 45 ft below the water mark; there is also a high gusty gangway for pedestrians which meant that the energetic no longer had to wait for the ferryman but for one penny could walk across the Runcorn Gap.

THE TOWNS

Runcorn suspension bridge ▶

Part of Halton village ▶

By the turn of the century it was becoming increasingly obvious that some sort of road connection would have to be built, and the result was the Transporter Bridge opened in 1905. This steel structure had a span of 1,000 ft with supporting towers which reached 190 ft. above the high water level, yet it soon became inadequate and was replaced in 1961 by the present elegant suspension bridge. This single steel arch bridge with suspended roadway has a span of 1082 ft., the top of which is 306 ft. above the high water mark; when built it was the longest steel arch bridge in Europe and the third longest in the world.

A unique transport system is also at the heart of Runcorn New Town, designated in 1964 with the aim of providing homes and jobs for 45,000 people. This transport system is composed of two elements — an Expressway and a Busway. The Expressway is 14 miles long, passing through the town's outskirts with inward access to the residential communities and outward access to industrial areas and the regional road system, while the Busway is a 12 mile route serving all parts of Runcorn and restricted to buses only. The emphasis upon public transport is demonstrated by the fact that in the new town area 90% of the residents live within a few minutes walk of a bus stop, while each residential estate also has social and shopping facilities within easy walking distance. One of the major elements of the New Town has been the provision of new housing, yet with a definite movement away from high rise flats and towards a wider variety of choice

between bungalows, town houses, single bedroom apartments and larger detached properties.

Yet Runcorn New Town is not all new and brash, since it incorporates within it the picturesque village of Halton. Here can be found some attractive 17th and 18th century houses, probably built with stone taken from the Castle after the Parliamentarian army dismantled it during the Civil War. Around The Green at the foot of the castle mound are some quaint stone cottages and the Norton

60

Cottages in Halton village ▶

NORTON ARMS
Greenall Whitley

Arms, dated 1758 and built on a solid sandstone foundation. A narrow cobbled pathway winds its way up to the castle from the village, ending in front of the Castle Hotel which was originally built as a court house and jail for the Duchy of Lancaster. The 18th century coat of arms at the front of the building helps to enliven the stonework of a rather austere looking frontage. Close by on the brow of the hill is St. Mary's Church, built by Sir Gilbert Scott in his well-used 13th century style, while a little further round is the rather grand stone vicarage dated 1739.

Doorway of Norton Arms ▶

Although the ruins of the castle itself are not open to the public, from around its walls there are some striking views of Runcorn and its monuments to the twentieth century, while from the village streets below the stark

silhouette of the ruins reminds us that the modern-day town is built around a much older historic core.

Looking up the hill to the Castle Hotel ▶

Chapter IV
THE VILLAGES

*— manorial patronage
and industrial heritage*

*The Watch House,
Parkgate* ▶

◀ *St. Michael's Church,
Shotwick*

One would be hard-pressed to think of a pleasanter place to live than a Cheshire village. Yet an even harder matter to determine would be that of choosing one in preference to another, for there are so many whose beauty and individuality press upon us for our attention, calling out for us to step aside from life's hurried journey and take our ease in their restful environs. These villages come in all shapes and sizes, a veritable pot-pourri of humanity and history. On one hand there are estate villages such as Eccleston and Rostherne, whose heart-beat has been governed by the dictates of the lord of the manor, while on the other hand there are industrial communities such as Styal and Langley which have flourished through entrepreneurial prosperity rather than landed affluence. Then there are 'down-to-earth' farming villages such as Great Barrow and Alvanley, as well as 'out-of-the-way' villages like Wildboarclough and Shotwick which give one the distinct impression of discovering places that no one else has found. Besides these there are of course the 'picture-postcard' villages of Barthomley and Eaton-by-Tarporley, not to mention the delightful village of Burton-on-the-Wirral. Each village is a world of its own, a unique amalgam of buildings and traditions and people.

THE WIRRAL VILLAGES

Present-day Cheshire could hardly be said to have its feet in the sea. Since the local government re-organisation of 1974, when most of the Wirral was 'abducted' from Cheshire and handed over to the newly-born metropolitan county of Merseyside, the closest one can get to a coastline now is the estuarine banks of the muddy River Mersey or the silty stretches of the docile River Dee. Yet almost as soon as you pass into the lower half of the Wirral Peninsula, perhaps turning off the A5117 which marks the southern boundary of this part of the county, there is a distinct feeling of being in an area which is very different to the rest of Cheshire, a definite sense of being close to the sea.

It may be the beautifully white cottages which create this impression of the seaside, conjuring up reminiscences of childhood visits to tiny fishing villages, or perhaps the salmon-pink sandstone aglow in the bright summer sunshine and evident everywhere you go. Perhaps it comes from the extensive views across the widening estuary of the Dee, glimpsed between the houses and trees as you travel further onto the Wirral, or possibly just from the stronger breeze in one's face. Whatever its cause, this feeling of the sea not only lingers but also produces a sense of expectancy — a sense of expectancy not disappointed by what is to be found here.

The village of **Parkgate**, tucked away in the north-west corner of the county, still retains the atmosphere of a seaside resort with which history has endowed it. There are delightful fishermen's cottages, some terraced houses which were built for the local coastguards, a pleasant promenade along the 'front', shops where you can buy fresh shrimps and ice cream, and a bracing wind. All that is missing are sand and sea, although even now an occasional high tide will send the water lapping up to the base of the promenade. Facing out to the Dee estuary, Parkgate has extensive salt marshes between it and the nearest permanent stretch of water, the result of continuous silting over the last 100 years or so.

Parkgate's history is an interesting one. Its name comes from Neston Park, which was a deer park between the 13th and 17th centuries. The river shore by Neston Park was one of several anchorages on the Dee where ships would unload their goods if they were too large to reach Chester. During the 18th century the village became firmly established, and was particularly important as the terminal for packet ships carrying passengers to Dublin. John Wesley crossed to Ireland from here, as supposedly did Handel in 1741 with a new Oratorio, the 'Messiah', packed in his luggage. Entertainment was needed for the waiting passengers, so assembly rooms were built for balls and gambling.

By the early 1800's Parkgate had become a fashionable bathing spa, although by this time its importance as a port was diminishing due to the gradual silting-up of the Dee. It seems to have been the most popular resort in the north of England, attracting a smart and fashionable clientele who came for the invigorating air and the sea bathing. Yet decline again set in with the development of New Brighton as an alternative resort, and Parkgate was left very much in the hands of the shrimp fishermen. In more recent years the fortunes of the village have again revived, particularly since it became recognised as an attractive residential area and as a very pleasant place for a day out — although The Parade may no longer be

THE VILLAGES

thronged with hopeful bathers, their place has been taken by cars on the promenade whose occupants are happy to gaze out to the Welsh hills across the salt marshes of the estuary while enjoying a locally-made ice cream.

Despite its changing fortunes, Parkgate still has a great deal to offer both the resident and the casual visitor. On the road down from Neston to Parkgate, just before the sharp right hand corner taking you on to The Parade, are a number of 18th century cottages. One of these, Dover Cottage, has achieved some fame as being the house where Emma Lyon, later to become Lady Hamilton and the mistress of Admiral Nelson, came to stay in June 1784. Around the corner and along The Parade itself is Mostyn House, originally the George Inn. It became a school in 1865 and is famous as the birthplace of Sir Wilfred Grenfell, renowned for his work as a medical missionary on the Labrador coast of Canada. The rather overpowering black and white frontage of the school dates only from 1932.

Further along The Parade and up Coastguard Lane, just beyond the small sandstone chapel, is a row of whitewashed cottages running parallel with the river. These are the Coastguard Cottages which were built in the 1850's – a coastguard station with a chief boatman and two or three men was maintained here until about 1875. Parkgate's marine heritage is further evident in the Watch House at the end of The Parade – this was used from 1799 to 1828 as a lodging house for customs officers since it was a convenient place for them to keep watch on shipping.

There are two particularly attractive groups of houses in the village which are worth seeing. Beyond the Watch House are Pengwern, Sawyers Cottage and Dee Cottages – the central three-storey part of this group is late 17th or early 18th century, making this the oldest building in Parkgate. The other group of houses, the most interesting in the village architecturally, consists of Leighton Banastre, Banastre Cottage and Brockleigh, set back from the bustle of The Parade in the quiet of their own park-like grounds. Leighton Banastre is one of at least three houses in Parkgate where it has been claimed that Handel stayed in 1741 on his way to Dublin for the first performance of the Messiah, even though it seems that Handel in fact stayed in Chester!

Going south towards Chester from this now far-flung corner of the county, one passes first of all through **Neston** with its intimate atmosphere of a small town. At the beginning of the 19th century Neston was the most significant place on the Wirral, flourishing as a market town and coaching station while sharing in Parkgate's prosperity. Nowadays, Church Lane is still very much a charming 'olde-worlde' corner and there are some attractive Georgian houses near the centre along Parkgate Road.

From Neston Cross one can take a right turn down a minor road towards the 'picture postcard' village of Burton. On your way there it is definitely worthwhile stopping off at Ness Gardens, the botanic gardens of the University of Liverpool. Here can be found one of the finest collections in the country of trees and shrubs. These beautiful gardens were planted at the end of the 19th century by Arthur Kilpin Bulley, a Liverpool cotton broker with an eye for conservation who was one of the first people to collect plants from more remote parts of the world. Since the gardens came into the ownership of the University of Liverpool in 1948 they have been greatly added to and improved.

Ness Gardens ▶

THE VILLAGES

Charming thatched cottage in Burton ▶

There are superb views of the Dee Estuary and the Welsh Hills both from Ness Gardens and from the bottom of Denhall Lane, which leads off the road to Burton just after you leave the Gardens. From this vantage point at the bottom of Denhall Lane one can see not only the rounded eminences of the Welsh Hills to the west but also the harsher outline of the Shotton steel works on the same side of the Dee, evidence of the fact that the Wirral has both rural and industrial aspects.

Denhall Lane runs parallel to the Dee for a short distance and then becomes Station Road, which leads into **Burton** village itself. This is probably the most attractive village on the Wirral, and certainly one of the best in Cheshire — along the main street which curves through Burton is a delightful variety of small cottages which seem to epitomise the very best in English village architecture. Some are built of the local red sandstone which is so characteristic of this part of the county, while others are constructed of local bricks; some are painted white with contrasting black timbers, while others have retained their natural colours; some are thatched and others are not. Many of the cottages are built upon the sandstone

Brick-and-stone cottages, Burton ▶

THE VILLAGES

rock which protrudes at different places throughout the village — it even acts as a footpath at certain points. The way in which the houses almost seem to be growing out of the sandstone gives the village an air of intimacy and permanence, as though it had been here for ever.

Interestingly enough, Burton was the biggest settlement on the Wirral in the Middle Ages and was the main port for Ireland in the 14th century — but the creeping silt put an end to that and there are now fields and marshes separating the village from the Dee. There are several genuine cruck cottages in Burton, the oldest probably being Barn End along The Rake with its predominantly wattle and daub walls and classic rolling thatched roof. The church of St. Nicholas was built in 1721 and has an unusual one-handed clock on its tower as well as an 18th century sundial in the churchyard. Burton's continuing charm as a village is probably due to the efforts expended by mainly professional and executive newcomers in restoring and maintaining the valuable properties here.

Just beyond the homely village Post Office on the main street is a narrow lane which wanders down through the fields to **Puddington**, an even smaller settlement than Burton. Life in this village was centred very much upon the Old Hall, even up to comparatively recent times.

The Massey family were the most notable occupants here residing as lords of the manor until they died out in 1715, although ownership of the whole village continued with one family right into the present century. The Old Hall is the most notable building in Puddington and although the exterior is not particularly exciting there is a delightful inner courtyard with timber framing and an open gallery. At the heart of the village is a tiny village green which was handed over to the Parish Council in perpetuity when the estate was being sold off. Puddington looks to its larger neighbour Burton for many of its community needs, since it has neither church nor school and boasts only of a small Post Office.

There are still many places in Cheshire which are largely unspoilt, and of those which remain the village of **Shotwick**, just below Puddington, must be one of the best. In many respects it is an exaggeration to call this tiny hamlet a village, since it has no Post Office, shop or community centre. Yet it does have a church and a venerable hall, both with their roots deep in history.

Despite being only a few miles from Chester, Shotwick is surprisingly hidden and isolated. It lies at the end of a narrow lane running off the main A550 to Queensferry, a cul-de-sac in every sense of the word. It is a place where time

Puddington ►

THE VILLAGES

seems to stand still — even the clock on the church tower has lost its hands! The executive and professional classes have yet to discover Shotwick, and until they do the farms and the cottages here will remain quaint and even old-fashioned, and the hens and bantams will still strut across the lane freely. The village peace is disturbed only by the barking of farm dogs, and those who live here have time to chat. There used to be a pub, but its absence now may be a blessing in helping to preserve the unusual peace and quiet.

Like the other Deeside villages, Shotwick was at one time an important port — it is said that the waters of the river reached the church walls, and to prove the point the local farmer will show you the iron rings on the walls where boats were tied up. Henry II left for Ireland from Shotwick and in 1278 Edward I embarked for Wales from here. Even before this period the village was a fording point across the Dee on a main trading route between England and North Wales, and Wales is still only little more than a stone's throw away from Shotwick over the fields.

The sandstone church of St. Michael, right at the end of the village lane, has a very interesting Norman doorway and porch together with a tower dated about 1500. The porch displays deep score marks in the stone where archers used to sharpen their arrows, while inside the church is an unusual three-tiered Georgian pulpit. Away from the cluster of church and cottages, up a narrow track leading to Puddington, is Shotwick Hall — of attractive red brick it was built in the shape of the letter E in 1662, its noble frontage facing onto a front garden with distinguished gate piers.

Despite the close proximity of the Shotton steel works and an industrial estate, Shotwick still retains that sense of seclusion which must have been a feature of many of the Wirral villages even up to comparatively recent times. Even electricity only found its way here in the middle of this century! The rambling cottages with their tidy gardens and well-worn cobble pathways, the historic church facing out to the Dee, and a hall which has seen generations of families come and go — all these are facets of a hidden gem which is well worth discovering. Go during the week and you may well find that you are the only visitor there.

By way of contrast, **Willaston** is a village which seems to typify the changing face of the Wirral. Although it is one of the oldest villages on the Peninsula, it has grown considerably over the last twenty years or so with a large number of new houses — this mixture of ancient and modern is particularly evident around the village green, now bounded by new flats and town houses as well as by the Old Hall and the Old Red Lion. The local guide produced by the

Shotwick Hall ▶

THE VILLAGES

Old Red Lion, Willaston ▶

Willaston Residents and Countryside Society points out that a feature of Willaston which is unusual in the Wirral is the development of the village in the form of a number of farm houses grouped around a large green. Two of these farmhouses are now banks, again demonstrating the changes which have overtaken the village.

Willaston has a number of fascinating buildings, several of which have been recently restored. The Old Hall is built of red sandstone and brick, with an Elizabethan frontage in the shape of the letter E — very similar to the hall at Shotwick. It is more likely that the hall was built in the 17th century, and not in 1558 as the datestone over the front door might suggest. Just at the back of the village green is the Old Red Lion, which was a licensed inn up to 1928 but since then has been a private dwelling. Only a few years ago this building was faithfully and lovingly restored to what must

closely resemble its original appearance — the date of 1631 on the front of the building does not seem early enough to be the date of construction of the oldest part, and in the view of Mr. E.C. Bryan (writer of 'Willaston's Heritage') it is probably the year in which the gabled wing was added or some other improvement made to the property.

Just down The Weind from the Old Red Lion is Corner House Farm, so called because of its position at the south-west corner of the village green until other buildings were erected. The gabled stone part of this house probably dates from the early 17th century, and there is a later brick wing built in the early 18th century. Another building with a similar history is Ash Tree Farm on Hadlow Road. This is a cruck-framed cottage which was originally of wattle and daub in a timber frame, dating back to the 16th century or even earlier.

Ash Tree Farm, Willaston ▶

THE VILLAGES

A little further down Hadlow Road the visitor has an opportunity for an excursion into the village's more recent past. Here can be found Hadlow Road railway station, no longer echoing with the sound of trains and passengers but rather a quieter witness to past glories. The station is now a feature on the Wirral Way, a twelve mile linear park created along the line of the old railway track which ran between Hooton, just to the east of Willaston, and West Kirby on the tip of the Wirral Peninsula. The platform, waiting room and ticket office have been restored and refurbished to appear just as they would have been on a typical day in 1952 — as the plaque on the station wall declares, only travellers and staff are missing. The scene has been accurately re-created right down to the last detail, with advertisements for 'Hignett's Smoking Mixture' at 4d per ounce — and without any mention at all of a Government Health Warning!

Willaston Mill ▶

Willaston's last feature of interest is its mill, now a private house and to be found, as one might expect, on Mill Lane. Built in 1800 as the successor to an ancient 'peg mill', it was the largest of the old Wirral flour mills and is a fine example of a tower windmill constructed of hand-made bricks. At the top it had five sets of grinding stones, driven by wind and used for grinding cattle food. On the ground floor were four sets of bigger grinding stones, driven by steam, for making wheat into flour. With the coming of large power-driven mills the making of flour became uneconomical, but this mill continued to produce cattle food until 1930 when a storm broke its sails and it ceased to function. No doubt the inhabitants of this rather unusual residence have some fine views of the Mersey estuary — even from a little further along Mill Lane one can quite clearly see Liverpool's two cathedrals.

THE METROPOLITAN FRINGE

Although the villages of north Cheshire could well feel threatened by the proximity of their metropolitan neighbours Merseyside and Greater Manchester across the county boundary, they scarcely show it. In many ways they have retained their individuality and charm despite the obvious pressures from commuters who wish to live here and the large numbers of visitors who find their way in from the nearby towns.

The village of **Hale** near Widnes is a newcomer to Cheshire — in the face of the threat of being embraced by the metropolitan giant of Merseyside in 1974, it ran a vigorous campaign to be included among the affections of Cheshire. It succeeded, but its namesake near Altrincham was not so 'fortunate' and is now within Greater Manchester. In many respects it is quite appropriate that Hale (near Widnes) should be firmly within Cheshire, for it is a village with many attractive cottages, a sense of history and a strong community spirit — elements which seem to typify many Cheshire villages.

Historically, Hale was a manor whose lord enjoyed various claims over the small agricultural community of serfs who worked on his land and where ceremonies and traditions existed which were characteristic only to itself. Although the present owners of the estate, the Flectwood-Hesketh family, are not officially lords of the manor they are still referred to as the squires of the village and in fact live in The Manor House with its attractive Queen Anne frontage (although this was originally the parsonage). An interesting tradition which has been retained right up to the present day in Hale is the election of a Lord Mayor, a ceremony which appears to go back to at least 1320. The office of Lord Mayor used to be held by the oldest tenant farmer in the village, but he is now elected from among the Freemen of Hale, of which there are about sixty. A Freeman is chosen by virtue of the service which he has rendered to the village and by the quality of his life — the oath which he takes confirms him as being:

"A fair drinker,
A thorough smoker,
A suitable companion,
A lover of the fair sex
And all things belonging thereto".

Perhaps the most notable inhabitant of Hale was John Middleton, better known as the Childe of Hale (1578 - 1623) who was reputed to have grown to a height of 9ft 3in before he was twenty. The whitewashed cottage where he lived still stands in the village, with its thatched

THE VILLAGES

roof and two small windows high up in the gable which faces on to Church End — but the local historian is quick to point out that there is no truth in the tradition that the Childe of Hale slept with his feet protruding from these same windows! The Childe's grave can be seen in the churchyard just up the road from his cottage, surrounded by iron railings and bearing an unusually laid out epitaph.

The village has a number of very interesting buildings, particularly its thatched cottages with some dating from the 1600's. These create that 'olde worlde' charm which one so easily senses in a place like Hale, and their influence is seen in the large number of more modern houses at the Liverpool end of the village which mimic the traditional cottages with their thatched roofs and overhanging eaves. At the other end of the village, along a narrow track running from Church Road, is Hale lighthouse overlooking the River Mersey. This lighthouse was first built in 1836 to help vessels negotiate their hazardous way around Hale Head, although the present structure dates from 1906. With the reduction in shipping over the years the lighthouse became obsolete and was closed down in 1955; it is now only a landmark, but is worth a visit for the excellent panoramic views from here across the estuary towards Helsby and Overton Hills as well as towards the contrasting chemical works.

Perhaps the most unusual feature of Hale is the 'duck decoy' on the Widnes side of the village, one of only a handful which remain in the whole country. This is a small wooded area standing in lonely isolation on marshy land between the village and the river — surrounded on all its five sides by a moat, the wood and the quiet pond at its centre can only be reached by a narrow swingbridge. The decoy had been in operation since 1631 up to comparatively recent times, ducks being lured from the pond along narrow channels into cages at the end where they were caught and killed. The area has now been taken over by the Cheshire Conservation Trust, who have been working to restore the decoy to its original condition after some years of neglect and are turning it into a wildlife sanctuary — no doubt the ducks appreciate this enlightened change of use!

Perhaps the last words about Hale can be left to Sir John Betjeman, who described the village so aptly in the following way:

"The Manor House, the Green, the Church —
From Runcorn to West Kirby
You will not find howe'er you search
So sweet a rus in urbe"

Across the Mersey estuary from Hale and up the Manchester Ship Canal past Warrington is

Lymm, verging on a town in size but still very much a village in character — even the signs from the main A56 road will direct you down along Eagle Brow to the 'village centre'. Here a focal point is The Dingle, an intimate tree-lined area alongside the small stream flowing down from Lymm Dam, with white terraced cottages on one side and the Spread Eagle Hotel on the other. Just around the corner is The Cross, the most significant feature in the village landscape — it has an aura of permanence and age-old stability due to its solid sandstone base raised above the village streets and the surrounding cobbled area. The steps which were cut into the sandstone foundation are now rounded and smooth through the passage of time and also the passage of many feet as visitors have climbed upwards to read the inscriptions around the three sundials on the south, west and east faces of the stone canopy. These inscriptions seem to be even more relevant in the light of the rush and bustle of modern life — 'Save Time', 'Think of the Past' and 'We are a Shadow' are the words of wisdom which the Cross still proclaims to the crowds around it.

The present Cross probably dates from the 17th century, with some alterations added in the restoration work carried out during 1897 to mark the Diamond Jubilee of Queen Victoria. Beyond this, even the locals are uncertain as to its age and function, although it seems that the original structure may well have been on the same spot in the fourteenth century. The guide to Lymm suggests that the medieval cross here could well have served as an open air preaching station, as an assembly point and meeting place for the villagers or to mark a small market space. Whatever its function, it seems to have been the main focal point for village activity over the centuries.

An enticing footpath from the bottom of The Dingle leads you up through the trees to Lymm Dam on the other side of the main road. It is quite a surprise to find such an extensive stretch of water so close to the village centre. Above the pleasantly wooded slopes can be seen the tower of the parish church, overlooking the dam in a maternal fashion and adding to the settled scenic beauty which this man-made feature has developed since its creation in the early 19th century.

Just across from the parish church is Rectory Lane leading down to Lymm Hall, one of the oldest and most significant buildings in the village. Although much restored and added to, the Hall is very obviously a fine E-shaped Elizabethan mansion with part of the original moat still in evidence. In the landscaped grounds can be seen two relics of past life here

THE VILLAGES

— an old 'ice-house', the forerunner of modern-day refrigeration, and two cockpits, reminiscent of a previously fashionable (if gruesome) leisure pursuit. There is also the very unusual Moat House with a strangely rounded roof, Dutch gables and 17th century facade — whatever its purpose in the past, it is now a rather distinctive dwelling house.

Although Lymm's roots have traditionally been in agriculture, it has nevertheless had an interesting industrial past. From about 1700 small industries such as tanning, quarrying and iron working developed here assisted by the coming of the Bridgewater Canal in 1765, while in the 19th century Lymm became an important centre for the fustian cloth trade. The cutting of fustian cloth began as a small domestic industry, and a number of small three-storey terraced cottages were built with the top storey housing the cutting benches and acting as a long workshop. Such cottages can still be seen on Church Road, and many of the older cottages and terraces in Lymm were built originally for workers in the fustian trade. The cloth itself was brought in to the village from Manchester, usually along the Bridgewater Canal. In the early years of this century a small but significant salt-working industry grew up, but this proved to be the last chapter in the village's industrial story.

Although Lymm is now primarily a residential dormitory for larger towns such as Warrington and Manchester, it still retains its independence despite their proximity and successfully maintains its village character even in the face of modern development.

Little Bollington is a small village just a few miles to the east of Lymm, connected to it by the Bridgewater Canal which provides a pleasant walking route between them. It had originally been known simply as Bollington, but the 'Little' came to be added after local government re-organisation in 1974 when it was included in the same district as its rather larger namesake near Macclesfield. The inhabitants of Little Bollington could rightly feel somewhat aggrieved at the change having to be made by them — their village is situated on the River Bollin as the name would suggest, but the Bollington near Macclesfield is on the River Dean and therefore to some extent could be regarded as an impostor. Despite this, the local people seem to have accepted the change happily enough.

Little Bollington is really on the 'back doorstep' of Dunham Massey Hall, just across the other side of the river and now lying outside Cheshire. Described in 1801 as 'one of the most beautiful residences in Cheshire' the

Hall stands in a very attractive parkland setting and most people find their way to the village by following one of the paths through the estate. At one time Little Bollington was a totally rural and self-contained community with a smithy, a joiner's shop, a wheelwright, a baker and a pumpman who maintained pumps for miles around. In years gone by there would have been quite a lot of freight activity on the Bridgewater Canal, with corn, coal and night-soil being unloaded at the Bollington Wharves. Nowadays, the canal is only seasonally busy with pleasure and holiday craft. The main village is essentially a neat collection of cottages and council houses at the end of a cul-de-sac running off the A56, with a popular pub called The Swan with Two Nicks and a dairy farm just across the road. The parish as a whole embraces a much larger area of the surrounding countryside, and down narrow winding lanes (such as Spode Green Lane) one can discover some old fashioned ivy-covered cottages, with some equally old fashioned inhabitants. Although not particularly obvious, Little Bollington does have some considerable antiquity about it — two pubs in the area (The Nag's Head and Ye Old Number 3) were coaching inns at one time, and some of the farms have Georgian houses, while White Cottage — the oldest building in the village — is Elizabethan. Its popularity as a stopping-off point for travellers has remained, but now these travellers arrive by canal boat rather than by horse-drawn coach.

One of the characteristic features of Cheshire is the estate village, where life was centred around the great Hall and where many of the local people would be dependent upon the 'lord' for their livelihood. **Rostherne** is a classic example of such a village, where until comparatively recently every single house was owned by the Egerton family of Tatton and where every person was employed on the estate. Even now the houses are in one ownership, although the estate was broken up a few years ago and the Hall is a National Trust property open to the general public.

Although many new people have come into the village, the older inhabitants are still full of stories about the Egerton family and their dominance in village affairs. There seems to have been an unusual mixture of benevolence and 'oppression' — although Lady Mary Egerton built a new 'square' of 12 houses in 1909 at the south end of the village for some of the local people, and philanthropically provided a common laundry (a unique feature at the time), she had the houses built without backdoors so that the women had no opportunity to spend time gossiping! Again, around the side of the church there is an

◀ *The Cross at Lymm*

Thatched cottages in the village of Rostherne

Gawsworth Church

King Charles' Tower, Chester

THE VILLAGES

unusual little area which was fenced off by Lord Egerton — it appears that one day he discovered a courting couple there and decided to put an end to the practice. Only a mile and a half away from Tatton Hall, Rotherne was very much the backyard of the Egerton family who regarded the people in the village their property as much as the buildings.

Rostherne is very definitely a haven of tranquility, despite being close to the M56 motorway and the busy main road from Altrincham to Northwich. The first hint one gets of the village is the delightful view across Rostherne Mere, with the square tower of St. Mary's Church peering over the trees from its elevated position on the far side. The Mere is 164 acres in extent and is now a protected bird sanctuary, so public access is limited — this is probably just as well since there are stories in the village of this being the scene of several suicides. Getting to the village is quite an adventure in itself, following narrow tree-lined country lanes for a short distance before alighting upon either the church at the north end or small terraces of cottages at the south end. Perhaps the most attractive features are the immaculately-kept houses, each one named after a tree or flower and proudly displaying their names in white lettering on the same grey slate. One of the prettiest is Apple Tree Cottage, possibly the oldest in the village, which outwardly is brick-built but underneath is made of wattle and daub. There is also a very unusual fire insurance plate on the front wall,

Looking across Rostherne Mere ▶

one of only two such plates in north Cheshire. Around the village one can spot the tell-tale signs of an earlier, less technologically advanced era — such as the hand pumps for drinking water which were in use before a piped supply was laid on. The church itself, mostly built in the 18th and 19th centuries through the generosity of the Egerton family, is beautifully situated above Rostherne Mere with some very extensive views across it from the churchyard. The site has been occupied by a church from the earliest times, and it was once the parish

Picturesque Rostherne ▶

church for Knutsford; the interesting and unusual lych gate at the entrance to the churchyard dates from 1640, but has been restored since. There is a post office in the village but no public house — it seems that two former inns, the Red Lion and the Grey Horse, were closed in the 1840's by the Egerton family 'for the benefit of the inhabitants'.

If Rostherne is a classic example of the way in which the traditional landed gentry have influenced and controlled village life in Cheshire, then the village of **Styal** must be equally important in demonstrating the benevolence of one of the more enlightened leaders of the Industrial Revolution. Sandwiched between Wilmslow and Manchester, within earshot of Ringway Airport, Styal village is a living monument to the better aspects of the early cotton industry and was developed by Samuel Greg for the workforce of his Quarry Bank Mill, built in the Bollin Valley just to the south of the village in 1784. Although the mill ceased cotton production in 1959, it has since been opened to the public and through various displays and exhibitions gives a detailed and lively account of life in the early industrial era.

Samuel Greg, originally from Belfast, was a pioneer of the factory system which largely replaced the cottage workshop, and his Quarry Bank Mill illustrates a turning point in British industrial and social history. He employed large numbers of boys and girls drawn from workhouses and orphanages, yet he was no harsh taskmaster — the community which he created here was based on an effective blend of humanitarianism and self-interest which was both innovative and exemplary. Most of the very attractive cottages in Styal village, with their homely porches and well-tended gardens, were built in the 1820's after a period of great expansion at the mill. The small school and the Norcliffe chapel also date from the same period, while the Methodist Chapel was developed out of a former barn in 1837. To the west of the main village group is Oak Farm, a beautiful black and white timbered farmhouse which is probably the oldest building in Styal. This had been acquired by Greg in 1802, enabling him to provide both food and lodging for his growing workforce. Prior to this he had already built the Apprentice House in 1796, situated between the mill and the village, although his first employees had been housed at Farm Fold, Shaw's Fold and cottages on Holt's Lane.

Styal village, now in the ownership of the National Trust, is an enticing place to visit because of the really delightful mixture of

◀ *Styal Village* ▶

78

THE VILLAGES

*How things used to be at
Styal* ▶

buildings to be seen here — rows of red-brick terraced houses with porches and handrails at their front doors, individual thatched cottages with their 'timber skeleton' picked out in black in contrast to the white painted brickwork, and two tiny chapels. Although the village shop is no longer in business, there is an interesting display of the food and products which would have been sold here at least a generation ago. The attractive buildings in the village are complemented by their surroundings, set in a picturesque frame of cobbled footpaths, colourful gardens and an immaculately kept 'village green'. Footpaths leading away from the southern end of the village, past the remains of an old cross, will take you through green pastures with grazing cows down to the river. The shady woodland on the banks of the Bollin is part of Styal Country Park, covering approximately two hundred and fifty acres of Samuel Greg's original estate and embracing the village, Quarry Bank Mill and woods to the north and south of the mill along the river banks. The walks through this pleasant wooded landscape, following the river, are justifiably popular — although one feature which may not be appreciated by all those who pass through is the unusual variety of hardwood and exotic trees which can be found here.

The Mill itself, like the village, is full of life — although its traditions may be rooted in the past, its heart is very much in the present. This museum-in-the- making for the cotton industry

is beginning to hum again, with a variety of textile workshops taking place in an early Victorian weaving room within the Mill. As well as being able to view the original Manager's Office and Counting House, the Water Wheel chamber and the Turbine Control room, one can discover more about the living and working conditions of the work force here through displays and reconstructions which bring the early cotton industry back to life. No doubt Samuel Greg, master cotton spinner and humanitarian entrepreneur, would have been very satisfied to see how his enlightened vision has been respected and embraced by our own generation.

Another village on the banks of the River Bollin is **Prestbury,** tucked away in the north-eastern corner of Cheshire and probably the best-known commuter village in the county, with at least half the working population travelling more than 10 miles to their place of employment. For some people this might detract from their appreciation of the village, reducing it in their eyes merely to a 'dormitory suburb' for those with the money to be able to live here. Yet that would be a very unfair evaluation of a handsome village with a long history and a variety of very interesting buildings.

Probably one of the most attractive features is the approach to Prestbury along narrow lanes which wind their way over undulating hills

◀ *Styal chapel*

THE VILLAGES

Norman chapel, Prestbury ▶

beneath an almost unbroken canopy of trees. This is particularly the case on the western side, coming into the village from Wilmslow and Alderley Edge. Here especially can be found those large, elegant modern houses upon which Prestbury's reputation is based. Like a number of other villages in Cheshire, Prestbury has a linear settlement pattern rather than the more traditional 'nucleated' one focussing on a village green, and the buildings along the main central street, well described in the literature produced by the local amenity society, are the key to understanding its history. The vernacular architecture which is evident here is a strong contrast to the newer housing estates which have been built to accommodate the demand from commuters.

The main street is broad and long, and from 1633 to the start of the 20th century it was the scene of twice-yearly cattle fairs which were famous for miles around. On these occasions it was thronged with animals and stockmen, and it appears that defensive measures had to be taken against these 'invaders' — residents boarded up their windows, while village children were given sticks and told to guard gates and beat off those animals which attempted to intrude into gardens. At the southern end of the street is Prestbury Hall, an impressive mansion dominating this part of the village, while next to it is the original village school. Built in 1720 'for the purpose of teaching ten of the poorest children in the township', it later became the Reading Room and is now a bank.

Just across from Prestbury Hall, on both sides of the main street, are some attractive early 19th century weavers' cottages with characteristic long horizontal windows in the top storey. It was in this top storey where weaving was carried out on hand looms — the weavers would walk to nearby Macclesfield for silk yarn, return, and after weaving walk back with the finished material. Such a journey was always known as 'padding'. Similar three-storey weavers' cottages can be seen at the northern end of the village just beyond the Bollin.

Along the main street in Prestbury ▶

The Legh Arms, on the left hand side going through the village, was built about 1580 and was originally called the Saracen's Head. Its unusual inn sign was a rather ill-informed attempt at depicting a Saracen — the resulting picture of a negro led the inn to be known as The Black Boy. A little further on is St. Peter's Church, a focal point in the village scene. This building has dominated life in Prestbury over the centuries, and it is in this area that one can find the oldest evidence of the village's history. The church itself, first built about 1220, was the 'mother' church for the surrounding area,

exercising ecclesiastical jurisdiction over 35 townships. It is an attractive structure, but even so one's attention is quickly drawn to the small chapel at the back of the churchyard. This is the Norman predecessor of the church, probably built on the site of a Saxon church in the late 12th century. The doorway with its rounded arch and sculptured decoration is an excellent example of Norman architecture, one of the few remaining in the county. Also in the churchyard are remains of a preaching cross dating probably from the 8th century, evidence of Prestbury's significance as a religious centre in Saxon times.

Just across from the church is a delightful 'black and white' timber framed building at one time called the Priest's House. Dating from at least 1448, it was originally a vicarage — marriage ceremonies took place here, and at one time the vicar was forced to address his congregation from the balcony when the church was closed. The building has been restored to preserve its unusual character and is now a bank.

Crossing over the river one comes immediately to Bollin Grove, a charming little 'backwater' with some terraced cottages which are an early

THE VILLAGES

example of housing for industrial workers — this part of the village was the site of an early corn mill which became a cotton mill and then finally a silk weaving mill. An unusual feature here is the way in which the bed of this river has been 'flagged' over — this was done to facilitate the flow of water to the mill. Pearl Street, running off Bollin Grove, was originally part of the main village street until the New Road was built — consequently the 'front' of the Admiral Rodney pub, at one time facing on to Pearl Street, is now regarded as its 'back'! Pearl Street is very much a 'hidden gem' of Prestbury, if one can excuse the obvious pun, and here can be found another row of weavers' cottages (dated 1686) with walls and slates of the fawn-coloured Kerridge stone. It is here, around Bollin Grove and Pearl Street, that one can experience the intimacy which is still to be found in Prestbury, and where the roar of traffic even on the main street can be left behind.

THE PENNINE BORDER

Beyond Prestbury, to the east of the A523 running south from Stockport through Macclesfield and on to Leek, the character of Cheshire changes quite noticeably. This is where the Cheshire Plain merges into the Pennine foothills, where the hills and valleys become more accentuated, where the trees begin to disappear, where the winding country lanes become less common, and where the village communities seem more tightly drawn together for security and protection. It is a marvellous place with unrestricted views which would do justice to the Lake District and villages which would flatter the Cotswolds. The main building material has traditionally been the buff-coloured carboniferous sandstone, used for both roofs and walls, which conveys a rugged appearance suitable for the hill setting of the area while at the same time creating a sense of intimacy and warmth.

The village of **Rainow** is prettily situated just above the River Dean, a few miles to the north-east of Macclesfield. Coming into Rainow is a delight whatever direction you approach from since the village lies tantalisingly at the foot of the surrounding hills, just waiting to be explored. From Kerridge Hill especially one has a bird's-eye view of this closely-knit settlement, and many of the older houses were probably built with stone quarried here. The seclusion and charm of Rainow betrays the impact which the Industrial Revolution had — at one time there were 24 mills in operation and cotton spinning, calico printing, silk throwing and engineering all flourished in the village. All the mills have now disappeared except for a few ruins. Also indicative of Rainow's industrial heritage are the many flagged footpaths leading across to Bollington and Macclesfield — these were used by the local inhabitants to get to their workplaces and it is an enjoyable experience for visitors to trace

Looking down on Rainow ▶

81

THE VILLAGES

their steps through the open fields and onto the hills to the towns beyond.

Rainow was originally a farming community before the Industrial Revolution and the earliest records show that during the medieval period several farms were already established here, possibly in Rainowlow to the north of the main village. This is a tiny secretive hamlet of farms and cottages very much off the beaten track but well worth finding.

James Mellor's private chapel ▶

One of Rainow's most interesting characters was James Mellor, a local preacher who lived in the village from the start of the 19th century. His home, Hough Hole House at the bottom of Sugar Lane, is a fascinating testimony to a man whose energy, inventiveness and practical skills appear to have known no limit. The house itself, probably built in the 16th century, was altered both by James Mellor and his father before him, and a water wheel was introduced to provide power and run an organ. The garden also bears the stamp of Mellor's character — there is a small private chapel which was built in 1844 and in which Mellor would conduct his own services, while around the garden are

Howling house, Rainow ▶

numerous stone slabs bearing inscriptions from the Bible which the preacher cut out with his own hands. Mellor's musical 'bent' is further evidenced by the unusual 'howling house' to be found in the garden — this small stone structure, resembling a garden shed in appearance, has a space in the rear wall for a stringed contraption called an 'Aeolian harp' which produces rather eerie howling sounds when the front doors are opened and the wind is allowed to blow through.

Outside the village the large parish of Rainow still retains some evidences of its great antiquity — of particular interest are the old tracks and bridle paths running across the parish en route to the Pennines and beyond. Some of these tracks were used by salt carriers in medieval times as they brought salt from places like Nantwich round the end of Kerridge Hill and then into Derbyshire. Jenkin Chapel, built by local farmers, stands at the junction of three such tracks or salters' ways, while an even older route passes nearby Saltersford Hall as it makes it way over the hills through Oldgate Nick. There are also evidences of much older Roman roads in this area.

Hidden over the other side of Kerridge Hill from Rainow is **Kerridge** itself, a tiny community which continues to maintain its independence from the much larger Bollington just to the north. The terraced cottages made of local buff-coloured stone are tightly grouped on the wooded slopes overlooking them, while the stone-flagged footpaths provide some delightful walks both around the houses and up onto Kerridge Hill with its extensive views stretching right across to Rivington in Lancashire and Shining Tor on the Cheshire border. Kerridge has more than its fair share of unusual monuments — from the Redway Tavern one can meander gently up to White Nancy, an unusual bell-shaped structure which was possibly built as a garden house by the Gaskell family in nearby Ingersley Hall, while on Redway Lane can be found William Clayton's castellated tower, built in 1837 as a ventilation shaft for prospective coal workings which never in fact materialised. Despite the threats to the village resulting from the continuous quarrying activities here, Kerridge is a lovely place to visit because of the attractiveness of the houses and the marvellous views of the whole of eastern Cheshire which you can get from the top of Kerridge Hill.

Just a few miles to the south-east of Macclesfield is the village of **Langley**, really the gateway into some very attractive countryside covering Tegg's Nose Country Park and Macclesfield Forest. The village itself is perhaps most notable for its previous importance in the

THE VILLAGES

silk industry, although the first 'industry' of any significance was button-making, first developed by Charles Roe who was so active in Macclesfield. Then in 1820 William Smith came to Langley from Nottingham and set up a silk processing works because of the pure water available from the River Bollin. In 1826 he built Langley Mill, which eventually grew to be the biggest silk printing, dyeing and finishing works in the world. A particularly characteristic feature of the silk printing process here was the use of wooden blocks bearing intricate designs which were created using thousands of metal pins — these blocks were still being used up to the time when the mill was closed down in 1964, even though screen printing had been in operation in Britain since about 1930. At the height of its prosperity the village had five mills, with three being driven by water wheels, and up to four hundred people were employed in the silk industry. Many of these were housed in the terraced cottages which line the main street through the village, and here again one can see the characteristic three storey dwellings with their upper garret rooms where silk weaving was carried out.

Away from the village and further into the hills the area takes on special significance for the natural historian — it is one of the best locations in the country for bird watching, and a number of rare plants (such as the Needle Spikerush and the Orange Foxtail) are to be found here, especially in association with the four reservoirs built between 1850 and 1929 to supply Macclesfield. These reservoirs also attract a great variety of birds, and one of Langley's most famous 'sons' was the famous

bird painter Charles Tunnicliffe. Other beauty spots worth seeking out are Tegg's Nose Country Park (with its superb views looking west to the Wrekin and the Welsh mountains, east to the Derbyshire Hills and south to Mow Cop), and the mysterious Macclesfield Forest, at one time a royal hunting 'forest' and now thickly covered with coniferous plantations.

A similar sense of mystery extends throughout much of this eastern part of Cheshire, developing an expectancy within the visitor as each new valley is entered and each hill surveyed. This is particularly true of **Wildboarclough,** situated in a sheltered fold of the Pennines between the Macclesfield to Buxton road and the A54. It really is a wonderful place to discover, following the bubbling Clough Brook down from the northern end of this beautiful valley along a twisting narrow road which continually opens up new vistas of the surrounding wooded slopes. Wildboarclough itself, described by Pevsner and Hubbard as 'the most beautifully placed of all Cheshire villages', is really little more than a scattered hamlet consisting of a few houses, an early 19th century hall which is occasionally used as a hunting lodge, a very attractive 18th century building which was originally part of the local mill and then became a post office, and a friendly pub called the Crag Inn. The Church of St. Saviour is a comparatively modern affair, being built in 1908. Yet it all contributes to a feeling of being in an area which is very different to the rest of Cheshire — the surrounding hills are impressive rather then daunting, particularly Shutlingsloe from which there are panoramic views over

The Old Post Office, Wildboarclough ►

THE VILLAGES

most of Cheshire, while the valley of the Clough Brook is much softer by contrast. The name 'Wildboarclough' stems from the way in which the Clough Brook can so quickly become a raging torrent after heavy rainfall — the parish clerk in the area is quick to point out that the claim for it being the scene of the last boar hunt in England is completely unfounded, even though this might seem to add to its 'romanticism'. To the east of the village are the bleak and frequently mist-shrouded moors which bring you out at the Cat and Fiddle Inn, at 1690 feet the second highest pub in England. It appears that the weather — nine months winter and three months bad weather, according to one local source — dominates the lives and thinking of most of the locals in the area, and during harder winters the Cat and Fiddle Inn can be completely buried in snow.

The parish covers a large area, touching upon Macclesfield Forest in the north and embracing four churches and four pubs — quite a number considering there are only 160 inhabitants altogether in the parish! One of the churches, St. Stephen's Chapel, was first built in 1673 without seats, so people who attended services there cut rushes on a certain date each year and before taking them into the church carried them in procession around the parish. This was called Rush-bearing, and although seats have now been installed the ceremony is still carried on (usually the third Sunday in August) with the rushes being strewn on the floors and paths.

Wildboarclough encapsulates the very heart of the Pennine landscape — fast-flowing streams, scattered farms and open views out to rugged moors from a gentle valley bottom. It is all very much part of Cheshire, even though many people might not have imagined that such places could be found here.

THE DEEP SOUTH

It is in the south of the county that one can discover some classic English countryside — gentle rolling pastures, narrow lanes with verdant hedgerows, brooks and streams which are in no great hurry, and the occasional copse of trees. In this area farming has reigned supreme over the years, undisturbed and untouched by the silk or cotton industries which found no reason to come here. It is an area where the village is very much a rarity — the multitude of farmhouses and cottages seem to keep themselves to themselves by preferring their own little spots well away from the roads, perhaps representative of a self-sufficiency which the locals have developed over generations. Away from Crewe, Nantwich and neighbouring Newcastle-under-Lyme in the Potteries, it is a secluded and 'private' place in which rural life is being lived out quietly and contentedly.

The village of **Barthomley** has many of these characteristics, being largely unspoilt and one of the most attractive villages in the county. Although only one mile from the M6 motorway and close to both Crewe and Newcastle, it is a place which epitomises the best in rural village life — delightful Jacobean cottages with welcoming garden gates and porches, a 'black and white' timber-framed pub which has been in business since 1614, a sandstone church which served the lords of the manor for generations, and large farmhouses. The unusually-named St. Bertoline's Church stands in an elevated position overlooking the rest of the village, its red sandstone tower dominating the scene particularly when the late evening sunshine falls upon it. It was built largely in the 15th century, although there is a Norman doorway on the north side of the church which is almost hidden from view; it also seems likely that there was a Saxon church on the same site, together with an ancient burial ground. The church's main claim to fame is a gruesome one — during the time of the Civil War some of the villagers fired on a raiding party of the Royalist Army and were forced to take refuge in the church tower, from which they were smoked out and a dozen of their number massacred.

At one time the village and much of the surrounding area was owned by the Crewe family, and they worshipped here in St. Bertoline's. As a result one of the most interesting features is the Crewe chapel, its dark recesses on one side of the church being entered through a fine wrought-iron gateway, and inside is a well-preserved late fourteenth century alabaster effigy of a knight (which was probably Sir Robert Foulshurst) resting on a chest with his feet supported by a rather bemused-looking lion.

Across the road from the church is the White Lion Inn, and between them they seem to have catered for most of the village's needs over the last three and a half centuries. The White Lion is an intimate and friendly building which

Alabaster effigy, Barthomley church ►

◄ *Sparkling Clough Brook*

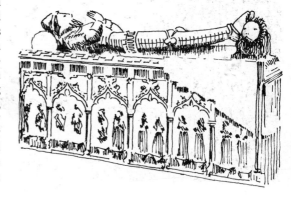

THE VILLAGES

White Lion Inn,
Barthomley ▶

◀ St. Bertoline's, Barthomley

offers a warm welcome — with the road running almost up to its timber-framed walls it quickly draws you in under its beautifully manicured thatch roof, although the stone cobbles outside the front door are pleasant enough on a hot summer's day. It has an interesting story to tell, for according to a plaque in one of the rooms the manor court rolls show that the parish clerks sold ale at least as early as the 16th century and old leases identify the White Lion as 'the clerk's cottage'. The date 1614 above an outer door commemorates the completion of the present building in the time of Sir Ranulph Crewe, whose family emblem, the silver lion, later gave the inn its name. It seems that for 200 years the twice-yearly Court Leet and Court Baron met here to administer justice for the manors of Crewe Green, Barthomley and Leighton, and in the early days the landlord's work was only a part-time occupation — landlords here have also been parish clerks, schoolmasters, grocers, joiners and wheelwrights. The White Lion is still very much the focal point of village life and during the summer members of the Barthomley Horticultural Society meet here every Friday night to compare the fruits of their labours, while in the winter everyone gravitates to the White Lion when the roads become blocked with snow.

Away from the pub and the church, along the main village street, is to be found the impressive Old Hall Farm, typical of what one would expect to find in such an important farming area with other black and white farm dwellings lying close by. The richness of the land in this area has produced a settled and stable life which is recognisable even to the visitor, and the largely 'private' ownership of Barthomley has helped to preserve it as a completely rural and unspoilt village with no significant new developments.

A few miles to the south-west is **Audlem**, the most significant village in the southern part of Cheshire and an exceptionally attractive one. It watches over the Shropshire Union Canal — known as the "Shroppie Cut" to boatmen — and a great flight of fifteen locks within a distance of two miles brings the waterway from Shropshire down to the Cheshire Plain. The nine locks between the Audlem and Swanbach bridges are called "The Thick", since they are unusually close together, and it appears that whilst the working canal boats went through 'The Thick' the women would hurry to the Audlem shops and return with their white aprons laden with provisions.

Audlem is a place with a very interesting history. The village first appears in the Domesday Book as Aldelime, the name being derived from Old Lyme or Alda's Lyme —

THE VILLAGES

Alda was a personal name and Lyme was the name of the forest which covered parts of Staffordshire, Cheshire and Lancashire. The yearly fair and weekly market were first held in the time of Edward I, but later on the place of the fair was taken by Audlem Wake which was marked by the offer of prizes to those with some rather unusual abilities: there was a prize on Wake Sunday for the first person to finish a plate of hot porridge and treacle, eaten whilst sitting on the church steps, and it was said that the first man to get drunk on Wake Sunday was called the Mayor of Audlem for that year.

The bear-stone at the foot of the twenty-six steps leading up to the church was the scene of bear-baiting during the Wake, and the mark of the large iron ring to which the bears were tied can still be seen. It was also used on cattle market days for tying up bulls. In those days one of the duties of the churchwardens was to go round the inns in the Market Place and turn out the people to come to church, where they were kept awake by the Beadle's staff which had a knot on one end for the men and feathers on the other for the ladies — it seems that human nature has always been the same! It was also the duty of the Beadle to put people in the stocks and to do any flogging ordered by the magistrates.

This sense of history continues to persist in Audlem, with its narrow winding roads and

The centre of Audlem ▶

THE VILLAGES

The Shroppie Fly, Audlem ▶

densely-grouped buildings which help to create an almost 'urban' settlement at the heart of the surrounding countryside. The most prominent building is undoubtedly the Church of St. James the Great, standing proudly above the rest of the village on a raised mound at the meeting point of the main roads running through Audlem. It is a predominantly 14th century building sturdily constructed of the characteristic red sandstone which has weathered at the edges to give a softened appearance. At the top of the church steps is a porch over the south doorway which looks as though it was a later addition but in fact probably dates from the late 13th century (according to Pevsner and Hubbard). Back on level ground by the road, immediately in front of the church, is the attractive 17th century Shambles with its solid Tuscan columns carrying the roof. It is open to the elements on all four sides and was originally a market building, although the less-enlightened and unobservant visitor may well think of it as a rather old fashioned bus shelter! Just in front of it is a cast iron memorial lamp dated 1877, which is unfortunately rather obscured by a collection of road signs.

Dotted around the village are a number of buildings which span a long period of architectural history. Along School Lane is the Old Grammar School (as one might expect) built of brick in 1652 but now somewhat

dilapidated, while down Woore Road is the Baptist chapel (1840) and a variety of other buildings from the 18th and 19th centuries. On the other side of the village by the canal is a Lock Keeper's Cottage, a typical piece of Telford architecture — with so many locks to manage the keeper's job here could not have been a very popular one! Just to the north-west along the canal is the Tudor style Moss Hall, a symmetrical timber-framed building built in the plan of a letter E, while a similar timber-framed house (built in 1615, just a year earlier than Moss Hall) is Highfields, situated well away from the village to the south-east. Then about three miles to the north of Audlem is Hankelow Hall, a once attractive but now sadly dilapidated early Georgian brick house which stands in the middle of green fields.

Following the county boundary to the west one comes to **Marbury**, another lovely Cheshire village which is just a few miles from Whitchurch. As at Audlem, the church is in an elevated position overlooking the village, but here the buildings are more informally grouped in an open setting with some delightful views to the surrounding countryside. The most important features of Marbury are its two meres, which are characteristic of Cheshire and probably resulted from the processes of glaciation. The smaller mere beside the village is surrounded by a fringe of willow trees with a border of bulrushes inside, frequented by the

THE VILLAGES

usual freshwater birds, coots, moorhens, swans and occasionally Canada geese, while the larger mere on the west side of the village is enchantingly bounded by the church, fields and beech woods.

There used to be several water pumps in Marbury, with the last one to go being that by the present school, and at one time there were five public houses, but only the Swan Inn has continued in its original form with the rest becoming farmhouses or cottages. Interestingly enough the Swan retained within it the remnants of a communal bakehouse.

The church of St. Michael is a fine 'battlemented' church built around the 15th century in a Perpendicular style, beautifully situated above the largest of the meres and within which can be found the second oldest wooden pulpit in Cheshire. Other features of this very distinctive village include Marbury Hall, built around 1810 in the Regency style overlooking the mere and the church, and an interesting group of Elizabethan 'black and white' houses.

This part of Cheshire is particularly beautiful because of the large number of meres to be found here. To the west of Marbury are the Quoisley Meres, another pair like those at Marbury with considerable landscape and wildlife interest, while to the east is the much bigger Comber Mere with its Abbey standing on the site of an old Benedictine monastery at the heart of a private park. Other meres, small and large, are dotted all around the area — at Norbury, at Baddiley and at Cholmondeley — bringing a rich diversity into the landscape.

THE WELSH MARCHES

Moving west from Marbury we cross the Llangollen branch of the Shropshire Union Canal and come to that part of Cheshire which could best be described as the Welsh Marches, an area in which historically the boundary between the Welsh and the English has been pushed backwards and forwards in accordance with their relative strengths. From just south of Malpas all the way up to Chester, along the line of the River Dee, there is a continuous chain of castle sites and fortified mounds on Cheshire soil indicating the very real unease with which Cheshire people viewed Welsh proximity across the border. Their concern for defence was justified as time and again marauding bands would sally forth to do their worst. Things are different now of course, but physical remains on the ground and names on the map are a continuing witness to less settled times. There are particularly impressive mounds and ditches (the remains of Norman fortifications) at Aldford, just behind the church and close to the River Dee, while at Pulford the motte rises from the little Pulford Brook which forms the county boundary there. A rather less spectacular mound can be seen just to the north of Shocklach village, at the appropriately named Castletown Farm, while another very good example is to be found at Malpas.

Tushingham is a scattered community of farms

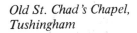
Old St. Chad's Chapel, Tushingham ▶

THE VILLAGES

and cottages along the A41 just a few miles north of Whitchurch, but within this community are to be found a number of interesting and diverse buildings. St. Chad's Chapel is the most intriguing, hidden in the midst of trees well away from the nearest road or track, the only approach to it being straight across the fields. It is a fascinating little building of well-worn brick and slate, with a miniscule tower and pyramid roof at one end, sheltering in the lee of several tall yews. The present building is largely the result of restoration work carried out in 1689-91, but it is known that a chapel has stood on this site since 1349 and at one time it was probably at the centre of a small settlement which has now disappeared. At the back of the chapel the land drops away quite steeply, and from beneath the trees one can survey the tranquil scene of green fields and hedgerows stretching out towards Shropshire. At the other end of the graveyard — with its headstones leaning at a variety of drunken angles — is a small building which houses an antique horse-drawn hearse constructed in 1880, an unusual carriage which must be one of the last of its kind. Inside, the chapel has as much to offer as on the outside — there is a Jacobean font, two family pews for the more well-to-do members of the community, wooden benches for the less-elevated folks, and a real three-decker pulpit.

At one time St Chad's Chapel stood in the grounds of Tushingham Hall about one mile to the south, but over the years the estate has gradually diminished in size and the link between Hall and chapel no longer remains. The Hall itself is a very stately affair, with its symmetrical front and Gothic-fashioned porch which were the result of rebuilding in 1814. Records show that in earlier years (at least 1645) it was an old manor house in the traditional black and white timbered style, and it must have been just as impressive then as now. To one side of the grounds at the front of the Hall is an ancient oak tree, possibly 700 years old and certainly one of the oldest in Cheshire with a massive girth of 25 feet. There is a large hollow at the base of the trunk, big enough for a man to stand in but where in fact geese used to be kept.

The other building of note in the area is the Blue Bell Inn with an attractive gabled porch at the front entrance which is indicative of its timber-framed heritage. The Inn goes back to the 16th century and is especially famous for its connections with a 'ghost' duck — perhaps the ale served here was even more intoxicating than many other places!

Further to the west of Tushingham beyond the small town of Malpas is **Shocklach,** an isolated village situated just above the River Dee, looking out over Wrexham across to the Welsh hills. It is a settled community full of friendly people and local traditions — but even those who have been here up to fifteen years still consider themselves comparative newcomers. The most notable building is St. Edith's Church, dating back to 1150 and probably the second oldest parish church in the county. A Norman building, it has a characteristic

St. Edith's Church, Shocklach ▶

THE VILLAGES

rounded-arch doorway of the time with the usual zig-zag decorations and an interesting double bell-cote at the west end. Built of large blocks of deep red sandstone, it has a very solid appearance — no doubt this has enabled it to survive the rigours of time and the elements, as the winds have swept across the flood plain of the meandering Dee. The church is situated in a wonderfully desolate spot at the end of a narrow lane running across open fields, within a beautifully kept churchyard which is obviously the pride and joy of the parishioners. Now actually 1½ miles from the centre of the village, it appears that as a result of the Black Plague the villagers moved away from around St. Edith's and settled where the village stands today.

Within the church are some interesting features worth discovering, particularly a message scratched on one of the leaded panes which reads:

"I, Robert Aldersey was here the 31st day
of October 1756 along with John Massie
and Mr. Derbyshire.
The roads were so bad we were in
danger of our lives."

How long they were there and the circumstances surrounding this message are unknown — but it does show that graffiti on public buildings is not just a modern phenomenon! Other features of the interior seem to span the centuries — there is a 14th century chancel arch, a 17th century baptistery and pulpit, and an 18th century communion rail.

The village of Shocklach itself is quaint and almost old-fashioned in the nicest sense, with its small village school, a Methodist chapel, a well patronised pub called The Bull Inn and one small shop which is open for just two hours daily and until a few years ago was the village post office. Although the present postal facilities are now somewhat unorthodox, with a retired postmaster from a nearby village coming to the pub every Thursday morning to dispense stamps and pensions to the villagers, it is an admirable arrangement which seems to be both popular and successful.

As with many Cheshire villages, Shocklach has its fair share of tales and traditions — one such tale is of a phantom coach and horses which is said to pass the top of the church lane (where the old village stood) whenever a death is imminent in the village.

Following the Dee northwards we come to an area immediately below Chester which has been owned and presided over by the Dukes of Westminster since the middle of the 19th century. There are five delightful villages to be found here within the Eaton Estate, all centred upon Eaton Hall which is the stately home of the Grosvenor family. These villages — Aldford, Pulford, Dodleston, Eccleston and Saighton — owe their existence largely to the efforts of the first Duke of Westminster who built farmhouses, cottages and churches for his estate workers. Due to the continuing care and concern of the Grosvenor family for their estate and the people who live there, these villages have largely remained unspoilt since they were first built in the 1870's and 1880's. From this part of the county, straddling the slow-moving Dee, there are some beautiful

Part of the Eaton Estate ▶

THE VILLAGES

views and panoramas across to the Welsh mountains in the west and the Peckforton Hills in the east, and the whole area is characterised by a balmy atmosphere of peace and tranquility as those who live here contentedly go about their daily work.

The village of **Aldford** has a considerable amount of the characteristic Eaton estate housing, much of it dating from the time of the first Duke of Westminster and designed largely by his architect John Douglas but with some cottages of the 1850's and 1860's which are typical of those built in the time of the second Marquess. Characteristic features to be noticed are the use of common bricks, low-pitched roofs and diamond-patterned windows. The church of St. John the Baptist was built in 1866 not at the expense of the first Duke of Westminster but of the second Marquess; it is again the work of John Douglas and is in a late 13th century style with a very distinctive tower and spire. The imitation of other periods which is such a feature of Victorian architecture can be seen in the former rectory to the east of the church since it was built in 1897 in an Elizabethan style, but it also has the characteristic blue brick patterning which is another feature of Eaton estate architecture. An evidence of Aldford's earlier history can be seen just north of the church, for the earthworks here are those of a motte and bailey stronghold which was known to have been in existence in the twelfth century.

To the west of Aldford is **Pulford**, again with the Eaton estate housing and also some particularly attractive farmhouses designed by Douglas in the usual brick, while further to the north-west just a mile from the border with Wales is **Dodleston**, very similar in style to Aldford and again an estate village with a church built in 1870 by John Douglas and many cottages dating from the time of the first Duke. To the south-east of the village can be seen Dodleston Lane Farm, a model farm which is typical of many more dotted around the estate, and in the grounds of the Old Rectory are the remains of another motte and bailey (said to be dated around 1086) while the house itself was the Cromwellian headquarters for the Siege of Chester during the Civil War.

Closer to Chester and just above the Dee is **Eccleston,** the most attractive of the Eaton estate villages. One could hardly imagine that such a quiet haven could be so close to Chester and the busy A55, yet it is. This village offers the best approach into the City, following the line of the straight Roman road through open fields on into the pleasant suburb of Handbridge and then over the river straight into the heart of Chester itself. It really is a delightful route, along a quiet country lane which takes you in ten minutes from one of Cheshire's best villages on the doorstep of the county's largest family estate through to the centre of one of Britain's most historic cities. Eccleston is really a quiet cul-de-sac which

Eccleston ▶

93

THE VILLAGES

Eccleston Parish Church ►

forms the gateway to Eaton Hall, and it has a charming mixture of cottages and other estate buildings. It is in a slightly elevated position above the surrounding countryside, hidden from the west by a protecting belt of trees and safeguarded on the east by the river. The village post office occupies an unobtrusive corner in a row of sandstone and brick-built houses at the centre of Eccleston, with an attractively-tiled pumphouse of 1874 just across the road. Close by is the huge parish church of St. Mary the Virgin, a fitting monument to the generous patronage of the first Duke of Westminster who rebuilt it at his own expense in 1899, the year of his death. The style is nominally 14th century, with the exterior characterised by an almost stark rectangularity (according to Pevsner and Hubbard). One of the most attractive features is the entrance, with some delightfully decorated wrought-iron gates which open on to an avenue of pleached limes bringing you up to the porch.

The gates and their rusticated stone piers with urns on top were originally from Emral Hall in Flintshire, dating from the early 18th century. Around the rest of the village there is a fascinating variety of buildings, mostly built by John Douglas and now predominantly private residences, including a school and schoolhouse (of 1878), a considerably earlier Manor House (dated 1632), and a number of brick and stone cottages built between 1870 and 1890.

The last of the Eaton villages is **Saighton**, again with a mixture of estate cottages and model farms including Saighton Lane Farmhouse with its unusually twisted chimney stacks, a feature which is to be seen on houses in some of the other villages too. The most important building here is Saighton Grange, at one time the principal country house of the Abbots of Chester. All that remains from the period during which they were in residence is the gatehouse, with the large house now attached to it being built in 1861 for the second Marquess of Westminster. The other interesting building is a 19th century castellated water tower which is raised above the rest of the village on top of a hill.

THE CHESHIRE PLAIN

That area of Cheshire popularly known as the Cheshire Plain is the part of the county with which outsiders are most familiar, for geography lessons in primary school have somehow instilled the idea that this corner of our fair and pleasant land consists only of the Cheshire Plain and little else. Yet this remaining area of the county has much more to offer than endless flat pasture land — among other things it has a significant range of wooded hills running from Frodsham in the north down towards Malpas in the south; it has forested areas, 'flashes' and meres; and above all else it has a tremendous diversity of villages which

THE VILLAGES

are alive and well and continuing to flourish as real communities.

Christleton is one such village. Although only just over 2 miles from Chester, it has retained its independent identity and by virtue of being on the right side of the ring road and the Shropshire Union Canal it has been protected from being engulfed in the suburbs of the growing City. It is a lively, charming place with a strong community spirit, a place which is truly representative of the best in English village life. Historically, Christleton (or 'Cristetone' as it was originally) was a large village even at the time of the Domesday Survey and may well have been the site of a settlement during Roman times, although very little remains of its earlier origins since the village was largely destroyed during the Civil War following the Battle of Rowton Moor in 1645 when King Charles' last major army was defeated by the Parliamentarians. The village we now find is a delightful blend of halls, cottages, farms and houses built over every generation since the middle of the 17th century. Largely hidden by trees from the main Whitchurch Road, one has to 'climb' over the canal bridge and pass along Pepper Street before coming into the centre of the village. Just over the bridge on the left hand side is Christleton Hall, an impressive building standing in its own grounds which was built in 1750 and is now a College of Law, while further along the road on the left hand side just across from Faulkners Lane is an unusual sandstone and brick 'tower' built into the garden wall. This is a 'gazebo', a magnificent type of garden house from which it is said that fashionable ladies of earlier days surveyed the landscape and watched the coaches passing by. Another gazebo is to be seen in the grounds of Christleton House, built in 1760 just across from the church. Pepper Street was a very fashionable area to live in Georgian times, with many of the houses being built for merchants

Ivy House, Christleton ▶

who had their businesses in Chester, and Ivy House on the opposite side to Christleton House is one such dwelling – dating from 1713 it has a very attractive three storey brick frontage with nicely decorated window surrounds and a semi-circular glass sunrise panel above the front door. Inside the house there is a Jacobean style staircase and a room with a peephole. At the centre of Christleton is the Village Green, a triangular piece of ground with trees which were planted to celebrate Queen Victoria's Silver Jubilee and a wooden-tiled pumphouse which was erected in 1886. Interestingly enough, the pump is outside rather than inside the pumphouse, which was actually built to provide shelter. As with all good English villages the church is across the road facing on to the Green, its present appearance largely a result of restoration in the 1870's but incorporating a 15th century tower. Next door to it is The Manor House, a picture of domesticity with its walls of local red brick, a cobbled footpath crossing the lovely front garden and a stone sundial watching over the passage of time. The porch is believed to date from Tudor times and the house was at one time thatched.

Across from The Manor House and slightly further up from the village green is The Old Hall, dating from about 1605 and reputed to be the oldest building in the village. It was originally a black and white timber-framed building which was later clad in brick to preserve it, and tradition has it that the house was occupied by the Parliamentarian General Brereton as his headquarters during the Siege of Chester in the Civil War. There is also a tradition that the tunnel which surrounds the whole building was at one time linked with Chester. Other interesting buildings are to be found to the south of the village green along the road leading out to Rowton Bridge,

'Gazebo' in Christleton ▶

Christleton's village pond ▶

including the Ring-O-Bells pub which was originally a coaching inn called the Red Lion; the Old Farm, a black and white building with the date 1653 cut into its timber frame; and a delightful terrace of cheery cottages (Primrose, Holly, Clematis and Rose Cottage) which are probably all over two hundred years old.

Perhaps the best spot in this thoroughly enjoyable village is the pond at the northern end, on the right hand side of Little Heath Road as one leaves Christleton. Thanks to the efforts of children and teachers from the local junior school, this former marshy area (the village 'pit' since probably 1400) has been cleared to create a beautiful village pond which is a haven for all sorts of birds and wildlife. Looking back from here towards the centre of Christleton the scene is prettily framed by encircling trees and the black and white almshouses which were built in 1868.

One can see why Christleton has been the place in which so many of Chester's Lord Mayors have chosen to live — although so close to the City in terms of physical distance, it is far removed in terms of the peace and quiet which is preserved here and the view one has of some pleasant open Cheshire countryside on the eastern side. The sense of history which embraces the whole village is complemented by the community spirit which has developed as the old and new have been woven together in a rich tapestry, creating a beautiful but thoroughly human environment. The way in which the old Smithy on Plough Lane is still working demonstrates how the traditions of the past have been brought right into the reality of the present.

Great Barrow (to the north-east of Christleton and still just a few miles from Chester) has always been a farming village and even now the continuing passage of dairy cows right through it makes wellingtons rather than shoes the order of the day. The number of farms at the centre of Great Barrow probably resulted from the need for communal protection against Welsh attacks which the earlier inhabitants feared, and even in the 1930's it was still a very busy farming community with its own railway station to which local farm produce was taken. Its tales and traditions tend to reflect the pre-eminence of those working on the land — it seems that the harvesting of early potatoes was carried out by different groups of Irishmen accommodated at either end of the village, with Saturday night being the usual time for fighting to break out between them, and there are tales galore of the old country characters associated with the area. Yet the settled life of the people here has not just been the result of their continuing pre-occupation with farming, for from the 14th century until the 1920's the village had been in the hands of just one family, first the Savages then the Rock Savages and finally the Cholmondeleys.

THE VILLAGES

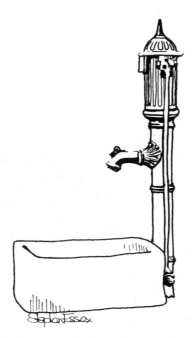

Water pump at Great Barrow ►

Petrol pump at Alvanley ►

The focal point of the village is the village pump, from which most of the locals obtained their water before a piped supply was introduced in 1936. Interestingly enough the pump was removed in 1946 but restored in 1977 to mark the Queen's Silver Jubilee, being replaced by the parish clerk whose uncle had removed it in the first instance! The cottages and farmhouses in Great Barrow, some dating back to the 17th century, are primarily of well-weathered, no-nonsense brick with a pleasant informality about them reflecting the down-to-earth nature of their inhabitants, while the parish church of St. Bartholomew is more shyly hidden at the back of the houses with its well-designed red sandstone tower of 1744 overlooking open fields. It has an interesting and unusual 'bulls-eye' window and inside there is a register of rectors going back to 1313. On the western side of Great Barrow (along Ferma Lane and then a grassy track) is Barrow Hill from where one can enjoy some striking views of Helsby Hill, the Stanlow oil refineries and Ellesmere Port, while just below here in the valley of the River Gowy is Plemstall Church, a largely 15th century building on a site which has been occupied by a church since the time of Alfred the Great.

The village of **Alvanley** is situated on rising ground just to the south of Helsby, on the edge of an area of meandering country lanes which weave their way over the central ridge running from Frodsham down to the Peckforton Hills. Like Great Barrow it has its roots very firmly in farming, and farmhouses still occupy prominent positions at the centre of the village. Yet it has the added attraction that many of the cottages here have been beautifully restored and would grace the pages of any colour calendar — the very names of Clematis

Cottage, Honey Tree Cottage and Rose Cottage seem to cry out for the passer-by to give them a second look.

Alvanley has had a long and settled history. In existence during Saxon times, it was noted in the Domesday survey and later on came into the ownership of the Arderne family, who held it until the Estate was sold off in 1922. This stability ensured that the village changed very little over the generations and that long-held traditions were maintained so that even less than 200 years ago fire dances were still held at Teuthill, a practice stemming originally from heathen fire worship, while a somewhat more homely custom called 'roping' was also practised whereby a rope held across the church gate forced newly-wed couples to pay a forfeit enabling all the locals to drink their health in the nearby public house.

The oldest building in Alvanley is the Hall, built in 1622 of the characteristic red sandstone and situated in majestic isolation to the south-east of the village. There is a tradition that a tunnel ran from the Hall to the church many years ago, but so far no evidence has been found of either an entrance or an exit. The church itself is a comparative newcomer to the village, dating from 1861 although there was a chapel on the same site before this, and so perhaps the 'medieval' style of the present building is an attempt to fit more easily into the history of Alvanley. It really is a place where the past is cherished and respected, and wherever you look you can discover buildings which are being lovingly restored to their former glories.

THE VILLAGES

Birch Cottage, Alvanley ▶

Birch Cottage looks like the classic English country cottage with its carefully thatched roof, its appealing porch, and the brilliant white walls which seem to intensify the sunlight as it cuts across the surrounding fields, while Rose Cottage really does have the roses which give it its name. Commonside Farm is another house with a thatched roof, together with the more unusual feature of some tiny four-paned windows and an end wall of red sandstone contrasting strongly with the white painted brick used for the other walls. It even seems that some people are not content with just restoring buildings which are already here — to the south-east of the village in the lee of Alvanley Cliff an entire Hall from the Nantwich area has been transported from its previous site and is being painstakingly rebuilt in its new location. Although really a 'foreigner' to these parts, this brick and timber-framed building should be a fascinating sight to walkers passing by on the Sandstone Trail which now runs through the parish. Yet Alvanley is not just a place where the past is venerated at the expense of the present, for farming is still an important feature of village life and the farmhouses themselves are attractive in their own right: Church House Farm is late Georgian with a particularly pleasing brick frontage, Poplar Tree Farm dates from 1684 (with its blocked-up windows being an indication of the 'window tax' imposed in former times), while Greenbank Farm has long been the home of one family who have farmed the land over many generations. The surrounding fields and woods in the Alvanley area are full of natural history, wisely and jealously guarded by a very active local conservation society, and there is a network of interlacing footpaths which open up endless possibilities to the walker. All in all, a delightful part of the county which typifies the best in village life.

Travelling eastwards up and down across attractive undulating countryside we come to **Great Budworth,** probably one of the best-known villages in Cheshire. This delightfully informal and intimate village was owned largely by the Egerton-Warburton family who lived at nearby Arley Hall, and their control of the village extended from 1469 when the first Hall was built right through to the 1940's when much of the estate was sold off. Great Budworth owes a great deal of its charm and character to the family's benevolent governance, and particularly to Rowland Egerton-Warburton who commissioned a number of distinguished Victorian architects to restore some of the houses and build others in a sympathetic style. Yet the village's history extends even further back than its connection with the lords of the manor at Arley — there was a priest here and probably a wooden church when Domesday Book was compiled, and before that a Roman road must have passed nearby on its way north to Wilderspool near Warrington, while the excellent visitors guide also points out that the village's name is a

THE VILLAGES

Saxon one meaning 'a dwelling by the water'. By medieval times Great Budworth was the main centre of one of the largest parishes in the country and the second largest in Cheshire, stretching from south of Northwich almost to Runcorn, and it is the church which is the oldest surviving building in the village.

The usual approach to Great Budworth is from the bottom of the village street which leads off the A559 to Warrington, a road which further south gives some striking views of the village raised proudly above the surrounding open fields. The best feature of the village is its narrow main street and the variety of houses and cottages which face on to it — no two houses are really alike, although many are built of locally-made bricks. Away from the main thoroughfare there are also some attractive little back lanes, and from either end of the village the scene is dominated by the tower of the parish church. At the foot of the hill leading up to the village is a pump and pumphouse, the source of drinking water until a piped supply was introduced in 1934, and looking up High Street from here one can just discern the first houses at the entrance to Great Budworth framed by the canopy of trees overhead. Entering the village along High Street one is impressed by just how varied and interesting the houses are — on the left hand side can be seen a lovely half-timbered black and white cottage on a sandstone base dated 1716, the dignified 17th century Old Hall behind its holly hedge, and a terrace of four houses (starting with Jasmine Cottage and ending with Rose Cottage) which were all remodelled by the Arley estate a century ago with decorative brickwork and steep roofs. On the right hand side at the brow of the hill is The Mount, a little cul-de-sac of cottages and gardens, and then the black and white Bakery

Cottage with some elegant decoration in its plaster work. This house was the place in which the village grocer carried on his business, and the old bakehouse remains at the rear. Next to it is the present Post Office and shop, whose pretty shuttered windows have not been altered in a century, and beyond that is a 16th century black and white building called Saracen's Head which was at one time a public house and then later on a farm. Further along the High Street is another cottage (called Noah's Ark), a pair of Victorian houses and then an old house called White Hart which also used to be a pub. At this point we are right at the centre of the village, with the church on one side and the George and Dragon pub on the other.

The Church of St. Mary and All Saints is one of the finest examples of the Perpendicular style of architecture to be found in Cheshire, with the oldest parts dating from the 14th century, a fine sandstone building in a beautiful village setting. Down the side of the churchyard is an inviting little lane called South Bank; at one end behind the church is a lovely terrace of Georgian cottages and at the other end are some equally delightful views of the placid Budworth Mere and then Northwich beyond that. More cottages, this time a terrace of 17th century timber-framed ones, can be discovered at the other side of the church along the cobbled School Lane which leads down to a beautiful long avenue of mature lime trees and from between these trees one can glimpse some fine views across the Cheshire Plain.

Back in the village, Church Street is similar to High Street in terms of the tremendously interesting houses which can be seen here. On the right hand side is a terrace of 17th century cottages with tall chimneys, which originally would have had wattle and daub walls between

Sign outside the George and Dragon Hotel, ▶ *Great Budworth*

THE VILLAGES

School Lane,
Great Budworth ▶

the timber frames but which over the years have been replaced by brick. Opposite, on the other side of the narrow road, is another lovely 17th century cottage which at one time was the Ring O'Bells public house. Further along Church Street numbers 46 and 47 are a fine pair of cottages which have remained almost unchanged since they were built in the 1780's. Church Street then continues along into Smithy Lane, on which can be found the 17th century Smithy and Smith's Cottage. Looking back towards the church from here one has a marvellous view of this half of the village, with the tiny cottages huddled together at a variety of unusual angles close to the road and the church tower demanding attention at the far

end. The road curves round to the right and one is drawn gently into High Street to discover some of the best village perspectives in the county, views along both High Street and School Lane.

Great Budworth is certainly one of Cheshire's most complete villages, incorporating all the elements which one would wish to find — an ancient but impressive church, cottages built in the style of their time from local materials, a tiny post office, extensive views out to the surrounding countryside, and a strong community spirit. It is certainly a delight to visit, and if you talk to the locals they will tell you that it is a delight to live there.

The Old Reading Room,
Great Budworth ▶

◀ Evening sunlight in
Great Budworth

THE VILLAGES

Lower Peover, 3 miles to the south of Knutsford, in many respects has much the same charm and beauty as Great Budworth but on a much smaller scale. In size it is really no more than a hamlet, but it has all the features of a charming and lively village including a public house which has been in business for centuries, a church which has been in business just a little longer, a nearby junior school, a narrow thoroughfare of pretty cottages and a scattering of farms. It seems a little reticent to make itself known to the world at large, but in many ways this makes it all the more exciting to find, for one only comes upon the centre of the village by following a discreet and ancient cobbled lane (actually called The Cobbles) from the road between Middlewich and Knutsford, or alternatively one can enter this oasis of beauty by way of Church Walk. The focal point of this marvellously compact area is the historic church of St Oswald, claimed to be one of the most beautiful churches in England. It is largely 14th century in origin although a chapel was known to have existed here in 1269, and it forms a very important example of a timber-framed church with the sandstone tower being a later addition of 1582. The most notable medieval treasure here is the oak chest, hewn out of one solid tree trunk, and tradition has it that local girls wishing to become farmers' wives had to lift the lid of the chest with one hand in order to prove their suitability for hard work.

Just across from the church and close enough to rub shoulders with it is The Bell's of Peover, an inn from 1569 and before that a hospice for visiting monks. Originally called the Warren de Tabley Arms its present name was taken from the surname of a landlord who kept the inn a century ago; contrary to popular opinion The Bell's of Peover did not derive its name from its proximity to the church, even though one could be forgiven for thinking that the terrace in front of the pub is merely an extension of the churchyard. Inside, one immediately senses a homely atmosphere created by the warm fires and a fascinating collection of Toby jugs in the 'snug'.

Only a stone's throw from The Bell's of Peover, just by the entrance to the churchyard with its ancient timber lychgate, is the original schoolhouse which is now a very attractive private dwelling. Built of warm red brick under the shelter of a stone flag roof, this tiny school was founded in 1710 by Richard Comberbach who had been a curate at the parish church. Up to 1874 the minister of the parish church was also the head teacher, and at one time in the 1860's there were as many as 168 pupils on the register. Although the building is now no longer a school, the noise of children running and shouting can still be heard around this corner of Lower Peover from the newer school which is just a few yards away, looking in on another side of the churchyard. So, standing at the centre of this little hamlet one can survey in a glance three buildings which catered for most of a person's interests in times past — church, school and pub. Or as the chairman of the local parish council so succinctly put it, here can be found salvation, education and damnation!

Over on the far side of the church from here is Church Walk, a cluster of houses along a delightful lane which wanders over Peover Eye, the unusually-named stream which acts as the northern limit of the village. At the top end of the lane and closest to the church is the former village shop, now a private house but

Old School House,
Lower Peover ▶

THE VILLAGES

with the old shop windows still very evident, while a little further down is the Old Church House which had been a pub prior to 1923. It appears that its closure was due to a disagreement which arose when pressure was being brought to bear on the landlord at that time to reduce his licence to six days instead of seven. It was claimed that there was too much noise coming from the pub on Sundays, but the landlord hotly denied this accusation and ultimately closed the place altogether. An unusual feature of the houses along Church Walk is the way their gardens are situated on the opposite side of the roadway — these gardens, together with the adjacent plots of nursery land, create a very picturesque setting for the church in the background.

Although the most interesting part of Lower Peover is the area around the church, beyond it there are some delightful farms and cottages scattered along the narrow country lanes, and some of the cottages in the parish are reminders of the time when it was possible to pilfer land from the roadside and build on it. This was allowed provided they were built in twenty-four hours, between sunrise and sunrise, the test being that a fire must be lit and smoke go up the chimney in that time. The Land Enclosure Act of 1870 put a stop to this unusual opportunity.

The village of **Swettenham**, between Holmes Chapel and Congleton, is another treasure of the Cheshire Plain, lying in peaceful seclusion above the valley of the River Dane. Approaching it from the south-east, one comes first of all to Clonterbrook House which is just inside the parish within the area known as Swettenham Heath. This beautifully restored house is the home of the Lockett family whose ancestors were here as far back as 1697. In earlier days it was known as "le Halle del Heath" (Heath Hall) and was used as a farm dwelling; in more recent times the house and adjoining barn have been restored to form two of the most attractive buildings in the area. They are complemented by the exquisitely laid out grounds — on one side is a placid pool surrounded by majestic trees while on the other side is a bubbling stream running through a delightfully wooded clough in which a profusion of daffodils and bluebells can be seen during spring.

A little closer to the village, past fields which are now cultivated but which at one time were covered by spinneys, one comes to Swettenham Mill. Here can be seen an old water wheel which is still in use sawing wood and occasionally grinding corn and the owner, Mr. Lancaster, tells of requests from Lower Peover church to prepare wheat for making the unleavened bread used in Holy Communion. Over the years Mr Lancaster and his family have planted thousands of daffodil bulbs in the valley through which the stream runs, helping to create a vista of fresh Spring beauty for which the area has become so well-known.

Daffodils herald the coming of Spring in Swettenham ▶

THE VILLAGES

At the entrance to the village is the front drive to Swettenham Hall, a 17th century house which at one time was the home of the lords of the manor. Although much altered by successive generations, it is still a very interesting building commanding wonderful views of the Dane Valley, the slopes of which are blanketed with snowdrops and primroses during the Spring months. Along the quiet and largely traffic-free road into the village one can see signposts to the left and right pointing the way to pleasant footpaths which wander through fields and meadows, and as one enters the village itself there is a pervading sense of timelessness. At the centre is the church, originally half-timbered and having a wooden spire but which in 1720 was found to be in such a bad state of repair that it had to be given a brick 'skin'. Records still exist of the cost of this operation, and heading the list is an entry for 100,000 bricks at a cost of £60. Within the church there is an old cross, believed to be of Saxon origin, which was built into one of the arches of the Tipping Memorial Chapel; a font in the north aisle is also thought to date from Saxon times.

Directly behind the church stands the Swettenham Arms with its 'olde worlde' decor, a brew of their own making, and a car park which must be one of the largest in Cheshire. Following the lane from the pub and the church one can discover a beautiful walk down into the valley of the Dane, where the vegetation is lush and the ever-changing course of the fast-flowing river is easily discernible. Yet thankfully Swettenham as a whole has largely resisted the fast-flowing waters of time and remains a quiet little village cul-de-sac set in the midst of a truly rural landscape.

Situated on the eastern boundary of the Cheshire Plain, the village of **Gawsworth** enjoys some panoramic views out towards Shutlingsloe and the neighbouring hills at the foot of the Pennines. Yet the exciting thing about Gawsworth is essentially what is to be found within it, for it is a very beautiful and historic place, and even if it lacks the small cottages and friendly farmhouses which seem to characterise so many of the Cheshire villages it more than makes up for it in terms of the grandeur of its Halls and church and the delightful landscape of pools and extensive grounds which encompass these historic buildings. The centrepiece of this historic tableau must surely be Gawsworth Old Hall, a classic black and white timber-framed house which has been the seat of the lords of the manor since Norman times. The building which can be seen today very largely dates from the second half of the fifteenth century, and now mellowed with age the Hall is a delightful sight when seen from across the fish pool which runs close to the church, while inside it is beautifully furnished, friendly, warm and thoroughly human in scale. It is still very much a family house, as it has been throughout the centuries. It has also been the scene of much pageantry which in former times was enacted around and within the Old Hall precincts, and one can still see the Tilting Ground where charging knights would practise their jousting skills as well as the amphitheatre in the walled park area where tournaments would have taken place in medieval times.

On the western side of the parkland an unobtrusive doorway provided the family which lived in the Hall with their own private access into the church, indicative of the close relationship which existed between the two. In fact the lords of the manor have always been patrons of the 'living' and continue to be so, and within the church the monuments to the Fitton family (who occupied the Hall from 1316 to 1662) and the special pews are further evidence of the dominant role which the lords of the manor played here.

The church is situated on rising ground just above one of the three fish pools which are a feature of the area — a fourth pool existed further below the church, where the land now drops away quite sharply, but the water drained away when the clay lining broke up. Dating from the 15th and 16th centuries, the church is an unusual mixture of both red and buff-coloured sandstone, evidence that Gawsworth straddles the dividing line which roughly separates these two types of rock strata which have been the source of so much of the characteristic building material in Cheshire. St. James' Church is also unusual in that it has no aisles, but rather a very wide nave, and there is no structural separation of the chancel from the nave. In the chancel are four monuments to the Fitton family which have already been mentioned — the one to Francis Fitton (1608) is rather gruesome in that it incorporates a skeleton below his effigy, while another features the figure of Mary Fitton who is commonly associated with Shakespeare as the 'Dark Lady' of his sonnets. Outside the church, but within the confines of the churchyard, can be discovered the Trooper's Memorial with its unusual inscription and then the chilling skull and crossbones which figure on the inside of the church gateposts.

Across from the church, separated only by the narrow road leading up to the Old Hall, is the Old Rectory. This is an excellent timber-framed house, one of the earliest examples of its kind and probably unique among glebe residences (having been the parson's house for several

*Gawsworth's
Parish Church* ▶

hundred years it is now privately owned). It has retained a timbered hall which is still open to the roof, and the south front which can be glimpsed from the gateway to the road is entirely original. The present Rectory, just by the churchyard, is another attractive building — built in 1707 as the school house it is a comparative newcomer to the scene, and it has a nice Georgian door surround which was introduced during restoration work carried out in 1949.

Of the same age as the Rectory is the New Hall, a large and stately Georgian building which looks out towards the Old Hall across the middle pool. It was built by Lord Mohun, who

with the Duke of Hamilton figured in the most famous duel in British history: since both had married co-heiresses to the Gawsworth estate a dispute about the property arose, resulting in a duel in London in 1712 when both were slain by the other. The New Hall is completely different to its older counterpart, being a large seven bay brick-built house with a hipped roof and no external decoration, but its pleasant landscaped setting enables it to complement its black and white neighbour rather than compete with it for one's attention. Just to the east of both Halls, beyond the higher pool which is still used for trout fishing, is an unusually-shaped building which was once called the Pigeon House and is now a private dwelling.

THE VILLAGES

The New Hall, Gawsworth ▶

Well away from this delightful Cheshire plot, encompassing historic Halls and a charming church within tranquil landscaped grounds, is the Harrington Arms. This good old-fashioned English pub can be found at the bottom of the lane running from Gawsworth, nearly half a mile away, as though it felt itself unworthy to be associated with such elevated company. Yet it is a very interesting building in its own right, being brick-built in three storeys with a stone-flagged roof, ivy growing up the front and cobbles by the entrance. In many ways the landlords seem to have turned their backs on 'progress' here, much to the delight of those who discover the place, for the rooms inside are small with lots of old-fashioned wooden benches and tables, the bar is tiny with barely

enough room to turn round in, and the beer is brought up from the cellar in jugs. The pub is also a farm house, with the farm buildings to be seen at the back, and it is probably the last remaining place in Cheshire where the two enterprises can still be found together even though in years gone by it was a very common combination.

Another little spot worth searching out here is a spinney (now a National Trust property) to the north of the church, along a lane off the main road to Macclesfield. Underneath the trees, known as Maggoty Johnson's Wood, can be found the resting place of Samuel Johnson who was the last professional court jester in England and who had lived at the Old Hall up to the time of his death in 1773. His eccentricity led him to be buried in unconsecrated ground and to compose his own entertaining epitaph which is recorded on his tombstone — a similar stone slab next to it has an inscription engraved upon it which is the work of Lady Harrington from the Old Hall, who is said to have been somewhat indignant about what had been written on Maggotty Johnson's grave.

Just below the 'new' Rectory at the foot of the church steps is the start of a footpath leading across the fields in a southerly direction via Shellow Farm and the Manor House to North Rode Church, a very attractive walk through open fields which offers some good views looking back towards Gawsworth. Even in the early part of the nineteenth century people

The Harrington Arms, Gawsworth ▶

A Cheshire copse in Spring

Lyme Hall and Gardens

THE VILLAGES

went out of their way to see the village, and it is recorded that the Manchester to London coach would often make a detour at the 'Warren' (just to the north) to give travellers a sight of the pride of Gawsworth — the corner of the parish by the silent pools. It is just the same today, for this is a really beautiful part of Cheshire which is worth making an effort to see and experience for oneself.

Situated on the eastern edge of the Cheshire Plain like Gawsworth, the historic village of **Astbury** lies just to the south of Congleton. It is a place which even motorists speeding along the A34 can appreciate since it lies within sight and sound of the main road. The attractive cottages grouped around a tiny village green make it particularly picturesque, especially in Spring when daffodils burst forth to create an extra dimension of fresh colour heralding the start of warmer times, while at night the ancient church with its very unusual detached tower and spire reaching heavenwards is dramatically floodlit to give it an even greater prominence than it has during the day.

Despite its proximity to Congleton and the textile industry there Astbury has traditionally been an agricultural area largely in the ownership of a branch of the Egerton family, and the dwellings to be found here were built for estate workers rather than as weavers' cottages. The village still retains this rural atmosphere, and it has some particularly interesting farms which furnish us with an insight into its history. Glebe Farm lies just behind the church, its name indicating that the rent produced by the land was a contribution

towards the parson's income, and it seems to have been the site of Astbury's manor house for there are remains of an old tilting ground, archery butts named The Longshoots and a large manorial fishpond. In 1704 the manor was bought by Dr Philip Egerton who combined the offices of squire and parson, and because he was called the rector (being entitled to collect tithes in the parish) the building became known as the Rectory. It was sold in the early part of this century and is now just a farm. A mile further up the road from the church is Peel Farm, occupying a very ancient site where the original building was surrounded by a moat. At one time the manor house of Newbold stood there (hence the parish name of Newbold Astbury), with perhaps the manor house and its barns being the 'new buildings' which the word 'Newbold' means. It appears that the manor of Astbury and the manor of Newbold were given together as one holding to the Earl of Chester who gave it to Baron Gilbert Venables; then in the 16th century the old manor house was demolished and a new one built which had a small square tower called a 'peel'. Once part of the empire of the Egertons of Ridley, the old house was taken down and the present farm built — although there is no tower it still has the moat behind it.

Astbury still retains a number of 'black and white' buildings which are such a characteristic feature of so many Cheshire villages, a style of construction which relied upon the use of timber framing for the basic structure of the walls in conjunction with wattle and daub infill panels. The fact that this type of building had virtually died out by about 1640 provides a

Astbury ▶

107

THE VILLAGES

useful historical indicator when looking at villages and settlement patterns. One of the best examples in Astbury is the very attractive cottage (originally three dwellings but now only one) at the top end of the village green next to the church. Stye Heath Cottage and Glebe Farm are other timber-framed buildings which have survived intact to the present day, and there are also numerous examples of timber framing being incorporated into later structures (Tenement Farm, Brookhouse Farm and even the church tower, which has sections of wattle and daub within its internal structure).

As with many villages in the county, it is the church which is the dominant physical feature. This is certainly the case here at Astbury, with St. Mary's being situated in a slightly elevated position above the rest of the village and capturing one's attention from the bottom of the village street when turning off the A34. The cottages and houses are dwarfed by its stature, and the narrow street seems to make a detour round the church in deference to its importance. Even the gateway into the churchyard is a solid stone structure, its castellated outline echoing the style of the church itself and providing an entrance which is totally worthy of this magnificent ecclesiastical edifice. The architectural historians Pevsner and Hubbard described this as one of Cheshire's most exciting churches, built in the Perpendicular style but with evidence of being older than its style suggests: the north tower and spire, for example, stands isolated from the nave and was probably built before it, perhaps in the late 13th century. The roofs of the church are particularly interesting, being characteristically low-pitched with camber beams, while inside the church is full of interesting furniture and decorations including a splendid Jacobean font cover and pulpit, an even more splendid chancel screen from the early 16th century, and an effigy of a late 14th century knight in the south chapel. Out in the churchyard there is an unusual canopied tomb with two stone effigies from the 14th century (their faces now totally unrecognisable due to erosion by the weather) and an ancient gnarled yew tree that has been a silent witness to the many happenings which have taken place during its 1,000 year life span within a picturesque village which has retained its beauty and character right up to the present day.

One of Peckforton's thatched cottages ▶

In the south-east corner of the Cheshire Plain are some comparatively little known villages which merit far greater appreciation and attention. **Bunbury** is one of these, situated a few miles south of Tarporley and within sight of the lovely Peckforton Hills just to the west. The area around the ancient parish church of St. Boniface is especially attractive, a winding road creeping up the hill and through the village with the impressive sandstone church on one side and some half-timbered cottages on the other side. The church stands cathedral-like at the centre of a large graveyard, almost aloof from the rest of this small village, its solid tower contrasted by the north and south walls which are lighter and much more decorative. It was built largely in the 13th and 14th centuries and inside there are a variety of monuments and effigies dating from this period, while just across from the entrance to the church with its 18th century gatepiers is the pleasant Dysart Arms pub, some pretty black and white cottages and a row of almshouses dating from 1874. To the south the ground drops quickly away to the stream valley which surrounds the village, and along the lovely lane which runs down in this direction one can see Church Bank Cottage, firmly built on its stone pediment, and the beautifully restored black and white Chantry House (half-timbered and built in 1527) leaning at a hair-raising angle as though ready to fall over.

Peckforton is a small estate village lying on the lower slopes of the wooded and mysterious Peckforton Hills which rise up suddenly and unexpectedly from the flat expanse of the Cheshire Plain. The area as a whole is secluded and relatively untamed, as though it belonged more appropriately to the Lake District rather than to Cheshire, and the presence of three castles here adds to the intrigue and atmosphere even though two of them are only comparatively recent structures of the 19th century. The village of Peckforton is quite a scattered affair but with some outstanding 17th century vernacular buildings which are a delight to find — small cottages of timber-framed and sandstone construction hiding beneath unruly thatched roofs, looking out onto the surrounding world through lattice windows. Such informal groups of intimate cottages along twisting country lanes are also to be discovered over the Peckforton Hills in the village of Burwardsley and further south in the villages of Bickerton and Brown Knowl.

THE VILLAGES

Eaton-by-Tarporley is probably one of the most unpretentious villages in Cheshire, a close-knit community which happily minds its own affairs. It has a wonderful array of old cottages and houses, a tiny village post office with a postmistress who knows everyone, a smithy which still shoes horses, a Cross at its centre, and farmyards with real farmyard smells. Its character has evidently been preserved because most attention has been focussed on its larger neighbour Tarporley, just two and half miles to the south-west, and it was only at the end of the 19th century that Eaton was provided with its own parish church — prior to that time it had been seen as part of the parish of Tarporley and a church of its own would have been something of a luxury. Even now Eaton is still very much off the beaten track except for those people on their way through to the Oulton Park Racing Circuit just outside Little Budworth, and the noise of passing cars is really the only thing that disturbs the peace and quiet of this delightful place.

The village was at one time largely in the hands of the Arderne and Oulton estates, and has traditionally been very much a farming community since the cottages here would have housed farm labourers and associated tradespeople such as the shoemaker, the baker, the blacksmith and the wheelwright. Thankfully Eaton still maintains this rural atmosphere, even though its links with the large country estates have been severed, and

although several old cottages have been knocked down over the years this village probably has more timber-framed and thatched cottages than any other in the county. Edgewell Lane on the southern side of Eaton is particularly attractive, with the traditionally-thatched Oak Tree Farm looking across the road to its black and white neighbour Well Farm which still has two very old wells by the corner of its front wall. Back up the road towards the Cross is Bay Tree House, a lovely restored cottage with a rare oak-mullioned window which probably dates back to the fifteenth century, while across the lane is another beautifully-white thatched cottage which used to be the village pub and which still retains the old bar.

Although the Cross itself at the centre of Eaton is not very old its stepped stone base certainly is, and it was probably the location of an old preaching cross. Looking westwards from this point one can see quite a variety of houses and cottages, each one uniquely made from local building materials — Hunter's Close is a black and white thatched cottage which used to be three smaller cottages dating from the 16th century, Stone Cottage is a later house made of large blocks of red sandstone, while the old School House with an inscription in the wall was built of red-brown brick in 1806. In the opposite direction is the village smithy, a small sandstone building on a little 'island' where the noise of a farrier's hammer can still be heard.

The village smithy, Eaton-by-Tarporley ►

THE VILLAGES

The Nun's Grave, Vale Royal ▶

The modern village sign just to the front of the smithy has a representation of the Delamere horn within it, signifying that Eaton was at one time in the Delamere hunting forest and that the Done family (who lived in nearby Utkinton) were the chief foresters excercising a great deal of power over the lives of the local inhabitants.

Just across from the smithy on Lower Lane is the village Post Office and shop, although only the red letter box on the wall and small sign by the door give any indication of the transactions which now take place within this former farm cottage. A narrow tiled path takes you through the garden up to the narrow front door which opens to reveal what is probably the smallest Post Office in the county. Behind the tiny counter the shelves overflow with stamps and groceries while the walls are covered with notices about the Women's Institute and the next church garden party. Its a lovely little shop, with barely enough room for two customers to be in it at the same time. Mrs Smith, the current post-mistress, will proudly tell you that the business has been run by her family ever since it first became a Post Office in the last century, when her great grandfather received one pound's worth of stamps which he thought he would never sell!

Further down the lane from the Post Office is Lower House, its weather-worn red sandstone exterior giving a good indication of its great antiquity. As well as the attractive buildings in Eaton there are also some very pleasant walks from the village including one from the Cross up the lane by the side of the Old School House and onto Luddington Hill, from where there are some extensive views across the surrounding countryside, and another from the lane west of Eaton through open fields and past the modern Arderne Hall into Tarporley itself.

The village of **Whitegate,** at the very centre of the present-day county, is an appropriate place to finish our journey through the villages of Cheshire. In some respects it is important to appreciate the unusual relationship which exists between Whitegate and neighbouring Marton, with which it has much in common: for a start, Whitegate has a church and is a large ecclesiastical parish but it is not a civil parish, while by contrast Marton is a civil parish but having no church it is part of the ecclesiastical parish of Whitegate. Yet despite the confusion the two communities work closely together and many so-called Whitegate Institutions are in Marton including Whitegate Recreation Room, Whitegate Methodist Church and Whitegate Way (a linear country park).

Whitegate was the estate village for the Lords of

Delamere, a branch of the Cholmondeley family who occupied the family seat at Vale Royal just a mile from the village centre. Although family occupation ended after the death of the last Lord Delamere in 1931 there is still evidence of Whitegate's role within the estate since the former estate office retains the name above its door. The village itself is very pretty with attractive thatched cottages, some larger estate houses and the parish church of St. Mary, all looking onto the central village green and a maypole around which children dance at the annual summer fete.

The most important feature of Whitegate is undoubtedly Vale Royal, the country house of the Lords of Delamere which was built on the site of the largest Cistercian abbey in the country. The abbey was founded by Edward I for the Cistercian Order in 1277 but unfortunately hardly anything is now visible above ground, although it seems that the church was about 420 feet long. One interesting little feature which can be seen in the midst of this former bastion of celibacy is the Nun's Grave, introduced at a later date on the site of the church altar and incorporating a 17th century column together with the head of a churchyard cross. The house itself was first built in the early part of the 17th century but since then has been extensively altered by succeeding generations. Although now empty and closed to visitors, the grandeur of former days is still evident from its proud and distinguished facade.

◀ *Eaton Post Office*

Chapter V

HALLS
AND HOMES

*— timbered survivals
and Gothic revivals*

Cheshire must have some of the loveliest homes in all England, ranging from the charming thatched cottages of humble 'artisans' to the magnificent mansions of aristocrats and landed gentry. There is a tremendous diversity of style as well as of scale and size — medieval timber-framed houses with their black and white patterning so characteristic of the county, elegant brick-built town houses from the Georgian period with their simple but unerringly beautiful proportions, and the classically-designed country residences of the more well-to-do which were expensively (and expansively) constructed of solid stone. Such lovely homes deserve to be complemented by their surroundings, and they have been - the domestic charm of tiny cottages is heightened as they nestle together at the heart of a village, terraced houses rub shoulders with their neighbours, while the halls of nobility maintain their splendid independence from within leafy landscaped parkland.

Cheshire has always been a very desirable place to live, as witnessed by the steady growth of its delightful market towns particularly in the 18th century, and this still holds true today — it is a refreshing refuge from the pressures of city life for many people who work in Merseyside, Greater Manchester and the Potteries, very definitely the place to be if one can afford the slightly higher house prices which accompany a Cheshire postal address.

Time and space prevent us from looking individually at the beautiful cottages and houses to be found down many a country lane or in the towns and villages — that must be left to the visitor in his own journey of discovery. Here we can cover just a few of those inspiring mansions belonging to families whose influence in Cheshire spans the centuries and who have seen fit to enable others to catch a glimpse of a bygone age.

Eaton Hall

Eaton Hall, the seat of the Grosvenor family, lies just a few miles to the south of Chester and is set in the midst of beautiful countryside close by the River Dee. Like many country homes, it has some delightful landscaped approaches through the surrounding estate - on the west side is the perfectly straight two mile driveway known as Belgrave Avenue while the northern approach follows the line of the old Roman road into Chester and is guarded by the picturesque village of Eccleston. For a family which can trace its ancestry back to the Norman Conquest, one might have expected Eaton Hall to have been a rambling mansion of great antiquity. Yet what one finds is a thoroughly modern marble-faced stately home built in the 1970's as a fine example of contemporary architecture. It seems that the Grosvenor family decided that what was needed was a real home to enjoy the present — not a pseudo-Georgian or strained Gothic design harking back to the past. The result is a stunning building of clean lines and modern materials which makes the most of its contrast with the neighbouring Victorian chapel by Sir Alfred Waterhouse and capitalises on the superbly landscaped gardens all around it.

◄ *The old and the new at
Eaton Hall* ►

HALLS
AND HOMES

Eaton's formal gardens ▶

The present Eaton Hall is in fact the fourth one to occupy the same site — obviously the Grosvenor family have never been afraid to move with the times. The first Hall had been built in 1683 for Sir Thomas Grosvenor with stone provided from the Norman border castle at Holt which had been conveniently wrecked by Cromwell some years earlier. Then in 1802 the Hall was redesigned by William Porden and transformed into what was described as "certainly the most magnificent mansion in Britain" — a Gothic styled palace which was reminiscent of York Minster and Chester Cathedral. Yet somehow even this building was exceeded in magnificence by the third Eaton Hall, completed in 1882 to the designs of the famous architect Sir Alfred Waterhouse. Built in the new Gothic style of the time, it had some amazing features — the exotic saloon, for example, measured 76 feet in length and had a domed ceiling as high as the average house. The works of art and other treasures which were to be found in its 300 rooms made it more of an Aladdin's Cave than a home, and it was even served by one of the country's first miniature railways which had been specially built by the Duke of Westminster. Sadly the deterioration which set in during the Second World War led to this classic example of Victorian munificence being demolished, and now only Waterhouse's red brick stable block and the family chapel with its separate clock tower remain. Yet even this latter structure is an example of the way in which the Victorians felt that if something was worth doing it was worth doing well — at 175 feet high with a four-faced

clock of vitreous enamel the tower is a striking 'miniature' of Big Ben in London.

The splendours of the architecture here at Eaton are matched by the loveliness of the landscaped gardens, the product of much thoughtful design by men like Capability Brown — the panoramic vista across the formal gardens at the rear of the house is largely his work, stretching out beyond the boating lake to the Peckforton Hills in the distance. Yet as well as the grandeur of such large-scale landscape design there are many smaller and more intimate gardens with a character of their own — the Dragon Garden, for example, is a beautifully-enclosed area named after its fountain centrepiece which was restored by the fifth Duke of Westminster. Here also can be found a sandstone temple flanked by two Roman columns recovered from ruins in Chester and housing a Roman altar dedicated to the nymphs and fountains by soldiers of the 20th Legion. Two distinguished and well known Victorian architects also had a hand in creating the idyllic surroundings which the Grosvenor family now enjoy and share with visitors on the several occasions during the year when their gardens are open to the public — the Italian Garden to the south of the house is based on a design by Sir Edwin Lutyens, while at the end of the Broad Walk is the intriguing circular Parrot House built in a classical style by Sir Alfred Waterhouse. At the other end of the Broad Walk is the sheltered Dutch Tea Garden with the simple but very attractive Tea House designed by John Douglas in 1872. All these

HALLS
AND HOMES

One of the carriages in the Eaton coach museum ▶

features are framed by a profusion of colour from the tremendous variety of flowering shrubs and beautiful trees which fill the gardens.

Eaton Hall also has a rather special influence over much of the surrounding countryside due to the fact that a great deal of it is in the ownership of the Grosvenor family and many of the buildings to be found in the encircling villages of Pulford, Eccleston, Aldford and Saighton are the result of the massive construction programme initiated by the first Duke of Westminster in the latter half of the 19th century. This is an area where domestic estate architecture can be seen at its best — a superb example of Victorian aristocratic patronage — and even today there are forty-seven tenant farms in the locality controlled by the Duke of Westminster and he is also the patron of four church livings. The Grosvenors have for a long time enjoyed very special relationships with their employees, no doubt helped by the fact that all who work on the estate live either there or in the villages close by — the interest which they have taken in their staff seems to have been a feature of the Dukes of Westminster over the years and is still very much in evidence today.

Arley Hall

Arley Hall can be found just to the north-east of Northwich, within a peaceful agricultural area enriched with woods and copses largely planted during the 19th century. Arley is perhaps best known for its beautiful gardens which have been open to the public for some years now, and particularly for the herbaceous borders which were among the first to be established in England. As well as these lovely gardens visitors also have the opportunity to

enjoy the Hall itself (more recently opened to the public), the Tithe Barn which is a fine example of a cruck-framed building and a walk through the historic estate ending at the cluster of cottages known as Arley Green. The Hall and its succeeding families have been inseparably linked with the beautiful estate village of Great Budworth three miles to the south, and one can still trace the route which the squires must have taken on visits to their tenants.

Arley has been very largely in the same family ownership for over 500 years now, with the earliest recognisable ancestor being Adam de Dutton whose great grandfather Odard the Norman was mentioned in the Domesday Book. Several houses have occupied the site, with the first being built in 1469 when Piers Warburton moved from Warburton to Arley. Although alterations were made by later members of the family, including completely encasing the original timber-framed structure with brick walls, deterioration had set in to such a degree that a new Hall was needed. It fell to Rowland Egerton-Warburton to embark upon this task of rebuilding in the 1830's, and the house and gardens which we see today, together with many of the buildings on the estate, are the fruits of his efforts during his long period of residence at Arley. Creative and artistic, affectionate and warm-hearted yet wise and practical, he was the best type of country squire, and in the poetic expression which came to be a characteristic of his life he wrote above the entrance to his house "This gate is free to all good men and true, Right welcome thou if worthy to pass through."

Proud of the history and antiquity of his inheritance, and influenced by the Romantic movement, Rowland wanted his new house to suggest something of the piety of the Middle

HALLS
AND HOMES

Arley Hall ▶

Entrance to Arley Gardens ▶

Ages as well as the grandeur of Elizabethan England. He also wanted it to be stately enough to reflect the family's position as important Cheshire landowners and solid enough to endure for several hundred years. The result was what his architect charmingly called the Queen Elizabethan style, in which every architectural feature had an exact model in some existing Elizabethan building. The materials for the house were all specially chosen — the red bricks were made on the site from clay dug to the north of the house, timber was brought from all over Cheshire and the stone was specially quarried and then cut and carved by masons. Although parts of this fine house had to be demolished in 1968, most of the very distinguished rooms which had so much time, skill and money lavished upon them were preserved. A particularly attractive feature of these rooms is their bold and beautiful ceilings, with those in the library, gallery and drawing room being especially elaborate. Other notable features include the oak panelling of the front hall, the excellent oak staircase with its panelled plasterwork and some delightful pieces of period furniture.

The private chapel associated with the house had been built in 1845 by Rowland Warburton to the design of the famous church architect Anthony Salvin. It had been Rowland's increasing interest in the Oxford Movement and his desire to have religious services regularly conducted in a more ceremonial style which led him to believe that he must have a Gothic chapel attached to his house. Then to service

his new chapel and provide for his tenants Rowland also founded the Arley School in an attractive setting at Arley Green, a mile away from the hall. The school was established in an old half-timbered barn and another eighteenth century building was adapted to form a terrace of Elizabethan-style cottages. The original farmhouse here was converted into the parsonage, now the home of the Flower family who are the present owners of the Arley estate.

116

HALLS AND HOMES

The beautifully laid out gardens to the south-west of the Hall are largely the work of Rowland and Mary Egerton-Warburton during the period between 1830 and 1860, and were very obviously a labour of love. Although one can see traces of Continental influence upon the design, with an English interpretation, the framework of the gardens was formed by the old brick walls which the Egerton-Warburtons inherited and extended and also by the yew hedges which they planted. Within those enclosures were created the gardens which exist today, carefully tended by a small but dedicated staff. There are three particularly outstanding features which ought to be specially mentioned — the long avenue of pleached lime trees leading up to the gardens, with their branches tightly intertwined from one tree to the next; the sumptuous double herbaceous border which was already in existence in 1846; and the quite remarkable avenue of 14 holm oaks planted in 1840 which have been clipped into the shape of giant cylinders. Some of the other parts are more recent developments: these include the Flag Garden, made in 1900 and planted with floribunda roses and dwarf lavender, the Fish Garden laid out in the period between the First and Second World Wars, and the Shrub Rose Beds set out in 1961. There is also a Herb Garden and a Scented Garden, planted with aromatic shrubs and flowers giving lovely scents throughout the year. Yet the gardens were not just for decorative purposes — they also provided fruit and vegetables. The large Walled Garden was originally one of three kitchen garden enclosures and at one time was run as a commercial market garden, while next to it is the present day Kitchen Garden, bounded on the north side by the Vinery which was built in the middle of the nineteenth century as a greenhouse for the cultivation of grapes and figs. Some of the fig trees which are to be found here even now are the original ones which were planted in 1860.

One cannot fail to appreciate the tremendous transformation which Rowland Egerton-Warburton brought about at Arley, for evidences of his creative talents are observed in every corner. One of his most endearing qualities was his ability to express his thoughts in poetic verse, and illuminated plaques on the inside walls of the Tea Cottage in the gardens carry verses written to his wife and the owners of seven neighbouring estates. Other verses are to be found on the estate sign posts, the one in the 'village' reading:

> *"Trespassers this notice heed*
> *Onward you may not proceed*
> *Unless to Arley Hall you speed."*

The visitor can even retrace Rowland Egerton-Warburton's steps along the Furlong Walk, for this 220 yard path on the edge of the gardens

The avenue of holm oaks at Arley ▶

The Tithe Barn, Arley ▶

was one of his favourite routes, particularly when he became blind in the later years of his life. The gateway to the house and gardens was also his work, created by removing the end walls of the fifteenth century cruck-framed barn and guarded by the clock tower above it which had been inspired by his travels in South Germany.

Tatton Park

Tatton Hall near Knutsford is one of Cheshire's best-known and most frequently visited stately homes, and with its parkland and gardens it represents all the features of a traditional country estate. The advertising leaflets emphasise the fact that here one can experience a thousand years of history in a thousand welcoming acres, and the origins of Tatton go back to a small homestead which was sited in a forest clearance by an Anglo-Saxon farmer called Tata. Over the centuries ownership of the land passed from one family to another, but eventually it came into the hands of the Egerton family who held it for 380 years up to 1958 when the line died out and the estate was bequeathed to the National Trust. The magnificent house and park which remain today are very largely the creations of this family, an expression of their considerable wealth which came from land owned in Lancashire and Cheshire as well as from investments in the factories of the region's industrial towns. Above all Tatton provides an opportunity to see how the other half lived —

as is evident from exhibitions in the house, the Egertons spent much of their time outdoors following the leisure pursuits of hunting, shooting, fishing and painting.

The present Tatton Hall was designed by the famous architects Samuel and Lewis Wyatt and completed in 1813, although the home of earlier lords of the manor (known as the Old Hall) still stands in the park surrounded by traces of a 'lost' medieval village which was removed as part of the landscaping work carried out in the late eighteenth century. It was John Egerton who was the first of the family to actually live at Tatton, and his house was built on the same site as the present house in the early part of the eighteenth century. Fortune smiled on the Egertons in the form of a wealthy legacy from another branch of the family, providing the money for the extensive rebuilding of Tatton in the late eighteenth and early nineteenth centuries — this was carried out in the Neo-Classical style by the Wyatts who were employed on the project from 1774 to 1825. Although Samuel Wyatt began the work, it was left up to his nephew Lewis to complete the seven-bay main block; he was also responsible for the interior decoration, and many of his furniture designs were executed by the notable cabinet makers Gillows of Lancaster. Between 1790 and 1812 two hundred pieces of furniture ranging from clothes horses to four-poster beds passed from Gillows' workshops to Tatton, and one hundred and twenty pieces are still in the Hall.

HALLS
AND HOMES

A tour through some of the rooms of this memorable mansion provides a fascinating insight into the family life of the Egertons during the nineteenth century. The main entrance hall on the north side of the building demonstrates the passion prevalent at the time for everything to be in a classical Greek style, with the marble floor and porphyry columns being particularly prominent. To the three owners of the last century this was the grand entrance, but to Maurice Egerton of the twentieth century it was the 'saloon' where he prepared afternoon tea. From the somewhat cold and restrained grandeur of the entrance hall one can pass into the warmer and more intimate surroundings of the music room and the drawing room, both hung with a cherry-coloured silk which is an Edwardian replica of the original wall-hangings. The doors between these two rooms would be folded back to make one large room when the house was full of visitors — a frequent occurrence in the 19th century, especially during the autumn 'shoots' and the Christmas festivities. As well as being the stage for glittering social functions, it was also the scene of much more mundane activities such as family tea which was served every day at five o'clock. The Drawing Room is probably the most ostentatiously decorated room in the house, with its ornate ceiling and beautifully finished furniture in the Continental style which became so popular during the early part of the nineteenth century. The sofas and chairs

in this room indicate the Egerton characteristic of following new fashions and tastes — with carvings on both back and front the furniture was designed to be seen from all directions, whereas in the previous century seats had been arranged around the edge of a room so that only the fronts were visible. The distinguished library was a particularly important room in the house, specially designed to accommodate a fine collection of books, engravings and atlases which give a valuable insight into Egerton tastes and interests over four centuries. In contrast to the extravagance of the other rooms, the more simple and restful decoration of the library sets it apart as a room to be used and not just admired. Most of the furniture is again by Gillows, including the beautiful bookcases with their brass trellis-work fronts. Adjacent to the library is the rather splendid dining room, the only surviving room from the earlier mansion which existed here before the work undertaken by Samuel and Lewis Wyatt was carried out. In place of the geometric patterns of the Neo-Classical designs in the rest of the house there are bunches of grapes, vine leaves and acorns which were characteristic features of the Rococo style of decoration which had been fashionable in the mid 1700's. The insistence which both William and Wilbraham Egerton made upon preserving this room within their classically-styled house underlines its obvious beauty.

Tatton Hall ▶

HALLS
AND HOMES

Upstairs are the family bedrooms which still contain so much of the furniture originally designed for them. The Silk Bedroom is the finest of the six guest rooms and twenty-four bedrooms in the house, and it is reputed to be the room where important visitors such as the Crown Prince of Siam slept. Most of the furniture was made by Gillows of the finest mahogany and ebony. The bedrooms also enjoyed some lovely views out to the surrounding countryside — from the Silk Bedroom is a view down Lady Mary's Walk to Rostherne, while the occupant of the Lemon Bedroom would have had a spectacular view through the rear portico across the park and gardens. Some of the bedrooms have now been converted into display rooms concentrating upon particular themes — the Victorian exhibition shows the social life and pastimes of the Egertons during the Victorian period, while the exhibition of architectural drawings demonstrates the tremendous amount of work that went into the mansion's design.

Another fascinating feature of Tatton Hall is the opportunity it provides to discover what life was like behind the scenes, for the servants' quarters are still very much as they were when the Egertons were in residence. The Butler's Pantry was the place where the butler took care of the silver and glass, while from her Sitting Room the Housekeeper would keep an eye on both the work and after-hours activities of the female servants. Her special assistant was the 'still room' maid who spent all her time in the 'still room' preparing teas and light meals. All the main meals were cooked in the kitchen itself, with most of the ingredients coming from the home farm or kitchen gardens — the enormous stove would have been a very necessary piece of equipment in the task of feeding the large household. The nearby scullery was the place where all the dirty work was done — cleaning and chopping vegetables and washing up. These tasks were the responsibility of the scullery maids, who would rub stains and soot off the cooking pans with a mixture of silver sand and lemon slices.

The gardens at Tatton are a blend of both formal and informal designs, with a good number of exotic features which probably stem from the foreign travels the Egertons embarked upon so frequently. In the late 1850's the formal manner in gardening was back in fashion, and Sir Joseph Paxton (landscape gardener at Chatsworth House in Derbyshire) was commissioned to lay out the terraces on the south front with flights of steps and vases together with a central fountain basin on the lower level. As a result of his work the Hall commands some spectacular views into the park over the Italian gardens and the more

The Knutsford entrance into Tatton Park ▶

informally planted woodland garden in the valley. The Fernery was probably also by Paxton — here one can find mossy rocks, a trickling pool and a mass of New Zealand tree ferns — while to the east is the Orangery, added to the gardens in 1818 by Lewis Wyatt and now full of citrus fruits and exotic climbers. Each part of the gardens has its own unique character — to the west of the Orangery are individual shrub borders with their own predominant colour scheme, while close-by is a sunken rose garden with a tea house flanked by a pergola. To the south is the Tower Garden, hemmed in by massive yew trees and full of primulas and hydrangeas, and in the midst of all the greenery is the Golden Brook, an attractive lake encompassed by azaleas and rhododendrons and encircling a small island upon which is a Shinto temple overlooking the exotic Japanese garden laid out in 1910 by Japanese workmen brought over specially for the purpose. Some of the other unusual features include an African hut, evergreen trees from America's Rocky Mountains, a 'handkerchief tree' from China and a giant rhubarb-like plant from Brazil, while at the centre of the whole garden and concealed by shrubs and trees is a small beech maze.

One must not overlook the importance of the stables at Tatton, designed by Samuel Wyatt in the 1790's and now converted to restaurants, since up until the early 20th century the Egertons depended upon horses for communication and transport. In the first half of the 19th century there was stabling for fifty horses here, and every day a groom would ride the three miles to Knutsford station in order to fetch newspapers and letters. A groom, two undergrooms and a helper took care of the horses, with the undergrooms sleeping in the lofts above the stables so that they were always available to prepare a horse for a ride or stable it on its return. In the sheds opposite the stables Tatton's own horsedrawn fire engine was kept, ready for any emergency in the surrounding area.

The crowning glory of Tatton must surely be its

HALLS
AND HOMES

Tatton Park ▶

parkland, with the eight mile long boundary enclosing a thousand acres which are open to the public and another thousand which are private farmland. It was Humphrey Repton who created the park by re-routing roads, sweeping away hedges and buildings and then planting thousands of trees and shrubs. His purpose was to use the land's natural features to show off the mansion to best advantage, while at the same time opening up some beautiful views from its windows. The success of his efforts can be gauged from the sense of freedom and remoteness which one experiences in the park from the seemingly boundless landscape — it was just such an experience which his plans strove to produce. The mile long Tatton Mere was already in existence by the time Humphrey Repton came on the scene, created when the monks of Mobberley Priory dammed the River Lily flowing from Knutsford in order to make a fishing ground some eight hundred years ago, whereas Melchett Mere resulted unintentionally from underground subsidence following the extraction of brine from beneath Tatton's green acres. Over to the eastern edge of the park is the Old Hall, a fifteenth century house which at one time was the focal point of Tatton. This was the home of the lords of the manor prior to the arrival of the Egerton family, but it fell into decline when

a new house was built on the site of the present mansion. Thankfully the Old Hall has been restored, the oldest part being the Great Hall with its high carved quatrefoil roof; a later wing was added in the sixteenth century, the improved conditions which it must have provided contrasting strongly with the more primitive standards which doubtless prevailed in the Great Hall. Close by is the site of what must have once been a thriving village, the hamlet of Tatton which flourished for 900 years until it was pulled down as part of Repton's landscaping work. Although there are no building foundations left, the outlines of houses still show, as do the peasants' fields and the main road through the village.

Although so much seems to have been packed into Tatton Park over the centuries, the lasting impression is one of tranquility and classical splendour. For the departing visitor the tranquility is epitomised by the sheep, cattle and large herds of red and fallow deer roaming across Tatton's wide open spaces, while the classical splendour is emphasised by the main entrance lodges — the Rostherne Lodge was modelled by Lewis Wyatt on a small classical temple and the Knutsford entrance was framed with a triumphal arch in the Greek tradition.

An intimate corner at Adlington Hall

Bollington from Kerridge Hill

Cottages in Parkgate on the Wirral

HALLS AND HOMES

Lyme Hall

Lyme Hall in the north-east corner of Cheshire has much in common with Tatton Hall — it is an impressive and majestic building set in the midst of lovely parkland and owned by the National Trust. Yet this is where the similarity ends, for it has a distinct character and atmosphere which gives it an identity of its own. Interestingly enough, although Lyme Park is actually in Cheshire it is leased from the National Trust by Greater Manchester Council and Stockport Metropolitan Borough Council, who obviously recognised its value to the people of the Manchester conurbation.

Lyme Hall is the largest house in Cheshire, and is also much earlier than that at Tatton — parts of the present building date from the late 16th century, although major alterations were carried out in the early 18th century which produced the house we see today. In medieval times King Edward III promised land at Lyme to Thomas Danyers for rescuing the Black Prince's banner at the Battle of Caen in 1346. Then in 1388 Margaret Danyers married Piers Legh and they became the first Leghs of Lyme; family ownership of the estate carried on right through to 1946 when Richard Legh gave Lyme Park to the National Trust. The earliest part of the present Hall was built in the 1570's and has been retained in the very unusually designed Elizabethan frontage on the north side with its interesting mixture of columns and pediments.

It is the south front of Lyme Hall which is its most impressive and striking feature, particularly when seen from across the open lawns adjoining it and complemented by its shimmering reflection in the placid lake. This frontage was the work of an Italian architect named Giacomo Leoni, whose design of fifteen bays in three storeys is drawn together by a portico of four giant columns bearing a massive pediment. The monumental appearance of this south front is quite original, although it has much in common with the Palladian style which was being developed at that particular period, while the use of local gritstone brought from quarries on the estate further emphasises the solid yet clean-cut approach of the architecture. Leoni at the same time redesigned the courtyard by giving it a rusticated cloister. Another architect with a hand in the Hall's final appearance was Lewis Wyatt, who added an oblong tower to the south front and also made some alterations to the east front during the period 1816 — 22. Inside, the house has some intriguing features, particularly the chimneypieces to be seen in the Elizabethan rooms — the drawing room has a huge stone overmantel with the arms of Queen Elizabeth, while in the small Stag Parlour the chimneypiece is decorated by a hunting scene with the Elizabethan house in the middle.

Other Elizabethan rooms include the Stone Parlour on the ground floor, with a huge stone chimneypiece, and the Long Gallery on

The monumental frontage to Lyme Hall ▶

HALLS
AND HOMES

the top floor with the most elaborately decorated chimneypiece of all. Next to the Gallery is the Ghost Room with yet one more stone chimneypiece. Other treasures contained within the house include some rare tapestries, pieces of period furniture and some remarkable Grinling Gibbons carvings in limewood.

Immediately around the house are some delightful gardens, including a sunken Dutch garden and an Orangery built in 1862, while the lovely setting is completed by rolling parkland extending to the north and south of the house. This is the home of herds of red deer which roam the estate, reputed to be the largest and most magnificent deer in the British Isles. There is also a herd of smaller but prettier fallow deer to be seen wandering among the trees, together with flocks of gritstone sheep, while there are numerous species of birds and waterfowl to be observed in the copses and woodlands. An unusual feature with an air of mystery about it is Lyme Cage, to be seen on the hill above the road coming down from the main entrance — a square stone structure with corner turrets, it was built as a vantage point from which to follow the stag hunt. Although its date seems uncertain, it probably comes from the Elizabethan period.

Perhaps the most attractive feature of Lyme Park's setting is its position at the foot of the Pennines, with the rising hills forming a dramatic backcloth. There are some excellent walks from Lyme up to these hills in the east

of the county, and only a mile away from the house one can discover the ancient Bow Stones which are believed to be the bases of stone crosses. From this point one can look back down towards Lyme Hall, mysteriously shrouded by the surrounding trees, and somehow become more attuned to the history and beauty of the scene.

Adlington Hall

Adlington Hall, between Macclesfield and Stockport and only a mile from the county boundary with Greater Manchester, is a much more homely building than either Tatton or Lyme and has at least some of the black and white timbering which we have come to rather expect of such historic buildings. It has been the home of the Leghs of Adlington from 1315 through to the present day, a delightful mixture with one half dating from the fifteenth and sixteenth centuries (the black and white timber framed portion) and the other half from the eighteenth century (a very handsome Georgian frontage built of brick and stone). Although it is certainly quite a striking building, particularly when viewed from the southern aspect, Adlington Hall lays no claim to be considered as one of the great country mansions of England. Always a small manor, it has nevertheless been important in the fortunes of Cheshire and nearly all of the Leghs have taken a significant part in the affairs of the county throughout a period of over six hundred and fifty years.

Adlington Hall ▶

HALLS AND HOMES

The Hall was originally built on the site of a hunting lodge which stood in the Forest of Macclesfield in 1040; of this building two oak trees rather amazingly still remain, supporting the east end of the Great Hall which was built between 1480 and 1505 by Thomas Legh. The rest of the house, built by another Thomas Legh in 1581, was almost certainly half-timbered thoroughout in the traditional black and white style. The Hall is essentially quadrangular in shape and at an early date was surrounded by a moat, but whether there were originally buildings on each side of the quadrangle is not certain — it is possible that the west side was open while on the south side there may have been a detached gatehouse with a bridge.

Significant alterations were carried out by Charles Legh in the middle of the eighteenth century when it was decided to add a new west wing and some additional rooms in the north-west corner. At this time the Georgian south front was built connecting the west wing with the old Elizabethan east wing — it is this south front which is a particularly pleasing part of the Hall, its two storeys divided into thirteen bays centred upon a four column portico which bears the date of 1757. These Georgian additions may well have been designed by Charles Legh himself, employing local builders to carry out the work; it appears that the bricks were burnt in kilns in the park and the flags with which the whole building is roofed came

A familiar figure at Adlington ▶

from the nearby quarry at Kerridge.

The most notable and historic room here at Adlington must be the Great Hall, built at a time when this particular feature of the English manor house had reached the height of its importance in domestic architecture. The Hall was the centre from which the rest of the present house grew, and it measures forty five feet long and twenty six feet wide. Its roof is an excellent example of the hammer-beam type, with fine mouldings and carefully carved angels at the ends of the six hammer beams. At the east end of the Hall are the two oak trees remaining from the original hunting lodge, while between this is an organ which is by far the largest and best preserved 17th century organ in the country. Handel is known to have played on the organ when staying at Adlington in 1741-42 and again in 1751. At the other end of the Hall is another lovely feature — an elaborate timber canopy which is the finest in Cheshire. This canopy is divided into sixty small panels which bear the armorial shields representing the chief Cheshire families; these are understood to have been painted in 1571, and above them is the heraldic insignia of the seven Norman Earls of Chester and of the eight Barons.

The other room not to be missed is the beautifully-furnished Drawing Room with its georgeous panelled walls and white marble fireplace which date from the late 17th century. Elegance is evident everywhere, particularly in the superb carving of the overmantel above the fireplace executed probably by Grinling Gibbons and bearing the usual bunches of fruit and festoons of foliage. The ceiling is of a simple geometric pattern with egg and tongue mouldings, while the wooden panelled walls are divided by fluted Corinthian columns standing on pedestals. The finishing touches are provided by the lovely English chandelier which was made in 1750 and the five portraits of earlier members of the Legh family.

The gardens at Adlington may not be as extensive as those at Tatton or Lyme, but they nevertheless contribute to the lovely setting of the house. They were laid out in the style of Capability Brown in the middle of the eighteenth century, and at that time there were a number of small temples, a Chinese bridge over the River Dean passing close by, a hermitage and even a mock castle. Today's visitors can explore the 'Wilderness' where they can see a Temple to Diana with its painted ceiling and also a Shell Cottage; besides these there is a fine Yew Walk and a Lime Avenue planted in 1688 to celebrate the accession of William and Mary to the throne.

HALLS
AND HOMES

Capesthorne Hall

No one passing along the A34 between Alderley Edge and Congleton can fail to have noticed and admired the remarkable sight of Capesthorne Hall across the Cheshire fields, its unusual turrets and distinctive facade enchantingly discernible through the trees. The home of the Bromley-Davenports, it is quite unlike other stately houses in Cheshire since it was redesigned by the Victorian architect Salvin in a Jacobean style, having been almost destroyed by fire in 1861. The earliest part of the present house was a Georgian building of 1722, part of which still survives at the back, but this was considerably enlarged and altered by Edward Blore (architect to William IV and Queen Victoria) in 1834. Then came the disastrous fire of 1861 which led to the rebuilding of the entire centre portion. Salvin's designs were very much in line with Blore's intentions, and consequently Capesthorne is quite an unusual example of two generations of architects developing the same theme at a time when Victorian architectural taste was undergoing considerable change.

The Bromley-Davenports can trace their descent in an uninterrupted male line from Ormus de Davenporte, a Saxon who lived at the time of the Norman Conquest, and it was only in 1822 when they succeeded to the property of the Bromley family in Warwickshire that this other name was added to their own. Lords of the Capesthorne manor mentioned in the Domesday Survey, the Davenport family were Chief Foresters in the Royal Forests of Leek and Macclesfield and they upheld the harsh forest laws which deemed the life of a man less precious than the game of these royal domains. Their crest, a felon's head with a halter of gold around his neck, denoted the power of life and death without trial or appeal. It is this family who now live at Capesthorne, and the thief's head can still be seen carved in stone on many of the farms and cottages of the estate as well as on the gates of the courtyard and the walls of the house itself.

The driveway from the main road through surrounding parkland provides a grand entrance to Capesthorne Hall, a great red brick house with its tremendous facade which is longer even than that of Buckingham Palace. As one approaches the house the land drops away on the left hand side to a chain of small lakes which are spanned by a graceful bridge of brick and stone, with the radio telescope of Jodrell Bank rising up above the fields and hedges in the distance. Immediately in front of the house is a courtyard which is guarded by two pillars, upon which are the somewhat sinister representations of a felon's head in stone reminding us of the family history. The gardens at Capesthorne lie between the house and the placid lakes, entered through some highly ornate Milanese gates which date from 1750; from here paths lead the visitor to the waterfall

Capesthorne Hall ▶

HALLS
AND HOMES

and lower pool or in a different direction past the Arboretum and the entrance to Mill Wood. The summer house which one can see in the distance was originally the bell turret for the Chapel, built with the earlier Georgian Hall in 1722. This simple but attractive building with a stone balustrade above has been in use as the family chapel right up to the present day, and fortunately was little altered by Blore or by Salvin. Inside the furniture seems to have been assembled from all over the Continent — the pulpit with its carved panels is Flemish, the crucifix is of Spanish or French origin (probably 15th century) and the candlesticks are Italian, as is the delicate font made of different coloured marble.

Entrance lodge at Capesthorne ▶

Collecting art treasures from across Europe seems to have been a pastime which the Bromley-Davenports greatly enjoyed, and the house is full of valuable works of art and items of beautiful furniture. In the Entrance Hall, for example, one can see two panels of 16th century stained glass which originated in the Low Countries, a French clock and two Flemish figures incorporated into the chimney piece, as well as a long oak Tudor dining table dated about 1600 and two portraits of Oliver Cromwell which are slightly later. Capesthorne even has its own sculpture gallery, with arched recesses providing for the best display of the collection. The 'marbles' which the gallery contains are typical of the antiquities which were considered necessary to complete the decoration of town and country houses, particularly after the middle of the eighteenth century when the re-discovery of Pompeii and Herculaneium stimulated enthusiasm for souvenirs of the classical past. In the Saloon, the scene of many dances and festivities, one whole wall is completely covered by the portraits of the Squires of Capesthorne with their wives and children; the unusual-looking settees and chairs in this room were made in Ceylon, while the collection of ancient vases was brought back from Italy. Adjoining the Saloon is the Drawing Room — like the whole centre part of the house this was reconstructed by Anthony Salvin after the disastrous fire of 1861. Of special interest in this room are the twin fireplaces, brought from the London house of the family in Belgravia and splendid examples of Coade stone. Each is dated 1789 and signed, with the one on the wall next to the Saloon being carved with Christian symbols representing Faith, Hope and Charity. Also to be found here are six carved and gilded Venetian chairs (from about 1760) and two French clocks.

The furnishing of the rooms upstairs is just as sumptuous as in the rooms on the ground floor. The State Bedroom, for instance, has some

beautiful Entre-Fenetre panels on the walls and an exceptionally fine Boulle commode whose base is early Louis XIV. The carved gilt chairs of Adam design were made about 1780, while the Coronation chairs are the ones in which Sir Walter and Lady Bromley-Davenport sat at the coronation of Her Majesty Queen Elizabeth II. Another very interesting room is the American Room, containing furniture which was made by American cabinet-makers in the 18th century and china which was made in England for the Colonial market. Although the pattern books of English furniture designs were circulated among Colonial craftsmen and carefully studied, there is an unmistakable native touch about this furniture which was made for homes where the danger from hostile Indians and the dread of massacre were never far away. The items of particular interest here are the desk and bookcase of mahogany, the panel of woven linen commemorating the Declaration of Independence and the oil painting of Washington and his family.

There is probably no place more suitable for showing off such a fabulous collection of treasures from distant lands than Capesthorne, for the house itself with its domes and towers has something of an Eastern mystery about it. This is particularly so just before darkness falls, when the unusual outline of the building is silhouetted against the fading sky. The unusual architectural character of this house leaves an indelible impression, a rich experience to be enjoyed by all who pass this way.

HALLS AND HOMES

Gawsworth Old Hall

Gawsworth Old Hall (to distinguish it from the nearby New Hall built in 1712) is a lovely medieval manor house situated within an almost idyllic setting to the south of Macclesfield, complemented by the neighbouring church and ancient fish pools. Five families have held sway in the manor of Gawsworth from Norman times up to the present day — the de Orreby family, the Fitton family, the Earls of Macclesfield, the Earls of Harrington and the Roper Richards family — with each in turn being both lords of the manor and patrons of the church living. The present Hall dates primarily from the fifteenth century and like similar buildings of the period was constructed on a quadrangular plan, but later alterations destroyed this traditional layout and also led to much of the original external timber framing being faced with brick. Even so the Hall still retains the character of a venerable timber-framed house, enhanced by the immaculate black and white paintwork of its exterior and the solid oak beams to be seen within. One particularly interesting fact mentioned in the guide book to the Hall is that the estimated weight of the stone slates used on the five different roof levels of the building probably exceeds 350 tons — certainly a tribute to the strength and permanence of medieval craftsmanship.

Gawsworth must be one of the most endearing Halls to visit in Cheshire, its warm and intimate atmosphere created by the comparatively small rooms with their low ceilings and lovely pieces of furniture. It is very much a family house, in sharp contrast to some of the larger 'stately homes' which are open to the public, and many of the rooms bear evidence to the succeeding generations which have lived here. The cosy entrance hall, for example, has the heraldic arms of the Richards family mounted on one of its walls with two suits of armour (one from the fifteenth century and the other from the fourteenth century) displayed in the corners of the room. Next door, the library with its closely spaced ceiling timbers contains probably the best collection of books about Cheshire to be found anywhere, with other important features being the richly carved Tudor mantelpiece above the fireplace and the heavy velvet curtains embroidered in gold thread which date from the late 18th century. Passing through the Long Hall, with its original fireplace and low Tudor ceiling, one comes to the Dining Room which has been largely unaltered since the late medieval period — the principal piece of furniture here is the fine 16th century refectory table with its characteristic bulbous legs. Through the Guard Room, with its three early Jacobean chairs, the visitor then enters the Drawing Room which has always been the main living apartment for the family and has remained unchanged since the late fifteenth century. Much of the glass here is original and the timbering throughout is largely unrestored. Gawsworth also has its own private family chapel, with documents indicating that this has been associated with the house since 1365 when a licence for a domestic chapel was granted to John Fitton. The present chapel is thought to be the third or fourth to serve the Hall and dates from the work carried out in 1701 — highlights to be seen here include some lovely stained glass windows and the beautifully carved altar table. Next door is the chapel conservatory containing a collection of marble sculptures by John Warrington Wood, evidence of the present family's desire to make its own contribution to the treasures of Gawsworth.

Like the rest of the house, the lovely bedrooms on the first floor are beautifully furnished and paint an accurate picture of family life at Gawsworth over the centuries. The main bedroom is the Hall Room on the west side, with its ancient stone fireplace and oak framing surviving quite unchanged from the last quarter of the fifteenth century when the house was erected by Sir Thomas Fitton. It was here that the Duke of Monmouth slept in 1684, and possibly his father King Charles II at an earlier date. The marvellous four-poster bed is the main feature of the room, dating from the time of William and Mary. Another four-poster bed can be found in the Griffin Room (on the north side of the house) with its Tudor squared plaster ceiling — the bed itself is 16th century and came to Gawsworth from Lympne Castle in Kent. From this room access is gained to the Billiards Room, in which one has the opportunity to examine more closely the exposed roof timbers. There are also numerous interesting old documents displayed on the billiards table itself, one of which is a petition by a number of Gawsworth farmers put before the Earl of Harrington in 1830 for a reduction in rent of 10% owing to the hard times. The Earl did in fact grant their request and rents were indeed reduced by 10%, evidence of the trusting relationship which existed between landlord and tenants.

The open parkland surrounding the house and gardens is encompassed by an ancient Tudor wall and has remained much the same as it was in the Middle Ages, when it would have been the scene of jousting tournaments and colourful pageantry. Gawsworth is one of the few remaining places to have retained its own medieval tilting ground and it is believed that the Fittons used the Tilting Ground as such until the end of the sixteenth century, with the

Gawsworth Old Hall

HALLS
AND HOMES

last jousts to be publicly held in England taking place in the reign of King Charles I. On the west side of the park was The List, a long rectangular piece of ground used by knights on horse-back to practise their skills. Here was located a wooden figure called the quintain — if hit in the wrong position by a charging knight the quintain would spin round on its pivot and crack the unfortunate rider sharply on the helmet as he passed by. No doubt this ancient parkland, with its beautiful views of Shutlingsloe to the east, would have provided a suitable setting for other entertainments such as archery and drama, and the amphitheatre which

is still discernible in the grounds must have been able to accommodate thousands of spectators.

Thankfully Gawsworth Hall continues to provide a splendid opportunity for twentieth century people to experience the chivalry and romanticism of the medieval period, not only through the beautifully-maintained manor house but also through the open-air productions of Shakespeare's plays which are enacted here during the summer months with the black and white timbering of the west front forming a period-piece backcloth.

Gawsworth Old Hall —
two faces of a beautiful
home. ▶

Little Moreton Hall ▶

Little Moreton Hall

Together with the radio telescope at Jodrell Bank, Little Moreton Hall just off the A34 south-west of Congleton must rank as one of the best known sights in Cheshire and every summer it continues to draw hoardes of visitors to it. Surrounded on all four sides by its own moat, it is a beautifully kept 'black and white' house which is a superb example of English half-timbered architecture – almost entirely medieval in style it is a building which exudes history in every way and even from a distance its great antiquity is made immediately obvious from the way its walls appear to lean at a variety of precarious angles. The architectural historian Nikolaus Pevsner has described Little Moreton Hall as 'happily reeling and somewhat disorderly', and this is precisely the case – but certainly is a most attractive and endearing fashion. Perhaps the special charm of this particular house is that it has remained largely unchanged from the middle of the 16th century, untouched by the accretions of later generations which could have detracted from its very distinctive character.

The Little Moreton lands were held by the Moreton family for over six hundred years, and it was Ralph Moreton who first began the present building in about 1480: an 'H' shaped house, it consisted of two wings on either side of a great hall which still forms the north side of the courtyard. A second stage of building was carried out by William Moreton II in 1559, and it was left up to his son to complete the east range and to build the whole of the south range with its projecting gatehouse and long

gallery on the second floor, so that by about 1580 Little Moreton must have appeared much as it does today. It seems that the house has remained unaltered largely because the Moreton family, strong Royalists in a county which gave significant help to the Parliamentarian cause, never fully recovered from the effects of the Civil War, and although the house ceased to be their home at the beginning of the eighteenth century and was then tenanted by farmers for two hundred years the family always ensured that it was well cared for. It was then passed to the National Trust in 1937, and although very few of the family possessions survived with the house the comparative emptiness of the interior provides an opportunity to appreciate the structural ingenuity of the medieval craftsmen whose carpentry, plasterwork and glazing here are all of the highest quality.

The house is set in the south-east corner of an almost perfect 'square' enclosed by the moat, built in a rectangular block with a cobbled courtyard which is open for about thirty feet on the west wide. On the south and east sides the moat runs close to the buildings, but to the north and west there is an area of about an acre which forms the gardens to the house. A Knot Garden was laid out here in 1975, and it is likely that a similar style of formal garden (based on patterns made by rows of dwarf box hedges) existed at Little Moreton in the sixteenth and seventeenth centuries. Knot Gardens were intended to be viewed from above, both inside the house and from mounds or raised terraces, and two such mounds are still evident (one within the area enclosed by the

132

HALLS
AND HOMES

An item of furniture in the house ▶

moat and one outside the moat to the south west). The present garden has been planted with herbs and flowers which would have been available to gardeners in the sixteenth century, and a hedge of hornbeam and thorn has also been laid out to enclose the lawns in a way which would have been similarly fashionable during the later Elizabethan period.

Standing at the centre of the attractively cobbled courtyard, one is able to appreciate from changes in the patterning of the timber framing just how this lovely house 'grew' into its present form during a hundred year period in the late 15th and early 16th centuries. Building seems to have begun on the north-west side and gradually moved clockwise to form the present irregular quadrangle which is open to the west, with the original 'H' shaped house of the late fifteenth century still forming the north side of the courtyard. The first addition was in the north-east corner, marked by the two-storey bay windows elaborately patterned with their leaded glass panes and erected in 1559. Later on the east range was extended southwards to provide a chapel and other rooms, with the third and final phase of building being the addition of the gatehouse range on the south side which completed the open courtyard to be seen today. Access to this courtyard is across the lovely stone bridge which spans the moat beneath and then on through the gatehouse with its overhanging gabled rooms above.

A tour of the house should most appropriately begin in the Great Hall, still very much the focal point despite having lost some of the importance which it had when the house was first built at the end of the fifteenth century. This massive room with its timber framework still open to view was the centre of the house socially as well as physically, since it was here that the Moretons would have entertained both their family and their neighbours — the great

size of the room relative to the rest of the house was not only functional but also designed to impress. At a later date an extra floor was inserted to provide greater comfort and more space for the Moreton family, but this has since been removed so that the room is now in its original condition. There are three handsome pieces of furniture here which are nearly as old as the house itself — a long refectory table, a round-topped table which may well have been specially made to stand in the bay window added in 1559, and a large cupboard holding numerous small drawers which might have been used for storing spices. Two other rooms contained within the original house of 1480 include the Withdrawing Room, with its fine panelled ceiling of moulded beams, and the Parlour with its wall paintings which consist of a painted representation of wooden panelling together with Biblical scenes and texts. Numerous texts are also to be found on the walls of the lovely private chapel which was built at the southern end of the east range as part of the second phase of building between 1559 and 1570.

A spiral staircase just to the right of the gatehouse takes the visitor up to first floor level and to a landing from which access is gained to rooms which were probably set aside for the use of guests. On the right hand side of the landing is the Guest's Parlour, a large room with windows to the south and west and a sliding panel which leads to an adjoining 'secret room' which was used as a cheese store in the nineteenth century, while on the left is the large partitioned Guest's Hall. Both of these rooms have access via passages to the garderobe tower (a sixteenth century toilet facility), on each floor of which there are two closets with their original wooden seats — the effluent from this and the other garderobes in the house was conveniently discharged into the adjacent moat. The spiral staircase continues up from the first floor to the very top of the house and into the

The inner courtyard of Little Moreton Hall ◀

HALLS AND HOMES

Long Gallery, with its almost unbroken line of windows right round the south range and its rather undulating floorboards. The walls of this sixty-eight foot long room are lined by timber panelling, with the plasterwork on the gables at both ends being decorated with designs which were taken from the 1556 edition of 'The Castle of Knowledge' (a treatise on the sphere by the mathematician Robert Recorde). Leading off the Long Gallery and occupying the top floor of the projecting gatehouse is the Upper Porch Room, with a very attractive fireplace in one corner which is decorated by the Moreton family arms flanked by the figures of Justice and Mercy; this room was originally a bedroom known as the Gallery Chamber.

One of the main features which undoubtedly sets Little Moreton Hall apart as being an unusually complete sixteenth century house is its timber-framed construction, evident from its black and white appearance and matched by some elaborate carpentry work within the building. Yet it is perhaps the patterned glazing of the windows which is most striking to the visitor, the patterns varying from one room to another with some rooms having windows which contain more than one design. The individual pieces of glass are very small and and where the glass is original one can see tints of green, yellow and purple due to metallic impurities. It is this house, protected in earlier years by its own moat and now by the National Trust, which perhaps more than any other sums up the character of Cheshire and represents the best in English medieval architecture.

Peover Hall

Peover Hall is the central feature of a lovely group of historic buildings standing in the midst of pleasant parkland within the parish of Over Peover, a few miles south-east of Knutsford. Hall, coach-house, stables and church are clustered together in a secluded spot well away from the main road, a site of considerable interest since it holds evidence of domestic occupation from early medieval times to the present day. Peover was the ancestral home of the Mainwaring family from the twelfth century through to the early years of this century, and the present house was built by Sir Ralph Mainwaring in 1585 to replace an earlier half-timbered structure which stood in a moated enclosure nearby. Peover Hall is essentially Elizabethan in character, built of deep plum-red bricks with stone quoins and dressings and exhibiting the usual features of mullioned windows and numerous gables. Although it has suffered many alterations over the years, including the addition of a Neo-Classical wing in the nineteenth century which was later demolished, the house as we see it now presents a pleasing and uncluttered appearance to the prospective visitor and its warm brickwork offers a very marked contrast

Peover Hall ▶

134

HALLS
AND HOMES

to the half-timbered structure of Little Moreton Hall which was begun a hundred years earlier. Two interesting features particularly worth noting are the heraldic panel of the Mainwaring family over a doorway on the eastern front, with the date of 1585 above it, and the four brick chimneys on the roof which are set diagonally on their bases.

The other buildings associated with the house itself are also of great interest. To the south-east lies the two storey stable block dating from 1654, built of brick with stone dressings and having stone-mullioned windows. The ground floor was originally divided into sixteen stalls by some richly carved oak columns, overlooked by a finely decorated plaster ceiling, while the upper storey above was in the form of a continuous loft which was lit by several 'bulls-eye' windows. The adjoining coach-house is also a very handsome building, constructed of slightly lighter brick in 1764 and again having circular windows on the upper floor. The roof is crowned by a small domed turret with its own clock which bears the date of the building.

This rather special architectural grouping is completed by the presence of the parish church of St. Lawrence to the north-west of the Hall, a church which is believed to date from the 14th century when it was built as a private chapel of ease by the Mainwaring family. This church bears many indications of the association of the Mainwarings, who were lords of the manor and patrons of the benefice for over 800 years. Although the main body of the church was built of brick in 1811 to replace the previous building which was beyond repair, there are some earlier parts which demonstrate the dominant role played by the Mainwaring family in church affairs. The South Chapel to the right of the porch was built in 1456 and contains a monument to Sir Randle and Lady Margaret Mainwaring from that period, while the North Chapel was built in 1648 and has a magnificent monument to Philip and Ellen Mainwaring. There are also two alabaster slab monuments here (dated 1573 and 1586), while the ceiling portrays the family arms. The effigies just outside the North Chapel are the oldest remaining monument from the original church, dating back to 1410, and they represent a John Mainwaring and his wife Margaret. These effigies are among the finest of their kind in the county, with that of the lady being the earliest alabaster effigy known to exist in Cheshire — neither the lack of the original medieval colouring nor the passage of more than 500 years can obscure the exquisite modelling of the face and head.

Cholmondeley Castle

Cholmondeley Castle in the south of the county is principally known for its lovely gardens which are open to the public during the summer months and for a family chapel which marks the spot where regular worship has taken place over a period of at least seven hundred years. The Cholmondeley family has been resident here since the twelfth century, with the estate passing directly through the male line since that time — quite a unique feature even within a county which has at least its fair share of families who can trace their origins back over many generations. The Cholmondeley influence has also spread to other parts of the country through different branches of the family which have uprooted themselves and moved elsewhere, and by the seventeenth century a genealogist was already noting that there were 25 different ways of spelling the rather unusual family name. Although the house itself was built only in the early nineteenth century to an imitation 'gothick' design, its towers and castellated parapets nevertheless give it a rather historic appearance, and when seen from a distance one can be thoroughly impressed by its stark battlemented outline. Coming closer one cannot fail to appreciate the beautifully variegated exterior of this 'castle', created by the many different hues and tones in the colours of the large stone blocks with which it has been built, and the lovely pointed arch windows with their elegant white frames.

The original site of the ancient home of the Cholmondeley family lies within the parkland close to the walled gardens, but this was replaced by a much more substantial house built by Sir John Vanbrugh during the reign of Queen Anne. This house was also replaced at a later date when it was decided by the first Marquess that a new house should be built in a more advantageous position on higher ground. At that time both the Baroque and Palladian styles were out of fashion, and so Lord Cholmondeley had the house built to his own design in the romantic 'gothick' style. Although the building was completed by 1804, Lord Cholmondeley later employed Sir Robert Smirke of the British Museum to embellish the outline by the addition of further towers — the 'castle' which we see now has remained largely unchanged since that time.

The delightful gardens at Cholmondeley, with their rich array of trees and flowering plants, were laid out early in the nineteeth century at the same time as the 1st Marquess of Cholmondeley was building his new home. Just about every conceivable scent and colour can be found in these gardens at some time during the year, the Rose Garden being particularly

HALLS
AND HOMES

Cholmondeley Castle ▶

lovely with its tremendous variety of roses intermingled with honeysuckle and underplanted with lavander. A gravel path takes the visitor from the Rose Garden through the Herbaceous Borders and then down towards the Temple Garden, with a beautiful blue Atlas Cedar on one side which dominates the scene. This is probably the prettiest spot at Cholmondeley, looking out across the two islands and their temples from the top of the rockery with its geraniums and dwarf rhododendrons. One of the temples contains a rather charming lead figure sculpted by Van Noss, while nearby is a beautiful small garden gate made in the mid-eighteenth century and bearing the Cholomondeley coat of arms. Another feature to be found here is a waterfall, with the nearby bridge being formed out of carved dolphins which were originally part of a fountain; likewise the Temple from which the garden is named was taken from the garden of the Old Hall at the time when the Castle was built. The path from the Temple Garden follows the stream up to a water garden and then on into an orchard planted with walnut trees; this eventually emerges onto the main drive, which draws the visitor back to the house through some elegant white gates and past banks of conifers, rhododendrons and azaleas. Around the house itself is the Terrace area with its abundance of brilliantly coloured plants, a moat garden laid out to commemmorate the Silver Jubilee and some superb views over the parkland towards Beeston Castle on one side and the Staffordshire hills on the other.

The beautifully-kept Cholmondeley chapel stands in this parkland, somewhat removed from the main house and fronted by a very attractive pair of wrought iron gates. It appears from the historical guide to this building that the first reference to the chapel was a grant from the rectors of Malpas to Hugh de Cholmondeley in 1285 allowing him to have 'a fit Chaplain celebrating divine service in his Chapel of Cholmondeley'. Such licences were usually the confirmation of an existing situation and consequently the chapel may well have been built as early as 1200. Over the centuries the chapel underwent a number of changes to its fabric, with the oldest part being the hammerbeam roof which survives from one of the earliest timber structures. A major restoration was carried out in the 17th century and the interior furnishings from this period are considered by Pevsner and Hubbard to be the most complete of their date in Cheshire. In 1717 the chapel was encased in brick and stone to match similar work being carried out on the old house, and then in 1829 the present cruciform appearance of the building was created by the 2nd Marquess of Cholmondeley who added the north and south transepts. From this time the chapel has changed very little, right up to the present day. The internal features and decoration of this building make it a very significant one in ecclesiastical history, largely because of the many items of church furniture which date from the middle of the seventeenth century. The Screen, for example, is dated 1655 and is probably the most

HALLS
AND HOMES

impressive feature of the interior, flanked on either side by the Commandment Boards which are also dated 1655. The chancel panelling, pulpit and reading pew are likewise of a similar age and match the rest of the woodwork in both quality and ornament.

Although this was first and foremost the domestic chapel of the Lords of Cholmondeley it has also been much used by inhabitants from the surrounding district. Documents show that a chaplain was appointed to take services at the chapel whether the family were in residence or not, and the additions to the building are evidence of a desire to accommodate a much larger congregation than just the household and its retainers. Services are still conducted regularly at the chapel and visitors have the privileged opportunity to admire this prim and elegant building with its very important interior.

Cholmondeley Chapel ▶

Chapter VI

CHAPELS AND CHURCHES

— meek and lowly, high and mighty

Churches and chapels hold a great deal of interest for both the casual and the more devoted 'treasure-hunter' on any ventures into Cheshire. From an historical point of view they may be particularly significant, often being the oldest surviving buildings in a town or village and as such being the key to unlocking the 'secrets' of an area and uncovering the story of its growth and development down through the years. Architecturally, an ecclesiastical building can be a marvellous physical expression of the thinking and aspirations of a particular generation — a rich experience in timber, stone or brick of the skill and devotion of both designers and craftsmen. Then equally churches and chapels can be fascinating from a more personal angle, providing some delightful insights into local traditions and customs, revealing the interests of local people and perhaps demonstrating the important role played by the lords of the manor. Here you can read about a few of these lovely buildings around the county which have been silent witnesses to the comings and goings of many generations.

St. Mary's, Astbury

The village of Astbury to the south-west of Congleton has had its own parish church for over a thousand years now, although the magnificent stone building which exists today dates largely from the 15th century. This church is immediately impressive not only by virtue of its size but also because the tower with its lofty spire stands somewhat removed from the rest of the building, a very unusual state of affairs which came about through alterations to the nave and chancel undertaken in the 13th and 14th centuries resulting in the creation of a particularly striking feature on the Cheshire skyline.

The earliest church for which any evidence remains was the Saxon one which was in existence at the time the Domesday Book was compiled, a building which would have been largely constructed of timber. This was followed by a Norman structure of which only the lower part of the tower and several carved sections of a doorway remain as most of it was replaced by a more ornate building of the early English period. This also was partly demolished to accommodate the magnificent chancel and nave added in the 15th century, since which time the structure has largely remained unaltered. The details and decoration of this building not only demonstrate the development of ecclesiastical architecture over several centuries but also reveal the progress of religious thought, for there is a wealth of symbolism within the church which underlines the importance of the Christian faith to the people of the time as well as their fight against the forces of evil, and the frequency with which the portrayal of devils appears at Astbury is a striking reminder of this.

Passing through the stone lychgate dating from the 15th century, there are a number of interesting features to be found in the churchyard including a canopied tomb which was probably erected in the 13th or 14th century, an ancient yew tree which may well be over one thousand years old and several gravestones whose inscriptions provide examples of rather grim humour. The present level of the churchyard, necessitating a decent into the church from the north side, is due to the large area formerly served by the churchyard and the length of time it has been in use for interments (nearly a thousand years).

The church itself can be entered through one of the five very interesting doorways to be noted at different points around the building. The Western Porch is the main and most impressive entrance, and above it are two rooms which were formerly used by the villagers as Peel or Refuge Chambers for the women and children during cattle raids by the Welsh. The spiral staircase by which these rooms are approached also gives access to the almost flat roof of the Nave, so that the 'refugees' were able to roam at will over the large area of the roof. The South Porch is a very elaborate affair, having a fine carved door and an exquisite four-panelled roof, and above it is the Priest's Room which contains a variety of ecclesiastical relics. This porch was in close proximity to the Manor House of Astbury, which still exists as the Glebe Farm at the south-east corner of the churchyard with remains of an old tilting ground, archery butts bearing the name of The Longshoots and a manorial fish pond.

The best view of the interior of the church is obtained from the west end of the Nave taking in the beautifully-carved ceiling and the delicate fan-tracery of the rood screen, both of which are largely 15th century in construction. Jacobean work also abounds in this building, particularly in the box pews with their intricately carved panels which reveal an amazing variety of detail, although both the lectern and the pulpit date from the Tudor period. The present Moreton Chapel and North Aisle to one side of the main structure were originally the chancel and nave of the church which had been built in the 13th century, and here can be found the recumbent effigy of Lady Jane Egerton who died in 1599 and a medieval stone font with a beautiful Jacobean canopied cover. Across on the other

St. Mary's, Astbury

CHAPELS AND CHURCHES

side of the church is the Lady Chapel and South Aisle, with its 15th century ceiling decorated with a variety of religious figures and the tomb of a 14th century knight (Sir Ralph Davenport, who held lands in Swettenham). The other major feature of the church is the Belfry tower, which owes its isolated position to the fact that when the Norman nave and chancel were demolished the builders of the Early English church moved over towards the south leaving only a narrow aisle on the site of the earlier Norman building. This process was repeated by the 15th century builders who deserted the Norman site altogether and thus left the tower standing alone, with a narrow passage between it and the church which was later roofed over.

Perhaps the best place to appreciate the gradual genesis of Astbury parish church over the centuries is the north-west corner of the North Aisle, for here one can see portions from each period of its construction — a Saxon capital resting on a ledge, a Norman doorway into the tower which is now built up, the first bay of the arcading of the Early English Church, some 15th century glass in the west window and a curtain wall which dates from 1862. This is undoubtedly an exciting church architecturally and one which has been beautifully adorned by succeeding generations of craftsmen who have left their indelible marks in both stone and timber.

St. Mary and All Saints, Great Budworth

Again impressively built of stone in the Perpendicular style, this parish church is beautifully situated at the centre of Great Budworth and occupies a prominent position overlooking the surrounding countryside. Largely complete by the 16th century, its battlemented appearance contrasts strongly with the domesticity of the surrounding village scene. The mention of a priest in the Domesday Book suggests that there was already a church here at that time, although no specific reference was made to one, but by Henry I's reign the tithes and patronage were being given to the Abbot of Norton. It was the Augustinian Canons of Norton Priory who were serving the church at the time of the Dissolution when Henry VIII gave the tithes to his new College of Christ Church in Oxford (1546), and today the Dean and Chapter are still the Patrons of the Living.

There are two family chapels contained within this church which are of special interest, the Lady Chapel to the left of the north aisle and the Warburton Chapel just off the south aisle. The Lady Chapel is largely a 14th century creation and contains the burial vaults of the families of Tabley House and Marbury Hall, as well as being the resting place for Sir Peter Leycester who was Cheshire's great sixteenth-century historian, while the Warburton Chapel on the other side of the church was erected in the 15th century and has been the family vault of the Egerton-Warburtons who resided in nearby Arley Hall. The oak stalls to be seen here are reputed to be the oldest ecclesiastical woodwork in Cheshire (dating from the 13th century) and there is also an alabaster effigy of Sir John Warburton who died in 1575.

Within the main body of the church the rows of arches on either side of the nave are particularly beautiful, and from the slight changes in style it appears that the building of the nave was spread over a number of years and that it progressed from east to west. As with other churches of a similar age, the piers and arches are decorated with some curious carvings and religious representations. At the far end is the 14th century chancel, while above the entrance with its decorated doorway is the tower which was probably built between 1500 and 1520 by the same mason who built St. Helen's Church near Northwich about twenty years later. This tower was constructed of three storeys and ornamented with the coats of arms of the Dutton family, the Priory of Norton and the Warburton family. Then finally there is the octagonal font dating from the 15th century and probably one of the best examples in Cheshire, the panels of its shaft sculpted with emblems of the Passion.

Outside the church are two features representing slightly different forms of discipline and correction which have been applied in days gone by — against the churchyard wall near to the lychgate are the village stocks, while to the north of the church but still within the churchyard is the former School or Reading Room, built of ancient brick with narrow mullioned windows and facing onto School Lane with its pleasing terrace of timber-framed cottages. Meanwhile on the south side of St. Mary's, and in a better position to catch the sunlight, is an 18th century sundial unobtrusively marking the passage of time within the peaceful environs of this very attractive church which has been the focal point in Great Budworth for five centuries or more.

CHAPELS AND CHURCHES

St. Oswald's, Lower Peover

Founded in 1269, St. Oswald's Church in the hamlet of Lower Peover near Knutsford is a timber-framed building and has a completely different appearance and atmosphere to the more substantial stone-built churches in Cheshire. By virtue of its method of construction it is a very important building, but it is also a very beautiful one in its own right with the crisp black and white patterning of the nave and chancel forming a sharp contrast to the weathered look of the sandstone tower. As with many churches some restoration work has been carried out over the years, but the timber arcades and octagonal piers of the interior are largely unchanged and probably date back at least to the 14th century.

Although Lower Peover was not mentioned as an inhabited place at the time of the Domesday survey in 1086, in the space of less than two hundred years it had become an area worthy of a separate place of worship of its own – in 1235 Richard Grosvenor from nearby Hulme Hall built a timber chapel on rising ground above the stream known as Peover Eye and by 1269 it was dedicated to St. Oswald after being linked with the Augustinian Priory of Norton. The method of construction for this church was not unusual in itself, since hundreds of timber-framed churches must have been built throughout Europe between 500 AD and 1400 AD owing little or nothing to the tradition of stone church architecture derived from the old Roman 'basilica'. The importance of this building at Lower Peover, however, stems from the fact that very few timber-framed churches exist today due to the ravages of fire or their replacement by more solid stone structures.

Research has indicated that the chapel built here in 1269 was probably pulled down and replaced a century later, and this is reinforced by the fact that the form of St. Oswald's is very similar to the church at Marton which was certainly built in the late 14th century. The chapel was most likely smaller and simpler at first with only one roof and narrow passages north and south of the arcades, having low side walls and low windows. There may well have been a half-timbered tower originally, as is still the case at Marton. The building was enlarged to its present width between 1450 and 1500, although the introduction of the separate roofs came at a much later date with the restoration work carried out by Salvin in 1852. Two of the interior features of the church originate from its earliest years and are particularly important: the oak chest hewn out of one solid tree trunk is probably the most prized medieval treasure to be found here and may well be even older than the church itself, while the stone font was introduced in 1322 but slightly added to in about 1600.

The original tower at St. Oswald's was probably a slightly tapered half-timbered structure

CHAPELS AND CHURCHES

similar to that still standing at Marton, but it was replaced in 1582 by the present very handsome stone tower which is really the only true Tudor part of the church. Among the furnishings, the oldest parts of the pews may also go back to the second half of the sixteenth century, but they are probably not earlier than the very end of the Elizabethan period; whatever their date they have been altered over time, since originally most of them would have had 'half-doors' in order to retain the straw or rushes by which feet were kept warm in winter. At the beginning of the 17th century the side chancels were developed by two families descended from the Grosvenors of Hulme — the Shakerleys of Hulme took over the southern chancel (now containing monuments to two members of this particular family), while the Holfords of Holford had their own chancel lavishly screened in the north-east part of the church. Jacobean features in St. Oswald's include not only the handsome screens separating these family chapels from the main body of the church but also the pulpit, lectern and font cover. It was the restoration work carried out by Salvin in 1852 which gave St. Oswald's the title of "the finest specimen of ecclesiastical edifices", a title which it has deservedly retained right through to the present day. As well as general repair work, the most significant change was the introduction of the three-gabled roof and the substitution of timbered masonry for brickwork throughout the length of the south aisle.

This church is very special to Cheshire not only because of its own outstanding elegance and charm but also because of its picturesque setting in an intimate enclave away from the main road. It has enjoyed a close relationship both with the Bell's of Peover, a public house since 1569, and the local school which was founded in 1710 by Richard Comberbach who had been a curate at St. Oswald's. Up to the time when compulsory schooling was introduced under the first Education Act (in 1871) the minister at the church also fulfilled the role of head teacher. Now the original schoolhouse is a private residence, but the newer building in which children are currently taught is still within sight of the church itself so that the old-established link between the two has been maintained. Both the pub and the school are still situated just the other side of the churchyard from St. Oswald's, as they always have been, epitomising the close-knit character of this tiny community.

Old St. Chad Chapel, Tushingham

The Chapel of Old St. Chad (to distinguish it from the Church of St. Chad built nearby during the nineteenth century) lies within the scattered community of Tushingham to the

Old St. Chad Chapel, Tushingham ▶

CHAPELS AND CHURCHES

south-east of Malpas and is as different to St. Oswald's as chalk is to cheese. A tiny but very beautiful building of brick and slate it stands completely on its own in the midst of green fields, bearing an air of dignified simplicity and seemingly unconcerned for the affairs of the world, while round it is a churchyard which is still the burial ground for the parish. As well as the occasional funeral service the chapel is still used once a month between May and September for Morning and Evening Prayer. Almost impossible to get to in winter but a delight to visit during the summer, the only approach to the chapel is straight across the fields from the end of a narrow lane running off the A41 between Chester and Whitchurch.

St. Edith's, Shocklach ▶

The present brick building dates from 1689 and probably replaced an earlier timber-framed structure which could have been on the site for at least three hundred years, since it is known that a chapel already existed here in 1349. What we can see now is still very largely a 17th century place of worship with its original furniture and other features which are very definitely characteristic of the period — the roof, for example, is quite an unusual example of its time decorated with carved patterns which were probably the design of local craftsmen. The pews in the chapel are also particularly interesting, with two family box pews at one end which were obviously reserved for the wealthier families and some rather simpler pews in the body of the chapel formed only of oak planking which were for the "ordinary folk" who attended St. Chad's. Then there is a panelled pulpit, supported on one side by the stump of a tree which also acted as a seat for the lesson reader, together with a moveable font made largely of oak which is elaborately carved and may have been brought here in the early 18th century. The guidebook to the chapel makes the point that this elaborate carving might suggest that the pedestal to the font could well have started life as part of a four-poster bed! The gallery at the west end of the building is also unusual in that it can only be reached by an exterior stone staircase in the north-west corner, the gallery and staircase being introduced in 1822 by the Vawdrey family who were owners of the manor, while the chapel is attractively finished off by a tiny four-sided bell tower under its own pyramid roof which is located above the entrance porch. Old St. Chad Chapel should be noted not only for its architecture and furnishings but also because it is one of the few remaining places to hold a Rushbearing Service, commemorating the fact that at one time rushes had to be brought into the building to act as a floor-covering.

St. Edith's Church, Shocklach

This is a small Norman church which must rank as one of the oldest ecclesiastical buildings in Cheshire, and like Old St. Chad Chapel it lies in a hidden corner well away from the village with which it was originally connected. It is actually situated at the end of a lane running down towards the River Dee just to the north of Shocklach, quite humble in appearance and partially hidden by trees but certainly an exciting place to come across. Built of red sandstone, its most important feature is the Norman doorway on the south side with a rounded arch which is adorned by the characteristic embellishments and carvings.

St. Edith's Church, Shocklach

It appears that the church was built about 1150 by the lord of the manor Thomas de Shocklach, whose castle was sited on a fortified mound a little further to the north. Physical evidence of the site can still be seen on the ground and some of the place names around here are further proof of the history of the area e.g. Castletown and Lords Fields. The nave is the oldest part of the church, dedicated to Edith who is presumed to have been a daughter of the Saxon king Edward the Elder (round about 924 AD), with the chancel being a later addition of the fifteenth century. Externally the church has a very simple appearance apart from the small but architecturally significant Norman arch with its iron-studded wooden door, although there is also a delightful unenclosed double belfry which forms part of the west wall. The two bells are rung by means of iron chains, and over the years grooves have been worn in the sandstone above the point where the chains pass through into the church. Also at the west

CHAPELS AND CHURCHES

end is a small baptistry which was created when the space between two buttresses was roofed over as part of the restoration work carried out in the seventeenth century; it is this baptistry which is very much a focal point of the interior of the church with its seven-sided font dating from the 15th century. On the flanking walls here can be found two large armorial oil paintings, one being the Royal Arms of George III (with a date of 1760) and the other being a 'hatchment' or mourning board. A hatchment was used to depict the family history of a deceased person and was generally placed on the front of his house for everyone to see; it would then be left in the local church where it would hang for 'at least a year and a day'. This particular hatchment relates to a later member of the Pulestons, a family who were patrons of the parish of Shocklach from very early days. Other features within the church include a pulpit dated 1687, the ornamented 17th century nave ceiling, communion rails from the late 18th century and some very early examples of stained glass in the baptistry.

St. Peter's Church, Prestbury

The name Prestbury is a Saxon one meaning "Priests' Town", and it was here that priests settled during the early Christian period to evangelise the surrounding area. Consequently a church must have existed here possibly earlier

West end of St. Edith's ▶

CHAPELS AND CHURCHES

Norman Chapel, Prestbury ▶

than any other place in Cheshire, even though Prestbury was not specifically mentioned in the Domesday Book. The Parish Church of St. Peter is probably the third place of worship to have existed in the village, superseding the earlier and far smaller Norman chapel (still to be seen within the churchyard) which must likewise have replaced an even earlier Saxon building. For most of its history the church in Prestbury was the 'mother church' for an extensive part of Cheshire, exercising ecclesiastical jurisdiction over thirty-five townships, and even up to 1878 marriages between people from these places could only be solemnised at St. Peter's.

The belief that there was a church here long before the time of William the Conqueror received confirmation in 1841 when parts of an ancient cross were found embedded within the chancel wall, the carvings on the stone indicating that it probably originated in the 8th century when it may have been erected to commemorate the founding of the Christian community here. This relic is now on display in a glass case within the churchyard. Also in the churchyard is the lovely Norman chapel (with its arched entrance which is reminiscent of the doorway at St. Edith's church) probably built on the site of the earlier Saxon structure towards the end of the 12th century. The west face of this solid-looking stone building is its most attractive and interesting feature, with a row of carved figures above the doorway and

above these figures an inscription in Latin describing how the chapel was restored in 1747 by Sir William Meredith of Macclesfield. Perhaps this is one of the earliest acts of architectural conservation to be seen in the county, since the tablet records that the building had 'become ruinous through age, part of it having already fallen.' The six windows on either side of the chapel are somewhat more recent, having been dedicated in 1977, and they illustrate the lines of a well-known poem which is to be found on an old grandfather clock in Chester Cathedral:

'When as a child I laughed and wept, time crept.
When as a youth I dreamed and talked, time walked.
When I became a full grown man, time ran.
And later as I older grew, time flew.
Soon I shall find while travelling on,
time gone.
Will Christ have saved my soul by then?
Amen.'

The existing Parish Church first took shape in 1220, and although there have been many additions, alterations and restorations over the years the appearance which St. Peter's presents now is that which might be expected in the traditional English village. It is a church which has always been strongly associated with the local squirearchy, and it seems certain that the Davenports of Henbury, the Pigotts of Butley

147

CHAPELS AND CHURCHES

and the predecessors of the Leghs of Adlington all contributed to its erection. Although the manor and church remained in the possession of the monks of St. Werburgh in Chester up to the time of the Reformation, they eventually came into the ownership of the Legh family at Adlington Hall, and the family have remained patrons of the church ever since. The important role which this family has played in the life of St. Peter's is evident from the many monuments and references to them which can be seen throughout the building, and on the south side of the chancel is a canopied arch marking the probably burial place of Sir Urian Legh who died in 1627. The family also have their own private chapel at the eastern side of the north aisle, within which is a monument to Charles Legh who died in 1781, while their heraldic arms are among those of old Cheshire families which are painted on the front of the gallery at the western end of the nave. The patronage of the Leghs is also evident from

inscriptions on the church bells, one of which has been rung as a curfew bell every day at 8 pm during the autumn and winter months since 1577, finishing off with the same number of strokes as the number of the day of the month.

There is also a wealth of other interesting items to be discovered in St. Peter's, including a series of paintings above the arches which represent the twelve apostles and the twelve tribes of Israel, a series of candle brackets on the piers of the nave remaining from an early system of artificial lighting, and an oak pulpit made in 1607. In the churchyard there are several tombstones of some historic interest, including one near the chancel door which rather strangely records the fact that Sarah Pickford "died a Bachelour in the 48 yeare of her age," while gathered together near the east end of the church are a number of carved stones which are portions of Gothic grave slabs from the thirteenth and fourteenth centuries.

Jenkin Chapel, Saltersford ▶

CHAPELS AND CHURCHES

Jenkin Chapel, Saltersford

The Church of St. John the Baptist (known also as Jenkin Chapel) is a simple but attractive building situated in a fairly isolated position on the slopes of the Pennine hills which form the eastern boundary of the county. Its solid walls and heavy slab roof were built to withstand the harsh climate of this more exposed part of Cheshire, an upland area with a fairly scattered population of hill farmers; the fact that its appearance seems more akin to a farmhouse than to a church came about largely because it was the ancestors of these farmers who built the chapel back in 1733 using their own hands and local materials.

The church stands at the junction of three roads which are in fact ancient trackways on the line of old pack-pony tracks or 'salters' ways'. From Roman times right through the medieval era salt was a very valuable commodity and dealers used a network of packhorse tracks to transport it across the county – the name 'Saltersford' arose because one of these ancient tracks passed right through the parish. The track system was later used by cattle drovers and sheep dealers, one of whom (Jenkin from Ruthin) is said to have traded from North Wales to Derbyshire in the early eighteenth century. By the crossroads at this point on the hills had stood an ancient track-marking stone which came to be known as 'Jenkin Cross' since he carried on his business transactions there, and the chapel which was built here in the early 18th century was named after him. Several footpaths also met at the crossroads, linking the farms with what was obviously the most important place in the area; this importance lasted right through the nineteenth century with a small market being held at the 'cross' for the convenience of local farmers who could easily drive their stock there. Not only did the farming population at Saltersford build their own chapel here, they also committed themselves to raising £10 each year for the support of their own minister.

The architectural style of Jenkin Chapel is very definitely a vernacular one, built rather like a farmhouse with two rows of Georgian cottage windows on each side as well as a chimney stack (a rather unusual feature for a place of worship) and a small tower which was added some twenty-two years after the building had been started. This tower contains the bell chamber which is reached by an outside flight of stone steps, while below is a rather cosy porch with stone benches on each side. Inside the church are the original box pews, a high octagonal pulpit and a carved reading desk. At the east end of the building is the chancel,

much smaller in scale than the rest of the church and from the outside having the appearance of a later extension which was 'tacked on' as an afterthought. Above the chancel arch is a modern stained-glass window with wooden boards on either side upon which are written the Creed, the Lord's Prayer and the Ten Commandments, while within the chancel itself is some more richly-coloured glass and a small stone font with an oak cover.

Local families have always been important in the life of Jenkin Chapel, as is evident from some of the other features of the interior. On the floor of the nave and chancel, for instance, one can discover four grave slabs relating to members of the Turner family from nearby Saltersford Hall, and it was Richard Turner who was one of the original trustees of this church. Then at the west end of the building is a small gallery on the front of which hangs the coat of arms of the Stopford family who lived at Saltersford Hall in the seventeenth century and remained chief landowners in the valley until 1947. An inscription on the wall above the entrance porch tells how the church 'was made sacred for the worship of Almighty God' in 1739 at the expense of John Slack, another of the first trustees, while the small churchyard partly enclosed by trees has many old graves which record the names of the families who lived in Saltersford when the chapel was built and whose descendants still reside in the area. Many of the early graves are unmarked, with only slight mounds in the grass indicating their presence, while one tombstone has merely the single word 'Here' inscribed upon it as though the family could not afford the full inscription. Probably most of these families would have had a hand in the building of the tower in 1755, their names appearing in the accounts as the providers of labour, materials and money, and in fact less than thirty surnames occur in all the early documents relating to the church.

Jenkin Chapel has been in continuous use since it was built and despite its rather 'out of the way' location services are still held regularly on the second and fourth Sundays of the month in the period between Easter and Christmas. Many of the churches in Cheshire have their roots deep within the local community, and this one is no exception: a building expressed in the architectural idiom of the locality, rather romantically located amidst windswept fields at the foot of the Pennines and continuing to serve the local farming populace as it has done faithfully for 250 years now.

CHAPELS AND CHURCHES

Marton Parish Church

This beautiful black and white church dedicated to St. James and St. Paul stands on a rise overlooking the A34 just to the south of the picturesque village of Marton. Together with St. Oswald's at Lower Peover, this is one of the oldest timber-framed churches in Europe having been founded and endowed in 1343 by Sir John de Davenport and Vivian his son. It is without doubt a superb example of a wood and plaster building, with a particularly interesting tower (made of timber uprights and roofed with wooden shingles) which was a slightly later addition to the main church. The entrance into the building is now through a doorway which faces on to the main road, passing into the nave from beneath the tower, although earlier entrances had existed both on the north and south sides. As with many other churches the chancel is also a later addition to the main structure.

Marton Parish Church ▶

Inside the church on the west wall are traces of some early medieval paintings, together with much later oil paintings of Moses and Aaron holding the Ten Commandments, while within the belfry are two stone effigies said to be those of the founder Sir John de Davenport and his son. These figures have been given the form of knights with their conical helmets, plate armour and pointed boots which were characteristic 'dress' for the period. Their hands are clasped in prayer in the usual way with their feet resting against an animal, and under the head of each is the Davenport crest — a felon's head with a rope around the neck, reminding us that this was the domain of the family which administered the harsh laws of the Royal Forests. Other items worthy of note are the pulpit with its coat of arms dating back to 1620 and an Elizabethan parish chest. The pristine condition of this lovely and important church is due largely to several restorations which have been carried out over the years, enabling its very marked 'magpie' appearance to be admired and appreciated even by the passing traveller.

Marton Parish Church ▶

CHAPELS AND CHURCHES

All Saints, Siddington ▶

All Saints, Siddington

Only a few miles north of Marton Church is All Saints' Church at Siddington, which by virtue of the black and white appearance of its west wall seems to be similarly timber-framed. On closer examination, however, one will discover that this is really just a pattern painted on to the brick exterior, and that in fact almost all the external fabric of the building is brick rather than timber. Yet this in turn is also something of a deception, for beneath the brick walls is the original timber framing of which the church was first constructed back in the 14th or 15th century. It seems that the weight of the heavy Kerridge flag-stone roof caused the nave walls to bulge so badly that by 1815 they had to be strengthened by an external cladding of local red brick which was painted to resemble the original timbers remaining underneath. This unusual state of affairs in no way impairs one's appreciation of this church, a very lovely building in a secluded spot just above the Snape Brook and far enough away from the main road to preserve an atmosphere of peace and tranquility. Fortunately the external timber-work of the chancel is the genuine article, consisting of two narrow bays with herringbone bracing in the walls, while the half-timbered south porch is also original.

Early records which have been found mention a chapel at Siddington in 1337 and 1474, this being consecrated for preaching in 1521 and then licensed for baptisms, marriages and to 'bury in ye chappell yard but not in ye chappell' in 1721. Most of these functions had previously been the prerogative of St. Peter's Church in Prestbury. Internally, the nave and chancel of All Saints are separated by a 14th century screen which still shows the indentations of the adze or cutting tool which was used to shape the wood, while the pulpit and reading desk are later additions of the 17th century. Instead of a tower or spire the church has a pretty bell turret which probably replaced a small steeple, and within this turret is a single bell which had first been installed in 1588 to warn parishioners of impending Spanish invasion but which in the event rang out in celebration of the defeat of the Armada.

The churchyard on the south side of the building is particularly beautiful, incorporating some interesting gravestones as well as many trees which have been planted in memory of those who worshipped here. The single yew tree at Siddington is probably at least as old as the church itself, these trees being a common feature of medieval churchyards since their branches were used to make longbows for the bowmen of England. Also, because their leaves and berries were poisonous to animals the churchyard was almost the only fenced area in the parish where they could safely be grown. The churchyard also marks the resting place of earlier members of the Bromley-Davenport family from nearby Capesthorne Hall, patrons of this church for many generations now, as well as being the burial ground for many other local people, although strangely enough out of over 2,000 burials recorded here it has only been possible to trace the whereabouts of some 1,000 interments in 350 graves.

◀ *All Saints, Siddington*

CHAPELS AND CHURCHES

Bunbury Parish Church

The unusually named Church of St. Boniface in the village of Bunbury has a history similar to that of St. Peter's in Prestbury, with the present Perpendicular-style stone church being the successor of earlier Norman and Saxon edifices. It is certainly a very impressive building which dominates the surrounding houses from within its extensive churchyard, with the battlements, pinnacles and large windows on both the north and south sides bringing to mind St. Mary's Church in Great Budworth. Although the Domesday Book only mentioned a priest at 'Boleberie' without specific reference to a church, there appears to have been a stone building erected here towards the end of the eleventh century which probably replaced an earlier wooden one. This church seems to have sufficed until the later part of the 14th century when Sir Hugh Calveley decided to establish a college and chantry here in 1386, resulting in a significant programme of rebuilding to accommodate this ambitious project. Much of the present building has survived largely unaltered from this period, with the only extension to the fourteenth century plan being a chantry built on the south side of the chancel in 1577 by Sir Ralph Egerton of Ridley. The church still contains a number of monuments from the fourteenth century, including an alabaster tomb and effigy of Sir Hugh Calveley located in the chancel and several other effigies depicting knights or members of local families.

Many of the other interior features of this church seem to have originated from the 17th century, a particularly important one being the decorated tomb of Sir George Beeston in the sanctuary. This notable gentleman died in 1601 at the ripe old age of 102, having been in command of one of the ships which fought against the Spanish Armada when he was 88. Still in the 17th century one can see the north

door dating from 1630, an octagonal font from 1663 and an early hatchment memorial in the south aisle which bears the date of 1669, while the tower contains eight bells which span the centuries from the early 16th century tenor bell to the last two which were added at the close of the 19th century. Of much more recent interest is the curtain in the chancel which actually came from Westminster Abbey and is made from hangings used at the Coronation of Her Majesty Queen Elizabeth II.

To capture the full historic flavour of this church one should also wander down the narrow lane to the south in order to see the very attractive half-timbered house built in 1527 for the chantry priest. This two storey black and white building must have been typical of the many which would have existed round about the church in connection with its important role as a college, providing accommodation for the small community of Canons and 'singers' in addition to the chantry priests.

All Saints, Daresbury

This church is famous not for its architecture or history but rather for its association with Lewis Carroll, the well-known author of 'Alice in Wonderland' and the creator of the Cheshire Cat. It was in Daresbury that Lewis Carroll (born Charles Lutwidge Dodgson on January 27th 1832) spent his early years, the son of Reverend Charles Dodgson who was the vicar here from 1827 to 1843, and All Saints is still the place to which all who appreciate his writings are inevitably drawn on their pilgrimage to his birthplace. A particularly lovely feature of the church is the stained glass window at the east end of the Daniell Chapel which marks his centenary, dedicated in 1934 and subscribed to by people from across the world. The largest part of the window is given over to the Nativity scene, but above this are portions depicting Carroll's life including the Cheshire Wheatsheaf, representing the county in which he was born, the shields of Rugby School and Christ Church in Oxford where he received his education, and a pair of compasses together with the Lamp of Learning which symbolise his considerable mathematical talents. Then at the foot of the window are some delightful illustrations of characters from Carroll's books including the Mad Hatter, the Queen of Hearts, the Doormouse sitting in the tea pot, the March Hare, the Mock Turtle and the inimitable Cheshire Cat.

The church itself is of a considerable age, its sandstone tower dating from the 15th or 16th century but with some evidence to suggest that a timber-framed building may have existed here

Bunbury Parish Church ▶

The Battle of Nantwich re-enacted

Cheshire Hills from Wildboarclough

Cheshire Plain from Alderley Edge

He WAS born At ✢ ✢
DAResburY PARSONAGE,
JAN. 27, 1832, AND DIED
At GuildforD, JAN. 14, 1898.

Part of the Lewis Carroll Memorial Window ▶

at least as early as 1159 and which probably gave rise to it being traditionally called 'The White Church of Cheshire'. Hanging within the Belfry beneath the tower is a board upon which is painted an intriguing rhyme from 1730, demonstrating that Lewis Carroll was not the only local-born person with some literary talent:

> *'Dare not to come into this Sacred Place*
> *All you good Ringers, but in awful Grace.*
> *Ring not with Hatt, nor Spurs nor Insolence.*
> *Each one that does, for every such offence*
> *Shall forfeit Hatt or Spurs or Twelve Pence.*
> *But who disturbs a Peal, the same offender*
> *Unto the Box his Sixpence shall down Tender.*
> *Rules such no doubt in every Church are used*
> *You and your Bells that may not be abused'*

It is surmised that this poem with its initial letters forming the word 'Daresbury' may have been Lewis Carroll's first introduction to the acrostic, a literary device which he was to later use many times. The church is also very proud of its unusually-carved Jacobean pulpit, dating from 1625, its fine timber screen beneath the East Window and the ancient yew tree near the main gate. Yet above all it is proud of Lewis Carroll, whose impressions of the lovely Cheshire countryside in his earliest years may well have produced his love of nature and been the inspiration for many of his famous stories.

St. Mary's, Nantwich

This church has been called the Cathedral of South Cheshire, and deservedly so, for not only is it one of the finest medieval churches in the county but also in England as a whole. It is a building which successfully incorporates the architectural styles of several different periods while at the same time preserving its unity and an atmosphere of reverence, as well as displaying so many intriguing features and decorations which are tell-tale signs of the life and worship from previous generations. The church is appropriately and distinctively cruciform in plan with a superb octagonal stone tower rising high above the meeting point of the nave, chancel and two transepts — a splendid combination of fourteenth century craftsmanship and Victorian restoration. Although its early history is somewhat obscure a church at Nantwich was mentioned in 1163, with the first recorded incumbent being Henry de Sondbach in 1259, and it appears that about this time a large church was built on a similar plan to the present one. For some reason this must have fallen into disrepair or out of favour, since the present church was constructed later in the fourteenth century based largely on the previous edifice and incorporating parts of it. By the nineteenth century St. Mary's had lapsed into such a bad condition that considerable repair and restoration work was

CHAPELS AND CHURCHES

St. Mary's, Nantwich ▶

necessary, and Sir George Gilbert Scott was brought in to direct this. The result was the present-day church which exhibits the Decorated and Perpendicular styles of medieval English Gothic architecture together with Scott's Victorian 'improvements' largely imitating the 13th century idiom.

Entering the nave through the fifteenth century porch on the south side, one passes beneath a room which holds a library of theological books established in 1704 together with the old church registers and a complete edition of the 'Sarum Hymns and Sequences' printed in 1506 by Wynkyn de Worde (a pupil of Caxton who set up the first printing press in England). The nave itself, spacious and well-lit by rows of windows high above the pointed arches, is mostly fourteenth century but with traces of thirteenth century stonework which can be seen on the lower parts of the walls, while at the east end the line of the earlier and steeper roof can still be discerned. On either side of the nave are the aisles with their flying buttresses, the additional shanks making them appear like pointed arches. The pulpit in the nave dates from 1601 and was originally constructed as a 'three decker' one incorporating a clerk's seat and prayer desk, but it was considerably reduced as part of Scott's restoration work.

At the eastern end of the nave is the 'crossing', beneath the tower which is borne by four massive stone piers and encompassed by arches from the thirteenth and fourteenth centuries. The second church pulpit is to be seen here, a particularly fine stone one which is among the best in the country, and then to the north and south of the crossing are the two transepts (again mostly of thirteenth and fourteenth century work) in which are to be found two small chapels and some lovely windows. The North Transept, for example, contains St. George's Chapel in which is buried Sir John Griffin who fought at Poitiers, while the South Transept has the Bromley Chapel which is said to be the finest piece of Perpendicular work in Cheshire. The lovely south window is also Perpendicular in style (with nineteenth century glass), while a defaced monument probably represents Sir Donald Cradok (1342 − 1390) who was a patron of the church.

The chancel is undoubtedly the most interesting part of the building, dating very largely from the late fourteenth century and depicting in its windows the transition between the Decorated and Perpendicular styles of architecture.

Overhead one can see the only lierne vault in Cheshire, which is comparable to that in Canterbury Cathedral, while the magnificent carved wooden canopies above the choirstalls are unsurpassed even by those at Chester or Lincoln. Beneath the Misericords (wooden ledges on the lower side of the hinged choirstall

CHAPELS AND CHURCHES

seats) are some intricate carvings which are pictures in miniature of medieval life and traditions; they include a wrestling match, a hunting scene, a woman reading, St. George and the dragon, a fox and many religious representations. The multitude of such carved figures is a characteristic feature of this church, to be seen around both the interior and the exterior, and possibly they were the means by which the builders and craftsmen sought to express some of their own ideas and interests. In the North Transept, for example, are several representations of 'Jack-in-the-Green', a popular ancient pagan fertility god who also appears on the external base of the tower as a face peering through leaves, while other carvings of people and animals are to be seen on the stone pinnacles around the church. Besides these there are a variety of bizarre-looking gargoyles as well as a sculpture of the Devil flying away with a woman caught with her hand in a money jar, whilst another scene depicts the Devil holding a man by the hair. Such details only heighten the interest of St. Mary's, underlining the fact that although the architecture in many ways is quite imposing and monumental the importance placed upon the decoration and ornamentation of the church shows how well it has considered its contribution to everyday life.

St. Oswald's, Malpas

The lovely parish church of Malpas is similar in age and background to that at Nantwich but somewhat smaller in scale. Dedicated to Oswald, king of Northumbria who died in 642, its origins are lost in the mists of time, but it is known that the present church was built in the second half of the 14th century on the site of an earlier building, although no remains of this have come to light. Improvements to the basic structure of the church were carried out as early as the latter part of the 15th century, including an increase in the height of the nave and the introduction of a flat camber-beam roof as well as the addition of larger windows. The unusual two storey porch to be seen on the south side of the building was also added at this time, with the upper storey forming a room for the priest.

The fact that Malpas is probably one of the lesser known places in Cheshire has meant that the beautiful features of its parish church are not as fully appreciated as they should be. On either side of the nave, for example, it has two particularly fine chapels dedicated to the Brereton and Cholmondeley families with each containing an alabaster tomb in an excellent state of preservation. The Brereton tomb shows

St. Oswald's, Malpas peering behind the cottages ▶

CHAPELS AND CHURCHES

Sir Randal Brereton with his wife and was actually made some eight years before Sir Randal died in 1530; with its smaller figures around the sides it ranks as one of the finest alabaster monuments in existence and is obviously a masterpiece of the carver's art. The Cholmondeley monument, erected in 1605, represents Sir Hugh Cholmondeley and his second wife Mary and is surrounded again on the base by figures of other members of the family. The distinct difference in style between this monument and that of the Breretons is due largely to its later date, although both are excellent examples of English monumental art and both would doubtless have originally been painted. Another equally outstanding feature of the church is the nave ceiling with its richly carved timber panels and angelic figures along the edges; although the ceilings of the aisles are a little less spectacular they are likewise decorated in a similar fashion.

Among the many interesting furnishings of St. Oswald's are a magnificent 13th century oak chest covered with elaborate iron scrolls and a 15th century octagonal stone font with an oak cover which was made in 1627. At the back of the church there are even a number of the early box pews (originally installed in 1680) while at the opposite end in the chancel are three 15th century choir stalls with their carved misericords, although admittedly somewhat plain in appearance when compared with those of St. Mary's in Nantwich. As at St. Mary's the exterior walls of the church exhibit numerous carvings in stone, some of which represent the arms of local families, although these are now well-worn due to the passage of time. Within its tree-lined churchyard the position of St. Oswald's is really quite delightful in itself, sited a little above the rest of Malpas on a raised mound which was once occupied by a Norman castle and which now provides the church with a prominence its history and beauty thoroughly deserve.

Chapel at High Legh near Lymm ▶

Chapel at Somerford near Congleton ▶

◀ *St. Oswald's, Malpas*

Chapter VII

THE COUNTRYSIDE

— coast to hills

For a county which has traditionally been associated in most people's thinking with the flat expanse of the Cheshire Plain, one of the most memorable features of its countryside is the opportunity to climb up to some high point on one of the many hills in order to enjoy panoramic views stretching out into the distance — an experience which is both mind-boggling and breath-taking at one and the same time. A snaking footpath traversing the wooded slopes of Helsby Hill will bring you out onto the rocky and exposed summit with its extensive views across the Mersey estuary, while the more open flanks of Beeston Crag are one's route to obtaining equally extensive views of the southern half of the county. The red sandstone cliffs of Raw Head (the highest point on the ridge known as the Central Highlands) look westwards across the border into Wales, while the table-top of Bosley Cloud offers views not only across the Staffordshire hills but also back into the Cheshire Plain, enabling one to pinpoint the white bowl of the Jodrell Bank radio telescope in the middle distance. For more intimate views one need go no further than Kerridge Hill, affectionately overlooking the town of Bollington in a secluded valley to the north and the village of Rainow at the foot of its southern slopes. Yet enfolded in the midst of these hills and valleys are some noteworthy buildings and features which will be accorded the prominence which they deserve in the following paragraphs.

Norton Priory

Not more than a few miles from Runcorn are the recently excavated remains of Norton Priory, an important and extensive Augustinian foundation (later to be elevated to the status of an abbey) which existed on the site from 1134 to the time of its dissolution by Henry VIII in 1536. The archaeological investigations carried out at Norton have revealed in great detail the life and times of the canons who lived here, and the story of the Priory together with that of the Tudor and Georgian mansions which later replaced it has been carefully pieced together in the new museum adjacent to the site. Here visitors have a unique opportunity to discover exactly what life in holy orders was like, as well as being able to wander through the woodland gardens which formed part of the Priory in the medieval period and then were formally landscaped in the eighteenth century.

The ground floor of the west range of the Priory is the most substantial portion to have survived to the present day, although the excavations have ensured that the overall plan can be clearly picked out from the foundations uncovered so far, and it has even been possible to produce a model showing what the Priory must have looked like back in the twelfth century. The surviving parts of the Priory had been incorporated into the Georgian country house which stood here until 1928, and a section of the undercroft (used originally by the canons for storage) became the entrance hall of the house when a porch was added to the west front in 1868. This porch made use of a magnificent Norman doorway which had probably been erected in about 1180 and which by virtue of its well-preserved carvings must be the finest to exist in Cheshire. A superbly decorated passage which linked the outer courtyard with the central cloister has also survived to the present day, one of the most elaborate cloister arcades of its date in England. To the north of the cloister was an enormous church which reached a length of 290 feet and which was used by the canons for their daily services; there was also a series of chapels added on to the church to accommodate the burials of wealthy local benefactors, and many of their sandstone coffins can still be seen. On the east and south sides of the cloister were other important buildings including the chapter house and the refectory, the former being the place where the canons would gather each morning to read a chapter from the Rules of St. Augustine and discuss the business of the Priory.

Norton Priory had been founded in the 12th century as a religious house whose brethren followed the teaching of St. Augustine, and for four centuries it flourished through hard work and the gifts of wealthy landowners. In 1391 the Priory became an abbey and it continued as such until the Dissolution of the Monasteries in 1536, when religious life was brought to an abrupt end. Then in 1545 the buildings and lands were bought by Sir Richard Brooke who built a Tudor mansion here which was subsequently replaced by a Georgian country house, this in turn being demolished in 1928. At the height of its prosperity the Priory would probably have accommodated twenty-four canons together with a number of servants looking after the manual side of the Priory's work, and there would also have been farmworkers tied to the land. The emphasis for the canons was very much upon the worship of God, so when it was decided to lay new tiled floors in the church and chapter house a group of tilemakers was specially commissioned to carry out the work — the tiles and the kiln for making them which have been discovered here are a unique feature of the Priory, and the excavations have produced the largest area of mosaic tiled floor to be found on any site in Britain.

The structure of the excavated tile kiln consists of two firing chambers which are linked to a stoking area (containing the fire) by small tunnels; hot gases would pass through these tunnels into the chambers and up through a perforated floor on which the tiles were stacked. It appears that the tiles themselves were cut from a bed of clay using a template and while still pliable decoration was applied by pressing a mould onto the surface of the tiles which were then glazed and fired. The new tiled floors were laid in the choir, transepts and presbytery of the church as well as in the chapter house, in the form of decorated bands along the axis of the church. Each band consisted of shaped and coloured tiles which fitted together to form a pattern, and many tiles were also given an impressed decoration of foliage or flowers. In some cases these designs would link up to form larger patterns made by several tiles being put together in larger blocks, and they are now once more open to view in the attractively laid out museum.

Norton Priory also has a quite unusual range of excavated sandstone coffins and grave slabs, since it appears that in exchange for gifts local benefactors expected to be buried here. In general only the more important people were given places of honour within the walls of the Priory, with the burial grounds for others being located to the north and east of the church. The sandstone grave slabs which have been discovered marked either the position of graves where the dead had been buried in wooden coffins or formed the lids of coffins made from stone. Altogether about 140 graves have been excavated so far, with the skeletons found within them providing some very valuable insights into the health, stature and life expectancy of Norton's inhabitants.

Having become thoroughly conversant with just about every aspect of Priory life back in medieval times, the visitor then has the opportunity to wander freely through seven acres of beautiful woodland gardens which were laid out in the Georgian period. Following the informal footpaths the visitor will come across two very pretty summer houses which have recently been restored, a replica medieval bell cast in 1977 using evidence from a thirteenth century bell mould discovered during the excavations, a lovely Victorian 'rock garden' and a stream glade planted with azaleas. The Bridgewater Canal forms the southern boundary of these truly delightful gardens which not only contain a host of interesting and unusual trees planted by the owners of the Georgian mansion but also attract a rich variety of wildlife.

Nether Alderley Mill

Alongside the A34 to the south of Alderley Edge is the lovely Nether Alderley Mill, a centuries-old corn mill in the ownership of the National Trust which has been restored to full working order. From the outside its most striking feature is the very long sloping flagged roof which reaches almost down to the ground, while within its dark recesses one is immediately impressed by the complex arrangement of wheels, cogs and shafts on several different levels which all operate together to produce flour on the occasions when the machinery is set in motion. A special characteristic of this particular mill is its two driving wheels, one above the other, which are powered by water channelled in from the mill pond at the rear of the building; this pool in

Summer house in the gardens of Norton Priory ▶

THE COUNTRYSIDE

Nether Alderley Mill ▶

turn is fed by a small stream and several field drains.

The present mill with its sandstone walls, half-timbered gables and internal timber structure probably dates from the 16th century, although there is evidence to suggest that a Saxon village mill had originally existed on this site at one time. Even though none of the machinery from the medieval period has survived, that which is in place now dates from 1850 or so and was in fact constructed in the traditional manner. The mill contains two sets of grinding stones (known as French Burrs) which are rotated by two big 'overshot' water-wheels each measuring 12 feet in diameter and 3 feet wide — to see and hear this machinery in action, with its drive shafts and hundreds of wooden cogs operating against the background noise of swirling and splashing water, is a fascinating experience. It is also fascinating to see how the end product was conveyed from the millstones through a system of trap doors and hoists down to the lower levels.

In the vicinity of this interesting old watermill is some delightful countryside which is typical of Cheshire as a whole, encompassing quiet country lanes and green fields as well as winding footpaths, restored cottages and lovely churches. Across the road from the mill, for example, is a black and white half-timbered cottage which used to be a one-time coaching inn named the Eagle and Child, after the crest of the Stanley family who were lords of the manor in this part of the county for almost 500 years up to 1938, while down the adjoining lane is the splendid 14th century parish church of St. Mary built of local sandstone. An unusual feature of the interior of this church is the Jacobean family pew of the Stanleys situated high up on one of the walls and decorated with the arms of various families into which the Stanleys married in the 17th and 18th centuries — a pew which is unique in Cheshire and one of the finest of its kind in the country. Just inside the entrance to the churchyard is the Old Schoolhouse built in 1628 together with a 19th century addition (which has since become the Village Hall) and a mausoleum for the Stanley family, making up one of the most attractive groups of sandstone buildings in the county.

Half a mile or so northwards from Nether Alderley Mill is Bradford Lane which leads past the Mill House and The Smithy to a narrow cobbled track called Hocker Lane, along which can be found the beautifully-restored Hayman's House (built in 1524 of a timber frame with wattle and daub panels). This in turn leads on to the rather appropriately named Cheshire Lane running across the fields towards Birtles Church, perhaps not quite so old as St. Mary's but equally attractive with its octagonal tower and 16th century stained glass. Back on Bradford Lane the cobbles eventually take us up towards Alderley Edge itself, a wooded

THE COUNTRYSIDE

sandstone escarpment standing high above the surrounding countryside and providing some superb views towards the Pennine hills on the east side of the county. It has a distinct atmosphere of mystery about it as well as an appearance of beauty, for here legend and history seem to have become inextricably interwoven, with tales of a Wizard and of sleeping warriors who are meant to be the Knights of King Arthur. It seems that the Romans probably mined the area for copper ore, and the whole of the Edge is honeycombed with small pits, caverns and tunnels as a result of further spasmodic searches for minerals over the centuries. These only add to the intrigue as one follows any of the interlacing footpaths beneath the dense canopy of beeches and pine trees, suddenly coming out on to the edge of the escarpment with its lovely views across open countryside. On the main Macclesfield road, opposite The Wizard public house, the pretty Artists Lane descends through a series of twists and turns back down towards Nether Alderley, passing several charming black and white cottages before it reaches the road to Congleton. Many of the cottages along this narrow lane are reputed to have been miners' homes built in the 17th century, and Welsh Row across the main road was supposedly named after Welsh workers who came to the area to work in the copper mines. A mile down the main road one arrives back at the Mill, passing en route the entrance to the 16th century Alderley Old Hall which had been one of the homes of the Stanley family.

Stretton Mill and Bunbury Mill

Cheshire boasts of two other restored water mills lying in the midst of its attractive countryside, both of which were used to grind corn up to comparatively recent times. Stretton Mill is to be found between the hamlets of Lower Carden and Stretton on the western side of the county, quite close to Farndon, occupying a picturesque spot on the banks of Carden Brook with a lovely mill pond edged by swaying reeds tucked away at the rear. The mill is partially covered with timber weatherboarding which together with the wooden window shutters gives it an almost Scandinavian appearance, but its Cheshire origins are confirmed by the use of red sandstone for large parts of the walls and the fact that beneath this mixed exterior is the timber framing of which the mill was first constructed.

It was Cheshire County Council which rescued Stretton Mill from the ignominy of dereliction it was suffering in the 1960's, restoring it as a working museum and opening it to the public in 1978. The information leaflet produced by the County Museum Service tells us that there had been a mill at Stretton since at least the fourteenth century and that in 1596 the mill passed into the ownership of the Leche family at an annual rent of £5, where it remained as part of the Carden Estate until Cheshire County Council stepped in with a timely rescue act. Although the function of the mill has always remained the same over its long history, its

St. Mary's, Nether Alderley ▶

THE
COUNTRYSIDE

Stretton Mill ▶

external appearance has been altered in order to accommodate expansion and necessary change. The mill started life as a timber-framed building with a thatch roof, but then during the 18th century the roof was raised and the thatch replaced by slates; at about the same time the timber framing was covered partly by weather-boarding and partly by a casing of red sandstone in large blocks. In 1777 a second waterwheel for the mill was installed on the west side of the building, and in 1819 the original wheel on the east side was enclosed by a stone extension.

Stretton Mill from below the mill pond ▶

Together with the internal machinery these two waterwheels are the most important features of Stretton Mill. Although the two wheels are of different types, the earlier one on the east side of the building being a 'breast-shot' wheel and that on the west side being an 'overshot' wheel, both rely on the weight of the water to drive them. The breast-shot wheel is probably unique in that it has a sluice mechanism permitting the entry of water at three different levels, and together with the overshot wheel this enables the mill machinery to be operated whatever the level of the pond. As at Nether Alderley, the operation of the machinery is both intriguing and fascinating — power is transmitted from the waterwheel via a horizontal shaft to the pit wheel which drives the great spur wheel above it, this in turn driving the spindle which powers the millstones on the floor above. Flour is actually produced as grain is fed into the eye of the upper millstone via a chute from the grain hopper.

Bunbury Mill is located on the other side of the Peckforton Hills from Stretton, at the eastern edge of Bunbury village. Restoration work here was carried out by the North West Water Authority which had inherited the mill when it took over the adjoining sewage works in 1974. It seems that the first mill occupying the site was a sandstone and timber-framed building erected in the 17th century, with timber machinery and elm buckets on the waterwheel

which would have driven the two pairs of millstones. In about 1850 a new mill of local brick was built (probably because the first one may well have burnt down) incorporating parts of the original walls and the waterwheel enclosure. For this new building millstones were brought from Birmingham and the local carpenter engaged to make many parts for the machinery from crabapple wood, oak and elm. In 1890 the tenancy of the mill passed to Thomas Parker, and he and his family continued producing flour here until 1960 when a torrential storm swept away the vital floodgate and thus emptied the millpond. With no water power to operate it the mill was abandoned, until the North West Water Authority decided to embark on the formidable task of restoration. This involved replacing 260 beechwood gear cogs (originally hand-made by millwrights), renovating the rotted base of an octagonal oak drive shaft and fitting the waterwheel with new elm buckets. Outside, the mill pond was re-formed and a new flood gate constructed. This programme of careful restoration work was completed by 1977, with a member of the Parker family which had last operated the mill opening up the sluice gate and once more setting the waterwheel in motion to usher in a new era of the mill's life.

Quarry Bank Mill, Styal

To come upon the elegant Quarry Bank Mill, so prettily situated within the wooded valley of the River Bollin to the north of Wilmslow, is an experience not to be missed — a small part of the Industrial Revolution which somehow found its way into the Cheshire countryside. Apparently it was the physical character of the site which persuaded entrepreneur Samuel Greg from Dublin to build his mill for spinning cotton in this location, particularly the good head of water to provide power for running his machinery and a nearby source of sandstone which could be used as one of the building materials. When the mill was first built in 1784 it was a four-storey building which accommodated 3,000 spindles, but as output increased and the mill prospered a fifth storey had to be added in 1795 and the whole building extended to twice its previous length. At first spinning was the only activity carried out here, but gradually weaving was introduced and after 1894 the mill was exclusively devoted to this.

Despite its apparently isolated location Samuel Greg had ensured that his Quarry Bank Mill was well-connected with the developing network of canals and roads which were so important in stimulating early industrial growth, and the yarn produced at Styal was transported either along the Bridgewater Canal (built by James Brindley in the 1760's) or along the main turnpike road which made its way through Wilmslow. By the early part of the 19th century more yarn was being produced here than at any other cotton factory in the country, and it was the importance of Greg's establishment which was significant in persuading the House of Lords to approve the Cheshire Junction Railway Bill of 1836.

Obtaining sufficient labour for the mill initially proved to be something of a problem, although Greg was eventually able to meet most of his needs from the local workhouses. Many of those employed here were young boys and girls who were accommodated in the Apprentice House to the north-east of the mill, and by 1847 when the apprenticeship system was ended over 2,000 boys and girls had been housed in this purpose-built home. The philanthropic approach which Samuel Greg adopted towards his business was also demonstrated by a concern that his other employees should likewise live close to their place of work and within pleasant surroundings, so consequently he built several terraces of houses in Styal village together with a shop, chapel and small school which all mingle very nicely with the older timber-framed farm cottages which existed here before Greg came. Even today it is obvious that he achieved his goal, creating a community (now mellowed with age) which was a convenient distance from the mill and separated from it by green fields and leafy woodland.

The energy and inventiveness which Samuel Greg displayed is evident in other ways too. To the south of the mill, for instance, is a dam which was built at the end of the 18th century to control the flow of the Bollin, while another feat of engineering was the tunnel made between Quarry Bank and Norcliffe for the purpose of increasing the speed with which water through the tail-race could escape into the river downstream, an operation which he himself directed. No doubt the lovely setting of the valley was as important to Greg as its physical advantages, for he built his own impressive mansion immediately to the north of the mill and had the manager's house built in a Regency style just to the south.

Hidden and enfolded by its own wooded valley, Quarry Bank Mill with its octagonal brick chimney reaching high above a lovely little bell turret on the roofline is a delightful place to visit, together with the associated buildings in Styal village which are largely the result of one man's vision to create a decent working environment for his employees.

◄ Quarry Bank Mill, Styal

Work is still going on at Quarry Bank Mill

Beeston Castle

Beeston Castle occupies one of the most impressive sites in the whole of Cheshire, its ruins romantically dominating the surrounding countryside from the top of a sandstone crag which rises up steeply from the pastures beneath it. Markedly separate from the long ridge of the wooded Peckforton Hills to the south, it captures one's attention from a great distance and draws you towards it as if through the power of some unperceived magnetic field. Although now only a dramatic ruin this one-time fortified castle demands a closer and more personal encounter, for it not only dominates the horizon for much of the surrounding area but also commands some spectacular views around the whole of southern and western Cheshire from its own elevated position.

Signposts from the main roads direct you along narrow country lanes through the pretty village of Beeston with its black and white half-timbered cottages to the foot of the crag, and from here a steep climb brings you up into the walled enclosure with its breathtaking views of the beautiful countryside spread out 300 feet below. From the earliest times this has been a natural vantage point for the south-west corner of Cheshire, its strident views encompassing much of the Wirral, the Frodsham and Helsby Hills, the Cheshire Plain and the Delamere Forest as well as the more distant hills of Derbyshire, Shropshire and Wales, so it was a natural choice for a castle site.

Beeston Castle was actually started in 1220 by Randle de Blundeville, the sixth Earl of Chester, but in 1237 it was taken over as a Royal stronghold and remained as such until the latter years of Queen Elizabeth I. Over the centuries the fortunes of the Castle fluctuated, and it was not until the English Civil War that it recaptured its former prominence when the Parliamentary forces which occupied Beeston in 1643 were remarkably and surprisingly defeated by the Royalists, who then held it for almost two years. It was only after the nearby Battle of Rowton Moor, when the Parliamentarians gained what proved to be their ultimately conclusive victory over the King's forces, that the Royalists were forced to surrender and Beeston Castle was very largely devastated, remaining the ruin that it then became up to the present day.

The original layout of the Castle, still discernible even now, consisted of an upper bailey or fortified enclosure of about three-quarters of an acre with a curtain wall further down the hillside which had seven towers and a gatehouse, embracing about ten acres of hillside altogether. Due to the steepness of the slopes no additional walls were built on the north or west sides, the main defences being strung across the south-western approaches to the hill and combined with a deep ditch cut in the rock.

Beeston Castle

Macclesfield Canal

A lane in Nether Alderley

Premises of Arighi, Bianchi and Co. in Macclesfield

THE COUNTRYSIDE

Another feature which made Beeston Castle particularly resistant to being overwhelmed by a siege was the well within the inner bailey which was sunk to a depth of 370 feet through solid sandstone to ensure that the garrison here always had its own water supply, and tradition has it that this could be the hiding place in which Richard II deposited a sum of 200,000 marks. At least two unsuccessful attempts have been made so far to clear the well (one in 1842 and another in 1935) with the aim of recovering this lost treasure, yet whatever happens in the future to solve this mystery we have the confidence that the 'treasure' we see in the ruins of Beeston Castle itself is already there to be enjoyed.

Peckforton Castle

This part of Cheshire seems to have far more than its fair share of castles, for just a mile to the south is Peckforton Castle hidden among the trees at the edge of the Peckforton Hills and almost competing with Beeston for our attention, both eyeing each other with suspicion across the narrow divide which exists between them. Yet Peckforton Castle is something of an impostor to the throne, a relative newcomer to the scene which was built between 1844 and 1850 as a country house for the first Lord Tollemache who owned extensive estates in this area. Constructed of locally-quarried sandstone it occupies an equally prominent position to its older neighbour, although perhaps a little too hidden by the surrounding woodland, and with its gatehouse, towers, turrets and moat it is a very accurate reproduction of a medieval castle on a grand scale. Pevsner and Hubbard report that its structure is characterised by 'overwhelming solidity and marvellous workmanship', features which are evident from the vantage point which Beeston Castle offers and which is probably the best place from which to admire this marvelous piece of Victorian architecture. It would make a wonderful 'set' for a film, and in fact now that it is no longer lived in it seems that it is being used for this very purpose.

Mow Cop

When considering 'reproduction' castles one ought not to forget the rather splendid ruin built on higher ground at Mow Cop in the south-eastern corner of the county, a mock castle commanding superb views from its dramatic and somewhat desolate position on top of a rocky outcrop. Consisting of a round stone tower together with an arch set in the midst of a thick stone wall, this structure was built by Randle Wilbraham in 1754 as a summer house and was one of the first English follies. Although new houses have encroached more and more upon the slopes of Mow Cop, the castle is still the eye-catching feature from below that Randle Wilbraham intended it to be, and from its lofty perch on the rocks there are far-reaching views which take in at least seven of the surrounding counties.

Mow Cop 'castle' ▶

171

THE COUNTRYSIDE

Jodrell Bank

Yet the single most impressive feature of the Cheshire countryside is also one of its most recent, the massive Mark IA radio telescope at Jodrell Bank between Withington and Goostrey. There are very few places on the Cheshire Plain where its huge white bowl measuring 250 feet in diameter cannot be seen, and from the surrounding hills this is the first feature to be picked out from amongst the flat expanse of fields and trees. This telescope, together with its much smaller neighbour the Mark II radio telescope, is the basis of the radio astronomy laboratories of the University of Manchester at Jodrell Bank, and their location in the midst of the Cheshire countryside is due to the fact that the electrically-quiet environment here (well away from Manchester) was most suited for the detection of radio emissions from outer space. Jodrell Bank first came to public prominence in the 1960's, not only because of the significant developments in radio astronomy which took place in this formerly little-known part of the county but also because it was deeply involved in the Soviet and American space programmes.

The Mark IA telescope (originally called the Mark I) was completed in 1957, its principal feature being a 250 feet-diameter parabolic bowl made of welded steel plates supported on a drum-shaped steel framework. This is held aloft by two massive towers of steel girders which are mounted on concentric circular rails with an overall diameter of 353 feet. By means of its structure the bowl can be rotated and turned in every direction, allowing the telescope to be pointed to any part of the sky in search of radio emissions. For more than a decade this pioneering instrument was the largest fully-steerable radio telescope in the world, being almost the same height as St. Paul's Cathedral in London. The name Mark I was changed to Mark IA following improvements to the telescope in 1970 and 1971, including the fitting of a new membrane of improved shape above the original bowl. The Mark II telescope stands just a quarter of a mile to the south of its larger 'brother', utilising a much smaller bowl which is elliptical in shape and designed to pick up radio signals of shorter wavelength.

To enable the lay-man to make some sense of all that is going on at Jodrell Bank, the Concourse Building close to the Mark IA telescope has an exhibition of explanatory diagrams, photographs and working models which describe the techniques used and the results obtained by radio and optical astronomers. Then once the visitor's appetite for galactic discovery has been whetted, the Planetarium with its 40 foot projection dome offers a presentation consisting of a descriptive commentary matched by a visual display of celestial bodies, while for those who want to enjoy open space as well as outer space there is

◀ *Jodrell Bank*
Radio Telescope ▶

THE COUNTRYSIDE

the 40 acre Granada Arboretum next to the telescopes, planted with a wide variety of trees and shrubs. Interestingly enough, botany rather than astronomy was Jodrell Bank's original use, for it was the University of Manchester's horticultural botany department which was first located on an eleven acre site here. Yet the exciting progress in radio astronomy made in the early years by Dr (later Sir) Bernard Lovell ensured that the Jodrell Bank Experimental Station was destined to become a permanent feature of the Cheshire countryside, a very visible and not unattractive symbol of Britain's contribution to the space age.

Footpaths

For the more active and energetic, Cheshire's long-distance footpaths offer not only something of a challenge but also an opportunity to explore the best of the county's countryside, keeping well away from towns and villages. The Gritstone and Sandstone Trails are particularly good since they traverse the two characteristic landscapes of Cheshire, each a unique product of the underlying rocks. Although both trails are similar in that they tend to hug the higher contours, the features to be seen along their routes are distinctively different — the Gritstone Trail passes through largely wild and untamed topography characterised by moors, hill farms and steep-sided valleys while the Sandstone Trail looks out onto the gentler and more settled landscape of the Cheshire Plain laid out over the red sandstone strata beneath.

Covering a distance of just over 18 miles along

the eastern edge of the county the **Gritstone Trail** is the shorter of the two routes and takes its name from the underlying gritstone, a hard rock which has produced the somewhat rugged character of the landscape and which in turn has influenced settlement patterns and man's activity in the area. The hills and valleys predominating here have resulted from the natural forces of erosion, with the more resistant rocks which cap the hills remaining in stark relief as the softer rocks between them have been removed to form gentler valleys. The northern starting point of the Trail is Lyme Hall, an imposing and regal house which was built largely of stone quarried from the surrounding estate, and from the parkland of Lyme the route climbs eastwards up to the Bowstones. These are the shafts of Anglo-Saxon crosses which probably acted as markers for the boundary of the Kingdom of Mercia and which may also have picked out the line of an ancient route over these dramatic hills. Just to the south of here this first part of the Trail is characterised by several old stone quarries which supplied so much of the building and roofing material used in houses throughout a large part of the surrounding area.

Skirting round the neat little town of Bollington the Trail passes through Ingersley Clough, a place in which many mills flourished during the 18th century when there was a massive growth in the spinning and weaving trades. From here the route ascends to Kerridge Hill with the unusual structure known as White Nancy marking its northern point, a distinctive bell-shaped landmark which is evident for miles around, and from it the footpath follows the

White Nancy on Kerridge Hill ▶

THE COUNTRYSIDE

line of the ridge opening up superb views on both sides. Even on Kerridge Hill one can discern the vestiges of early industrial activity in the form of old stone quarries and the pits of previous coal-workings, the latter being clearly picked out on the eastern slope from nearby Rainow in periods of dry weather. Although now a quiet little village Rainow was at one time a busy place which supported twenty-four cotton and silk mills, but now all that remains today are a few crumbling ruins and the occasional chimney.

Passing through fields used largely as grazing land the Gritstone Trail wends its way up to Tegg's Nose Country Park on the east side of Macclesfield, encompassing another one-time quarry which was the largest in the area. At the foot of the quarry face is a display which shows how the stone was obtained and used, while a 'viewfinder' on the hill above picks out some of the features on the skyline which can be seen from this point along the Trail. Southwards from here nature seems to make its voice heard more strongly than man, since the footpath passes alongside several reservoirs in the vicinity of Langley which are important for the birdlife attracted to them, while over to the east are the tree-clothed slopes of Macclesfield Forest. Making its way south again past lovely stone-built farmhouses and cottages the Trail draws the walker up towards the Post Office Telecommunications Mast which stands 286 feet high on Croker Hill, re-asserting man's authority in this remoter part of Cheshire. From the heather-clad slopes of Croker Hill and Bosley Minn the route meanders down towards the lusher slopes of the Dane Valley and the end of the Trail which lies just across the Staffordshire border.

An ancient 'plague stone', not far from the Gritstone ▶ *Trail*

The **Sandstone Trail** is thirty miles long and stretches almost the length of Cheshire, from Frodsham in the north to well beyond Malpas in the south, and running along the top of the ridge of higher ground which bisects the Cheshire Plain it offers unmatched views of the whole of the county. This ridge was formed through earth movements which took place ages ago in geological time, remaining unaffected by the glacial deposits which were left on the surrounding Cheshire Plain at the end of the last Ice Age: as a result the cliffs and crags which mark the edges of this central ridge stand out in stark contrast to the flat, pastoral lands below. The Trail begins from just below the summit of Overton Hill, from which there is a superb panorama of the Mersey estuary embracing many features of the modern industrial age: the Stanlow oil refineries, cooling towers, the Manchester Ship Canal, chemical industries across the water in Widnes and the M56 motorway which seems to thread its way delicately across the flat expanse of the flood plain stretched out below. Yet in just a couple of miles the Trail takes us back in time thousands of years, passing alongside the remains of Woodhouse Hill Fort which was built in the Iron Age as one of at least seven fortified sites on the central sandstone ridge which would have offered protection to some of Cheshire's earliest inhabitants. The families living here would probably have been housed in crude wooden huts protected by stone and earth ramparts.

From this point the Sandstone Trail tiptoes around the peaceful villages of Alvanley and Manley before entering the shady depths of Delamere Forest along its western edge. Delamere Forest today is managed by the Forestry Commission and as such is really quite a recent development, but it covers just part of the area which would have formed the ancient Forest of Mara and Mondrum and which probably extended in Norman times from Frodsham to Nantwich. To the south of the modern plantations the route of the Trail passes through an area rich in history — here is the hill known as Old Pale which was enclosed from the forest in 1338 to protect the king's deer, while a little further on a disused quarry known as the King's Chair is said to have been the source of stone for the building of Vale Royal Abbey between 1277 and 1300. The footpath also passes over the line of the old Watling Street, the road which Roman legionaries would have marched along when crossing from Chester to Manchester.

Gradually and almost imperceptibly the northern section of the central ridge peters out, and the Sandstone Trail drops down onto the flatter farmland of the Cheshire Plain just to

THE COUNTRYSIDE

the west of Tarporley. Almost immediately one is confronted by Beeston Crag rising up sharply from the valley of the River Gowy, its dramatic castle ruins guarding the approach to the southern half of the sandstone ridge with Peckforton Castle echoing this defensive stance on the next rise. The Trail respectfully edges between the two castles and climbs up onto the pleasantly wooded slopes of the Peckforton Hills, passing close to the hamlet of Higher Burwardsley and eventually coming out at Raw Head by way of Bulkeley Hill. At 746 feet Raw Head is the highest point on the Trail, its deep-red sandstone cliffs which have been etched and eroded by the elements acting as a superb vantage point giving some extensive and breath-taking views. These cliffs are honey-combed with caves which have been hewn out of the comparatively soft rock, and tradition has it that these were the hideouts for bands of robbers who roamed the surrounding countryside.

Descending from Raw Head the Sandstone Trail crosses the road which connects Nantwich to Wales and then makes the ascent up onto Bickerton Hill, a large expanse of heathland forming the southernmost part of this central ridge which the route has faithfully followed all the way from Helsby. In the south-west corner of this sandstone outlier is Maiden Castle, another fortified Iron Age settlement which was originally protected by a timber and earth rampart but which now remains only as a pair of earthbanks. From this ancient site the path tumbles downwards on its final descent to the

Cheshire Plain, making its way more gracefully to the end of the Sandstone Trail at Grindley Brook on the Shropshire border. En route it passes a number of prosperous farms and houses which typify this part of Cheshire, including Larkton Hall with its farm buildings grouped in a rectangle (a feature found in many 18th and 19th century dairy farms), Manor House Farm with its cobbled yard, and the beautiful timber-framed house known as Hampton Old Hall which was built in 1591. Just before the very last leg of the Trail which runs along the Shropshire Union Canal the footpath draws near to greet Old St. Chad Chapel, standing all alone in the midst of the surrounding fields with only swaying yew trees to keep it company.

THE COUNTRYSIDE

For those who prefer walks of a less-strenuous nature there is the Whitegate Way and the Wirral Way, both following the line of former railway tracks and somewhat shorter in length than either the Gritstone or Sandstone Trail. **Whitegate Way** runs for a distance of six miles from just north of Winsford through to Cuddington, along the route originally taken by a railway built in the 1880's to transport salt from the mines at Winsford up to a junction with the Manchester — Chester line. Now the track which formerly guided railway engines belching clouds of smoke as they hauled their wagons of salt has been removed and in its place is a lovely linear walk with a firm cinder path underfoot hemmed in on both sides by trees and bushes. Nature seems to be taking over once again in this small part of central Cheshire, creating a very enjoyable recreational feature for both walker and horse rider (a three and half mile section of the route is also open as a continuous horse ride) Among the most attractive features of Whitegate Way are the meres and pools to be seen on either side, former sand pits which have since been filled-in with water and which now draw a tremendous variety of wildlife. This is also an important historic area where much of the land was at one time owned by the Cistercian Abbey at nearby Vale Royal, and many of the place names such as Abbots Moss, Nunsmere and Knight's Grange point back towards this period. Close to Whitegate Station, the major access point onto Whitegate Way, is the site of a 13th century Cistercian farm and fishponds, while Newchurch Common to the north-west was originally common land used for grazing farm animals in the Middle Ages but which now appears as an extensive lake due to the excavation of sand which has taken place here in more recent times.

The **Wirral Way** runs a distance of 12 miles between Hooton and West Kirby, and as such acts as a link between the northern and southern parts of the Wirral Peninsula — a distinction which came about when Cheshire lost the northern half of the Wirral to Merseyside with the advent of local government reorganisation. As at Whitegate the route follows the line of an old railway track, providing a continuous path for walkers which passes through pleasant farmland as well as along the sandy banks of the Dee Estuary. Not every evidence of the former railway line has been removed though, for one of the special features of the Wirral Way is Hadlow Road Station at Willaston which has been restored to appear just as it would have done in the 1950's — one could almost be forgiven for looking up and down the platform expecting the next train to appear! Other features of this rather unusual linear country park include picnic areas, fishing ponds and nature trails.

Hadlow Road Station on the Wirral Way ▶

THE COUNTRYSIDE

The canal at Middlewich ▶

Canals

Although Cheshire was never heavily industrialised, its rich salt deposits and an important position between the Midlands and the great commercial centres of Liverpool and Manchester encouraged the growth of a significant canal network in the 18th and 19th centuries. The 2,000 miles of canal which cover the county focus on two main destinations, Runcorn and Ellesmere Port, linked by the strategic Manchester Ship Canal which is the main commercial waterway. It is to this part of Cheshire that most of the canals make their purposeful journey: in the north, for example, the Bridgewater Canal cuts its way through from Manchester to Runcorn and joins up with the Trent and Mersey Canal which passes right through the salt-producing towns of Middlewich and Northwich on its journey up from the Potteries. Running parallel to this latter canal is the Weaver Navigation stretching from Winsford to just south of Runcorn — due to the demand for Lancashire coal used in heating salt-pans and the increasing cost of pack-horse transport, an Act of Parliament of 1721 led to the River Weaver being made into a navigable waterway along its lowers stretches. The Shropshire Union Canal links the southern part of Cheshire with Ellesmere Port, passing through Chester en route with branches running off to Middlewich and Llangollen; this is probably the most attractive of all the canals since its rather circuitous course travels over some of the most picturesque parts of the Cheshire Plain, particularly where it picks its way through a gap between the two sections of the central sandstone ridge just north of Beeston. Then on the eastern side of the county is the Macclesfield Canal, running southwards from its junction with the Peak Forest Canal in Marple through the cotton and silk towns of Bollington, Macclesfield and Congleton on its way to Kidsgrove in Staffordshire where it joins up with the Trent and Mersey Canal.

Nowadays commercial traffic on Cheshire waterways is primarily restricted to the Weaver Navigation and the Manchester Ship Canal, with other canals being used for pleasure trips. Whereas the Shropshire Union Canal is the best for leisurely plying through beautiful countryside and then into historic Chester, the Cheshire Ring is a circuit which links up the Macclesfield, Trent and Mersey and Bridgewater Canals enabling the county's industrial heritage to be explored in one memorable journey. Along the way there are so many interesting and historic features to be discovered which are peculiar to the Canal Age — locks, bridges, canalside wharfs, lock-keepers' cottages, warehouses and tunnels. One of the more unusual structures to be seen is the Anderton Boat Lift near Northwich, built in 1875 to transfer boats between the Trent and Mersey Canal and the Weaver Navigation which is 50 feet lower. The two tanks embodied in the lift, each containing 252 tons of water, were initially raised and lowered by hydraulic rams, but in 1907 it was decided to change to the electrified system which is operated now — even though the total weight moved is about 570 tons the power is supplied only by a 30 horsepower electric motor, an eloquent testimony to an impressive feat of engineering.

Ellesmere Port was the focal point for much of the early canal activity in Cheshire, but it experienced a marked decline as alternative means of transporting goods began to flourish and many of the buildings and warehouses which had grown up around the basins constructed by Telford fell into disuse. Now some of these are being brought back to life through the Boat Museum which has been established here to recreate a traditional canal port of the 19th century, enabling restored barges to be displayed to the general public and providing an appropriate 'home' for all kinds of canal memorabilia. Among the thirty or so canal boats in the collection are small weedcutters, a Worsley mine boat, a tunnel tug and a range of narrow and wide boats.

Country Parks

Much of Cheshire's countryside consists of well-kept farmland in private ownership, the hedge-lined fields devoted to crops or pasture giving that settled and prosperous look which is so characteristic of the county. However, there are several areas where the public are able to wander more freely and so enjoy the scents and sounds of the countryside at their leisure. One of these is **Delamere Forest,** already noted as being traversed by the Sandstone Trail which ambles down the central ridge from Frodsham. The 'forest' as we see it now is a massive pine

THE
COUNTRYSIDE

Delamere Forest ▶

plantation created by the Forestry Commission for commercial timber production, but which has also been opened up for recreation in conjunction with Cheshire County Council. Scattered throughout the area are parking places and picnic sites with criss-crossing footpaths which very quickly take you into the secluded peace of forest depths, although for those who prefer to avoid the possibility of getting lost there is a network of waymarked walks set up by the Forestry Commission. Delamere Forest is also a sanctuary for wildlife (as well as the harassed motorist), with a fascinating variety of fauna and flora which can be discovered even with a modicum of patience and observation.

Yet animals in this part of Cheshire have not always experienced the measure of protection which they enjoy now, for in Norman times this was a royal hunting ground for the Earls of Chester who pursued wild game across an extensive area of native woodland, heath and rough pasture. This was brought to an end from the Middle Ages onwards as the need for more farm land led to the clearance of large areas of the forest, with the Forestry Commission stepping in during the early part of this century to initiate an intensive programme of tree planting and woodland management on some of the land that was left. Now one can walk for miles with a carpet of pine needles underfoot and a canopy of branches overhead, every so often coming across the occasional clearance which allows the sunlight to penetrate just a little into the shady forest glades. One of the

179

THE COUNTRYSIDE

prettiest spots is Hatchmere on the northern side, a small stretch of water edged with reeds and the occasional fisherman hoping to entice an unsuspecting resident from the rippling waters.

Another area where one can roam without let or hindrance is **Tegg's Nose Country Park**, away on the eastern side of Cheshire at the half-way point of the Gritstone Trail. By comparison with Delamere Forest one is now in a completely different world, a world of exposed rocks and open moors as opposed to sheltering trees and secluded glades. Tegg's Nose was originally a large quarry and an important source of building stone, but it eventually ceased operation in 1955 and then in 1972 became the centre of a small country park. One of the features here is a display at the base of the quarry showing how the stone was prised away from the rock face and to what uses it was then put.

Perhaps the best approach onto the ridge overlooking the former quarry below is a climb up from the reservoirs which lie just to the north of Langley village, skirting along the edge of Tegg's Nose Wood and then climbing further until the windswept top is gained — a breath-taking experience in more ways than one! Yet it is more than worth it, for from the summit one can enjoy some superb views in all directions: the Cheshire Plain away to the west with the radio telescope of Jodrell Bank standing proud in the middle distance, and the Pennine hills over to the east with Shutlingsloe comparatively close at hand.

Marbury Country Park near Northwich is different again to both Delamere Forest and Tegg's Nose, a flat green expanse prettily hemmed in by belts of trees and bordered on its north side by the extensive waters of Budworth Mere and on the south by the Trent and Mersey Canal. The parkland once formed the grounds and gardens of Marbury Hall, built in the early 19th century along the lines of the French royal palace of Fontainbleau but sadly demolished in 1968, a family seat which had been occupied for 800 years by the Marburys, the Barrys and the Smith-Barrys. With the new Hall came a new landscaping scheme, more fortunate than the house in surviving to the present day and evident in the formal avenues of lime trees and the informally-planted woods with their large variety of species, including more exotic ones such as the Chile Pine and the Portugal Laurel. These woods are also rich in wildlife — foxes, rabbits and squirrels as well as birds, moths and butterflies.

Beyond the woods lies Budworth Mere, which in the Middle Ages was used as a fish hatchery to supply nearby streams and even now is well-stocked with bream and pike. The way in which the Mere developed in the first place has been subject to debate, some suggesting that it arose due to subsidence connected with underlying salt beds while others believe that it is a water-filled depression which was formed at the end of the last Ice Age. Whatever its origins the Mere provided an interesting approach to Great Budworth for the Smith-Barry family — an unusual 'back-door' entrance to the village and church, with which the family was closely associated. Now the boats crossing the Mere belong mainly to local anglers, while the reeds at the water's edge provide a home for a colony of Reed Warblers in what is one of the most north-westerly breeding grounds in Britain for the species. Budworth Mere is also an important gathering place for Great Crested Grebes, with sixty-four pairs being the largest number seen at any one time.

Quite close to the shore of the Mere are the remains of two features which have long since passed into history. One is the lower half of an ice house, the progenitor of modern refrigeration, which during winter would have been packed with blocks of ice and insulating layers of straw; this ice would then have been available for use in the hottest of summers, and in some cases it could be preserved for up to two years. The other feature is a hollow known as the Grotto which could well have been a cockpit, possibly used by the 'sporting' Smith-Barry family even after cockfighting was made illegal in 1839. Both the ice house and the cock pit would have been essential 'equipment' for most large country estates in the 18th and 19th centuries.

Marbury Country Park also has its industrial connections, for it was within the confines of the estate that the first rock-salt mine was sunk in 1675. Then on the southern boundary is the Trent and Mersey Canal, which had been built in the 18th century to allow china clay to be transported from Liverpool to the Potteries and finished goods to be brought in the opposite direction. Obviously the canal also encouraged the further growth of the salt industry in this part of Cheshire, but the two were not always completely compatible — the extraction of salt below ground often produced subsidence at the surface leading to the frequent collapse of the canal banks, with the worst occurrence taking place in 1907 when the canal bed caved in and all the water was lost.

◀ *Marbury Country Park*

THE COUNTRYSIDE

Salt and Cheese

One could hardly complete a chapter on the Cheshire countryside, let alone the book as a whole, without making more specific reference to those two famous products of the county which have been so important in its overall character — salt and cheese. Although salt has always lain beneath the surface, its extraction and consequent subsidence has produced a unique landscape of pools and meres, especially in the Northwich area, whilst cheese is the product of a dairying 'industry' established upon the lush pastures of the Cheshire Plain. Salt, in the form of brine, has also been the raw material for the very important chemical industry which has grown up in Cheshire during the 20th century and which has spawned its own characteristic 'landscape' of pipes, tanks and chimneys.

It has been estimated that about 400,000 million tons of salt lies in the saliferous strata beneath the Cheshire-Shropshire basin, and ever since Roman times man has been extracting all that he could of this precious commodity. The original method of producing salt was by open-pan evaporation, whereby natural brine obtained from surface salt pits would be fed into large pans or tanks and heated from beneath until the salt crystals formed. These would then be raked to the side, packed into tubs or baskets to form blocks of salt and then left to dry for two weeks or so before being ready for use. This method was used by the Romans and continued to be used in small-scale salt production up to the middle of this century, but only one works (the Lion Salt Works at Marston near Northwich) continues to uphold this traditional method of making salt. Now more modern industrial techniques are the order of the day, such as those practised at British Salt Limited's factory in Middlewich whereby brine is fed into a line of six evaporation 'vessels' after having the magnesium and calcium impurities precipitated out of it. As the water is boiled off a salt 'slurry' is formed in the vessels which flows down the line of evaporators until it reaches the last one, when it is extracted for further concentration in centrifuges. The salt is scraped continuously off the centrifuge basket to fall onto a conveyor belt, at which point in the process it contains 2½% moisture and is suitable for industrial use. Salt for the food and allied industries is further dried (to a moisture level of 0.03%) and is then sieved and graded in an intricate system of conveyors, distribution points and hoppers. This modern method of production also makes use of a modern method of extraction, controlled brine pumping, whereby water is pumped down into the salt deposits below ground and then pumped back to the surface as a salt solution. The beauty of this method is that the shape of the underground cavity can be controlled, so that if sufficient rock salt is left above a cavity and between adjacent ones subsidence will not occur.

Salt is also obtained by mining, a quite dramatic operation for those who are fortunate enough to witness this being carried out at ICI's Meadowbank mine at Winsford, the only working salt mine in the country. Here shafts descend hundreds of feet to a nether world of underground roads leading to enormous caverns where the rock salt is extracted using heavy machinery, drilling equipment and explosives. Huge lorries then ferry the salt to conveyor belts which are miles long, ultimately bringing it to the surface and the light of day. The salt obtained by this method is used mainly for treating icy roads in winter and in the production of fertilisers.

Cheese is the other famous product of Cheshire, and probably the first thing which people associate with the county whenever you mention its name. It is one of the products of Cheshire's important dairy industry, an industry embracing about 140,000 cows which yield 150 million gallons of milk each year. Cheshire has been a great cheese-making area for centuries now, a result of the simple need to make the best use of excess milk, but in recent years the number of farms making it has dropped considerably as factory production has increased, to the extent that there are probably now no more than a dozen farms making cheese in the traditional farmhouse fashion. Those that are, however, are making use of tried and tested procedures to come up with a product at the end of the day which is highly valued. One such farm is to be found at Mollington Grange near Chester, where the daily cheese-making process gets underway at 5.30 am when the boilers are switched on and the milk in three 1,000 gallon vats is heated until it reaches a temperature of 83°F (about three-quarters of an hour later). At this point a carefully prepared culture of lacto-bacillus bacteria, known as a 'starter', is added to the milk. This increases the acidity of the milk by breaking down the milk sugar to produce lactic acid, which gives the characteristic cheese flavour. The temperature is held around 86°F while this ripening occurs, and if coloured cheese is required a vegetable extract is added.

Once the correct acidity is reached rennet is added, causing the solids in the milk to lump together and form curds at the top of the vats; these curds are then chopped into small pieces by rotating blades. Afterwards, the remaining

THE COUNTRYSIDE

liquid whey is drained off, first for the fat to be separated out for butter making and then to be transported to the piggeries for pig feed. With raking and turning the curds gradually become firmer and drier, and when the desired acidity is reached they are salted (2½ lbs of salt to 100 lbs of curds) and then milled into even smaller pieces. These are then packed into large cheese moulds, weighing about 65 lbs altogether, and taken to the Press Room where they are put into horizontal presses which exert a pressure of between 5 and 6 cwts. After two days any remaining whey will have been squeezed out and the now firm cheeses are removed, bandaged with calico and taken to the adjoining Warm Store where they are left to dry out at a temperature of 66°F for two to three days. They then go to the Waxing Rooms where a thin coat of wax is applied to seal in the flavour, and from there they are moved to the Cold Store where they are kept at a temperature of 48°F. Its a long process, but the end result is a tasty cheese which Cheshire can be proud of!

Typical Cheshire countryside — hills and pastures ▶

INDEX OF PLACE NAMES AND FEATURES